PRAISE FOR *MAR*

Eugenia is the *fourth* person I have met who has conscious memories of some past lives. The first person was twentieth-century hypnosis legend and author Ormond McGill, PhD. When I met him in 1986, he put his left hand on my shoulder while shaking hands with his right hand and said, "So good to see you again, my dear friend." He claimed that we were friends in many past lives. The second person was the daughter of a minister, who tried to "spank" what he thought were demonic fantasies out of her during childhood. The third was a former Methodist minister who had a client spontaneously go into a past-life regression—and when the minister prayed for answers, he did some research. His research was followed by acquiring conscious memories of several of his past lives. What makes Eugenia unique from the other three people is that she wrote about several of them in *Marlene and Me*. Many of her memories are of sadness and loss; but instead of feeling sorry for herself, she chose the path of spirituality. She even remembers her spiritual masters who help her gain wisdom from the periods of life between lives. One of the three other people I mentioned above also remembered one of the spiritual masters in-between lives. If you are ready to consider new paradigms of possibility, read her book.

—**Roy Hunter, DIMDHA, DAPHP, Published Author and**
Hypnotherapy Instructor

What an exceptional experience you will find in the pages of this fascinating journey that spans multiple lifetimes. Eugenia tells the tale of her intimate journey with her inner guides and the profound experiences of connection that weave and unravel her story through multiple lifetimes. I was enthralled with her story and the many pieces that explain current life challenges, opportunities that rose and lessons learned throughout her expressions of life. You will be too!

May you take away not just a great story, but really feel into the intent of what is real beyond this realm we currently experience. How do we make sense of the things that inform and invite us into greater knowing and trust? The life experiences do not necessarily become easier, but they are definitely more understandable. The lessons are received with love when we allow the possibility of a benevolent universe, of a loving God. This book will test your beliefs and invite a new perception. Let it expand your horizons and awaken your own inner awareness.

Thank you, Eugenia, for sharing your wisdom and the wisdom of the guides.

—Reverend Kyra Baehr, Minister, Unity Bay Area Houston, and Spiritual Coach & Mentor

Eugenia is and has always been a beautiful inspiration and comforter for many people. She doesn't just observe people when they are troubled. She actually helps them—even when she is facing dire circumstances herself. As a member of our Toastmasters club, Eugenia's speeches are always exciting, motivational, and soothing. You will love reading about her experiences and her compassion in this extraordinary fascinating book. You'll even learn important history. There are many stories within Eugenia's story. This book should become a great movie.

—Pamela Williams, Distinguished Toastmaster, Vice President of Education

I enjoyed reading this book and found it fascinating that the author could bring forth so many details of past lives and relate them to later lives. This is an interesting process of healing that could help many people.

—Dan Bridge, PhD, Environmental Science

MARLENE
and ME

I Discovered Spiritual Healing Through
Resolving Past Life Traumas

EUGENIA AFANADOR

DEDICATION

To my beautiful mother, Donelia. You have always been my
inspiration and I will always love you.

My mother, my dear, how much I do miss you!
Terms of endearment from your lips forever are sealed
I saw them immobile, but their wisdom in my heart is a shield
When in solitude I pretend to see you, your kindness in memories appears

I often wondered where did you go?
I heard a sweet answer from some place far above
"I am with the Masters in a flowery garden in peace and in bliss
So, daughter, continue your journey and please let me go!!"

CONTENTS

INTRODUCTION

Dear reader, this is a mystical book that is intended to take you to another reality. It will help you see your universe from another perspective. I encourage you to walk through this door and go with me as I narrate to you my own amazing journeys.

I wrote down my personal mystical experiences with past lives and with the Masters of the universe and celestial helpers who descend from another plane to help me when I request their help. This book is the reflection of my personal trials, struggles, and triumphs. They manifest according to my personal choices, contracts I made with loved ones in the past, or injuries to my spirit caused by others in the past of this life or past lives. By the same token, I believe that the lessons we enjoy or endure help us grow emotionally, intellectually, and most of all, spiritually.

We can remember past lives with the aid of the Masters. We have the intuition to remember our earlier experiences and acknowledge these helpers. They are ambassadors from God that manifest on Earth to help us remember our past and to guide us when we are in a place of suffering, turbulence, or decision-making. These guides also celebrate our triumphs and accomplishments with us, sending us clues that can be described as "aha" moments.

I've had a close relationship with my Masters since I was four years old. They have sent me the confirmation that memories of past lives were latent in my subconscious mind, and it was up to me to retrieve them and use them as tools to heal and achieve soul growth.

As time went on, the latent memories became vibrant and connected with an array of emotions described in detail in this book.

The memories became palpable when I discovered the art of creative writing. As I composed poems, I found places, history, and characters utterly unknown to my young mind.

Because of the poems I wrote, I understood that those stories were not part of my current reality. I used to go to my "safe place" when I was a little girl to remember other lives and other places. I knew at that time I needed to prepare myself for the day when I would have the tools to write about them in a book, and that is what I have done here. I chose four of the lives I've remembered since childhood and wrote about them.

Traumatic memories from past lives finally settled down in my mind, and I accepted them as a distant reality that could not haunt me anymore. I finally realized that we learn from each experience we enjoy or endure. Furthermore, I analyzed my past lives and became aware that everything happens for a reason. We can learn from all kinds of failures, injustices, torments, and even achievements when we awaken our subconscious mind. Overall, we live and learn, as the old cliché says. And this is a fundamental reason for our existence.

The book alternates between my past lives to my current life and back to past lives. I focus on one past life in particular, the story of a little girl named Marlene who was born in Czechoslovakia to a Jewish family during World War II. I have narrated Marlene's story in five chapters, using this sequence, and continued writing about three other past lives using the same method.

It was very hard to be a small child of four, five, or eight years old and remember all these things that happened to me in other places and countries. Smells and scenes on the street often triggered memories from my past lives that were still engraved on my eternal soul. I slowly came to understand that each of us living now is the product of past experiences from our fellow human beings who walked on this plane before us. Their pains, sorrows, happiness, adventures, discoveries, and triumphs stay with the dynamics of new civilizations. Our ancestors are present in our history, epics, art, dreams, and aspirations. According to Lynne McTaggart in *The Bond*, we are not alone because we are the product of the missions and achievements of past generations. Our mission is to discover our *togetherness* from all times in history. We are the continuation of the creations of the beings that came before us. Paradoxically, it could be us again, living in here and now. Hence, what we did, discovered, sacrificed, and invented in the past is what we are enjoying now, and we are continually enriching history. This is us, humankind.

We are in a web of energy that connects us with our fellow beings through time and generations. We come back to complete unfinished business and leave the world a little better for us and future arrivals at planet Earth.

In a similar way, Brian Weiss, MD, reveals in his book, *Messages from the Masters*, that the Masters are almost tangible beings. They are souls with personalities who have walked on Earth before us. When they reach the status of mastery, God sends them to the world to help us. They manifest as ideas, intuitions, premonitions, déjà vu, and other feelings like this.

We may ask ourselves, how is hypnosis related to past lives and the Masters? It's a reliable tool to help individuals find themselves. Traumas of the past may become engraved in our subconscious mind due to abandonment, neglect, abuse, and harmful residues in our inner selves from earlier lives or from old memories of our current life. The manifestation of these traumatic events can be projected as physical ailments, unexplainable sadness, anger, anxiety, and feelings of doom. However, because we are mindful beings, we can intensively concentrate on helpful clues that are stored in our spirit. If we achieve this insight, we may carry out the enlightenment we need to conduct self-hypnosis and to find solutions to our problems.

A prestigious psychologist, Dr. Edith Fiore, is the author of *You Have Been Here Before*. She writes a series of client stories showing that hypnotherapy is efficient. Hypnosis is a tool that helps us to be in contact with our spirituality and our innate eternal ability to heal ourselves.

I have come to understand that we need to love ourselves in humility and acknowledgment of our efforts, strengths, and talents. Once we reach this state of mind, we will be better equipped to look at our spirituality, soul energy, and unique light that connects us with the infinite, with God. Once we reach this state of awareness, the subconscious mind will communicate with us. It will present us with the tools we need to address painful episodes of our current life or issues that we left pending in a past life. When we move toward healing, we are on the way to self-growth.

Other brilliant teachers have walked through life while unveiling the mysteries that lie on the other side of the fence. Charles Tebbetts's statements in *Miracles on Demand* clarify how fortunate he was for the opportunity to learn from great teachers of the art of hypnosis and spirituality. He mentions Dr. Milton Erickson, Carl Jung, Fritz Perls, and other gifted individuals. These mental health professionals contributed to self-discovery of the mysteries of the mind. They also emphasized the veracity of hypnotherapy.

I was fortunate when I met Roy Hunter, a former pupil of Mr. Tebbetts. I recently had the honor to receive his training in *Parts Therapy*, a hypnosis modality Mr. Hunter learned from Mr. Tebbetts back in the early '80s. In addition to Mr. Hunter's teachings during the International Association of Counselors and Therapists, 2022 Hypnosis Expo Conference, he introduced me to two of his books. I am fascinated with Mr. Hunter's ability to captivate the reader with his insights. The books' titles are *The Art of Spiritual Hypnosis* and *The Art of Hypnotherapy*.

I have lived other lives; I remember them with clarity and with descriptive details. I can no longer consider these memories unreal or the product of my imagination. I am also convinced that the ambassadors from God on Earth, the Masters, have protected me since the time I was an infant and while I was living other lives in the past. They have taught me to look at life as an experience to my soul; hence, my soul is living a new experience in my current body.

As you find yourself in the story, you might be inspired to discover your own Masters. These beings are available to everyone and they can guide you through the past, bring you to the present, and help you with mental, physical, intellectual, or even spiritual issues that you might have from other lives.

I have reached the conclusion that whether a person accepts or rejects the belief in reincarnation, one factor is indisputable. We are the reincarnation of our human history. Experiences such as happiness, sorrows, bliss, and torments are imprinted with our "togetherness." Our present time is the result of how we lived and the trials we endured. The stories of our ancestors are the core of our existence. Those memories are embedded deep in our DNA, and in the deep forest of our subconscious mind.

CHAPTER ONE

TALENTS

ABRAHAM, 1847

POET

Oh, the intangible soul of a great poet
Whose verses brought emotions to many
His essence with his poems once departed
But in his eternal soul, the lyrics found their shelter

MY BIRTH IN IRELAND

M other is screaming, "Abraham, my husband, why did you have to die?" It's 1847, and there is hunger in Ireland. My mother is giving birth to me in some cabin in the middle of nowhere. She is calling for my father, but to no avail. During one of his outings, my father passed away when he was desperately looking for food to feed my mother and me.

Mama is hungry, and I'm being born. Why am I choosing a life of calamity again? Wasn't the destitution of the little boy in Mahashan enough? I know that my soul is in search of peace and self-forgiveness.

Wait a minute! I have the same Masters I had during other lives. Their names are Yahim and Tarboo. Goodness, I'm happy to see them. Yahim is good at uplifting me, giving me support, and assuring me that the terrain matters are not permanent. It's what I learn during each life I live. Nothing in life is permanent, and all shall pass in due time after we learn from our own experiences. Yahim is looking at me with his sweet melancholy eyes. He is, as usual, wearing his purple tunic. He told me once that he seldom changes it because it portrays his wisdom and dignity. His wavy black hair falls to his shoulders, showing that humans' roads are never straight; instead, they fall in unpredictable patterns. He never ages. He has olive skin, a color that stands for peace and harmony. And his eyes are green, the color of ingenuity.

Tarboo, on the contrary, hasn't been with me throughout some of my earlier lives. He's the poet, the sad soul who always manages to inspire me, especially in the art of writing. I see him next to me. He is wearing a green tunic as he often does. The green is the color of literature and poems, and boy, he's a *poet*. Tarboo is taller and skinnier than Yahim. He has white skin and long cinnamon hair. His hair is usually covered with a vivid green turban. Both of my Masters tell me not to fear since my beginning in life as Abraham will be more challenging, but it will get better with time.

I'm back to human reality. The Masters cannot distract me any longer, and I have to face my new life. My new mother is trying her best to help me with the task of being born. I'm out, and I see her. I helped my mother during labor by following the rhythm of her breathing because the midwife didn't arrive on time to help us. My mother sees me and tells me she's going to name me Abraham, like my father.

My mother has plenty of milk. Hence, I'm growing to be a strong lad. But everyone around me complains about the potatoes. My mother too. She fears we will not have any potatoes to feed us next season because the Irish depend on potatoes to stay alive. Their main source of food is turning black and ill inside. I cannot worry about these things yet, but she cries a lot, and I cry along.

My first years as Abraham

My mama is trying very hard to make ends meet, but there is simply no food. I go wherever she goes. She cries and cries. I'm eighteen months old, and I'm already sensing her pain and desperation. All I have is my mama's strong back to hold me. She walks, and I feel her hunger. Mama suddenly stops on the road, and someone gives her bread and water. She's happy and sits down. I'm on her lap, and Mama smiles at me. She talks to me as if I can hold a conversation with her. She says, "Son, the man who gave me bread told me he's a landlord who has his land near here, just down the road. He said to go by, and a farmer in charge will give me a job and a place to live."

My mother works hard, and I'm always with her but she doesn't have time to cuddle me. The only time we spend close together is when she feeds me from her bosom. Today is cold and windy. We're approaching fall, and it's cold outside. She works in the field, and I watch her. I'm hungry, and she hears my laments, but she stays there, down on the ground, looking at the potatoes that she digs up, but they have the blight. She cries because she's desperate. I cry because she cries.

Suddenly, I'm not there anymore. I'm in a deep sleep, and I don't remember anymore.

I'm six years old, and the landlord likes me. He sometimes calls me and teaches me the letters of the alphabet and the one-digit numbers. I'm playing in the meadows, and he calls me from the house's wood rails.

I haven't seen my mother for two days. One of the farmers told me she's sick with typhus and is in a place far away where authorities keep sick people, away somewhere. I'm sad because I miss her. But I console myself when I play in the meadows and see the blue sky. I wish I could go there and meet Jesus.

I run to the house, and the landlord tells me that Mama has gone to Heaven. No wonder I want to go there. I want to be with Mama. The man tells me she's not coming back, and I'm confused about it. I ask the man if I'm ever going to see Mama, and he says, "You will see her when you meet her in Heaven." The man distracts me with a small wooden train toy. I have never touched a toy before in my life.

It was yesterday when my mother left for Heaven. Today I'm with the landlord. He says I need to earn my living; therefore, I have to shine his shoes every day. I comply. This is an excellent way to make a living. We're in a big boat, and all I see is the blue sky almost touching the blue sea.

The man lives in England and has a huge house there. He says that I have to behave, and if I do, he will teach me to read and write. He's old and his hair is salt-and-pepper. I sleep in a cot in his room. When he wakes up in the morning, I do too. He teaches me to write and read poems and forces me to memorize them. But I don't mind that because poetry is how I express my feelings to him. I write poems to my dear mama, who I barely remember, and to my papa, who died before I arrived in this world.

The landlord reads to me and helps me understand poetry influenced by great poets and playwrights such as Geoffrey Chaucer, Dante Alighieri, William Langland, John Gower, and William Shakespeare. My master is a sad man who sees the tragedy of life and living.

Several years have gone by, and I'm older. I think I'm twelve, or so the landlord tells me. He's growing older and weaker, and I still sleep by his golden bed on a mat. When he takes his boots off, I wipe them with a white cloth and help him place them on his feet again. I follow him around like a devoted pet. I don't mind that because I have plenty to eat all the time. I eat bird meat, poultry, and an abundance of all kinds of wild fruits brought to England from the Americas.

I'm a fluent reader, and I have a way with words. My master keeps reading poetry to me every evening and quizzes me to find out how much I can retain, and I learn a lot. I now can write my poetry and narrate to him my own stories.

I'm sixteen years old, and I have decided to go away and discover the world. The old man is all I know and all I have. But I'm curious about the many places to the east of England. He has learned to love me, and he respects my decision. Before I leave him, he makes sure to let me have my salary. I have been earning a living since he rescued me from the infamous place where the potato famine took place, my native country, Ireland.

I'm twenty-three years old, and I want to go even further. I already visited France, and it was chaos. When I saw that country, the Franco-Prussian War was going on. The sadness of the peasants and the empty valleys motivated me to write stories and mostly poems.

I went through Germany and ended up in Ukraine. It's a beautiful country with forested mountains full of mystery and magic. Any time I visit a new place, I write poems and stories.

Ukraine is an exotic place. And I usually sit by Saint Sophia's cathedral and watch people go by while I write effortlessly. The poems that I write have the magic of my younger years and the endearing touch of my mother, who left me on this plane as an orphan when I was too young to understand the concept of death.

It has been two years since I left Ukraine. I manage to stay alive because I work when I can, and because I have found the love of my life. We're going to get married, and she helps me find a job in the synagogue. I'm a Catholic, but I have no restraints. I'm a free soul, and I see the world with the eyes of the poet. Since I don't have a last name, I will adopt hers, Margotski.

I tell my future bride that I must see the old man in England for the last time because he's getting older. She doesn't oppose my plans. I'm on the train that is taking me toward the English Channel. Nothing is new to me when it comes to traveling.

It's late spring, and I have arrived at the big house in London. I go inside, and a woman dressed in black, his maid, tells me that my master died last winter from some ailment. She believes he died from old age. He was seventy-six years old, and very few people live that long. The woman asks me to follow her to the dining room and presents me with a beautiful well-carved wooden grandfather clock. It has a compartment in the back. To my surprise, I find several thousand pounds, a poem I sent to him that I wrote when I was in Ukraine, and a note. The note says that he followed my adventures throughout my letters and collected the poems I'd sent him throughout the years. The message also reads, "Treasure the grandfather clock and pass it down to generations yet to come." He didn't have any heirs, and I was the only one close to him.

I'm back in Poland, and I'm a wealthy man. I can offer my bride stability. She's twenty, and I'm twenty-six years old. We buy a house in Warsaw with all the conveniences available in the market. The grandfather clock I brought from England has given me the idea to open a grandfather clock shop. I know of fine carpenters who work the wood to make beautiful boxes for the chiming clocks.

The business flourishes and guarantees the family name and prestige. The beloved grandfather clock sits in the living room's right corner by a recliner where I usually rest as I read poems from famous poets. When it chimes, it reminds me of when the church bells tolled on the day when my lord told me that my mother had died.

It seems to me that it was yesterday when we married, and four years have passed. My wife just had our second son. Their names are Jakub and Richard, and they bring lots of joy to our home. Today we are sad because Richard transitioned this morning, and he was only two years old. I feel guilty because my secret is tormenting me more today than any other day. I am very sad because I do not have Richard, my youngest son, anymore. I love my wife and Jakub, but I miss my freedom and long for my days of being a bohemian, especially when I try to write about issues concerning my sadness. My poems were better expressed when I was free, roaming the world and nature.

Jakub is nine now, and he likes to play with pieces of wood. Jakub admires our clock and pays attention anytime it chimes.

I'm thirty-eight years old, and I'm fading away. I recited my poems to people I met during my years of traveling. I remembered then, and I remember now. I'm the little boy in the poem I'm thinking of right now. I will remember it forever.

Mystical Notes: Talents

I'm transitioning, and I'm asking my wife to place some of my poems inside the coffin, under my hands, where the remains of the flesh will rest for a long time. Yahim is here by me and says, "Abraham, your soul has the eternal DNA of a poet. Poems have the magic to share wisdom and understanding with the reader. When we come to this world, we come with gifts under our armpits. These are talents. It is wise to recognize them, accept them, embrace them, and refine them."

Tarboo shows up singing and laughing! He says to me, "Life is a rose with precious petals. It's also adorned with its painful thorns. Humans will be happier if we appreciate the rose as we learn to deal with the painful thorns that come with the rose's beauty. We should learn to express our feelings and emotions with the aid of God-given gifts, our talents."

I am impressed with the endearing way Tarboo expresses himself, and I am asking him for a favor, "My dear Tarboo, would you be my voice when I communicate with Yahim? You're eloquent, and I want to borrow your eloquence." He smiles with humility and tells me that he will be my voice whenever I have serious matters to express to Yahim. Yahim is returning and is approaching me with a question, "My dear Abraham, what is the most important lesson you learned from the life you're about to surrender?" Tarboo is reading my thoughts and expressing them in the inclusive first-person plural to include me as the speaker. He says, "We may want to choose to carry the petals of our rose, our beautiful experiences, and use the thorns as the tools to create art to allow our talents to shine. Just as pianists use the piano to display their emotions, and painters use canvas to pour out their secret eternal memories, so poets use words to connect reality with unreality. And the list of talents goes on. They come in all shapes and forms."

Tarboo has finished talking and is reading my mind. I am remembering the time when I was months old and was crying because my mother was crying. I fell asleep on the grass. I was the boy whom leprechauns took to the land of plenty to comfort and show that there is always light after a dark tunnel. I acquired my writing talent, then developed my poetry when I was among the leprechauns in the magic land. Tarboo is impatient because he wants to recite the poem he read from my subconscious mind.

LEPRECHAUN

The young mother wipes her tears with weathered hands
Shelter, food, toys she wants for her lad
Not an easy task to harvest those potatoes
Laboring, her only way to calm desperation

The boy is sad, cannot understand
Few steps from Mama, he sits and wants
Her arms to hold him, her milk, her warmth
The grass where he sits is dried cold; his cheeks are blushing

The boy is crying, and his nose is running
The wind has blown away his scarf, the skill to grab he doesn't have
His age is tender, eighteen months, perhaps
His tears are no more; listen, he's only crying

The misfortunes are many; intangible they are
The child only senses the cold and his hunger
Suddenly, a wave of warm breeze has come to calm him
It cuddles him in love, comfort, and happiness

He follows the call from someone in the distance
Goodbye, he waves to his beloved mum
And the wind to other arms transports him
A place of abundance, love, and peace he encounters

And mother below screams and cries and begs him
"Purposeless, my arms without my baby are now
My sweet boy, I love you. I left you behind just for a little while
Why did you leave? Your home is in my bosom"

For months and months, the woman cries
"Oh, my little boy, so much, I wonder
Who took you from me, or who do you follow?
I miss you, my darling. My arms demand to hug you now"

It's Christmas, and her tears are absent
Hard labor and resignation are keeping her from fear
That his absence forever will be for real
Then, again she exclaims, "My little boy, please come, I'm here"

Suddenly at the grass, she stares
"My sweet boy, is this you? Are you here?
If the gift of speech you have, tell me now
Where have you been? Are you for real?"

"Mama, I have gone to lands with caves and mountains
A leprechaun took me to a land of plenty
Where Christmas is forever present
I was happy but miss your hugs, my mama, dear"

"Are the gifts all yours, the train, the bear, the money?"
"Yes, Mama, yours, and mine, I was amongst an abundance
They're for us because in the past you dreamed of them
The leprechaun told me that from now on for us, he will care
Because your love for me is as real as Christmas"

CHAPTER TWO

REMEMBERING

MARLENE, 1928

OH, MY SOUL!!

What is in my future, and what was left behind?
Enjoy the present and let go of the past!!
The Masters are telling me,
Laugh at my sorrows and embrace my new path.

A GIFTED BOOK

It's May 2006, and my daughter Elizabeth is coming to visit me at my home in Houston, Texas, from Florida International University. As she opens the door, she exclaims with her youthful voice, "Mom, I brought a gift, come look at it." It's titled *Many Lives, Many Masters,* by Brian Weiss. She continues talking, "That book has many answers to the many experiences you have had throughout your life."

I smile because I know my three daughters know my quirks and some of my inner secrets. I thank her for the book, and I read it while remembering events of my past life. My name is not Eugenia. It's Marlene, and my mother is Hilda. These are old memories from my soul.

MARLENE'S FAMILY TREE

It's the late nineteen-thirties in Czechoslovakia, and Hilda Margotski lives with me (her young daughter, Marlene), and Alfred, her husband, in a house at Sternberk. She's a tall, stocky woman with rosy cheeks, long reddish hair, and a sweet demeanor. Our home has beautiful furniture, all carved with expensive oak wood. My father Alfred is a carpenter. People who visit Papa and Mama's home admire his grandfather clock. The tall clock has been in Papa's family since Abraham inherited it from his master. Jakub, my grandfather, inherited it from his father, Abraham. However, its chiming reminds me of my great-grandfather because his essence lives in me. The clock chimes every hour, and it sounds like it has the voice and persona of Abraham. His soul and mine are one.

HILDA'S MEMORIES

My mother Hilda is gardening in her spacious backyard; she remembers her childhood. The Hardwicks, her parents, are farmers. They cultivate the land and work hard for their five children—four boys, and Hilda, their youngest. The parents are devoted Catholics with high standards of discipline and morality. The farm is close to Sternberk, about two kilometers away; hence, many of their fellow parishioners come to their gatherings and celebrations.

Mr. and Mrs. Hardwicks' constant coughing keeps Hilda awake at night since her bedroom is next to theirs. She's only eight years old and feels powerless because she cannot go to their room or attend to them in any way. They are sick with typhoid. Hilda's parents die two days apart. She and her brothers Maurice (nine), Mark (eleven), Henry (fourteen), and Patrick (eighteen) are orphans now.

THE CHILDREN AS THEY GROW UP

Martha, their nanny, has become a second mother to the children ever since their mother died. Hilda goes to parochial school in Sternberk as their late mother wanted that for her. She never misses school and is very smart, especially in math. By the time she's thirteen years old, she does the farm's bookkeeping. There are usually gains instead of losses in the farm business.

HILDA'S NINETEENTH BIRTHDAY

The Hardwicks are celebrating Hilda's nineteenth birthday in the company of family and friends. There is plenty of food and fresh homemade beer during the celebration. Hilda has combed her long reddish hair with a ponytail laid to the right of her face. She's wearing her favorite purple velvet dress with black-pattern flat shoes on that day. Her eldest brother Patrick has invited fellow parishioners from church, friends, and relatives from town and from other nearby villages. There are at least thirty people in their house celebrating the birthday girl.

MEETING ALFRED

The party is going full blast when Hilda opens the door to a stranger. People are drinking fresh beer and dancing to the region's folklore music. It's 6:00 p.m. as Hilda opens the door. She expects it's the last guest at her party.

A man standing before her is slightly shorter than her and in his early forties, with tanned skin, brown eyes, and receding black hair. The man asks for Mr. Henry Hardwick. Her second-oldest brother, Henry, had bought a grandfather clock in Munich from Alfred's clock shop, and he's there to deliver it.

The four brothers come to the door a few minutes later. Henry declares that he found out about Alfred's excellent clock shop in Munich from an ad he heard on the radio. He has told his brothers many times he wanted to have a grandfather clock for their living room. The men reach for their coats and Hilda for her blue shawl. The crew walks to the black station wagon where the clock is. Mark and Maurice use their strength to bring the heavy piece of furniture into the living room. It's a beautiful grandfather clock, carved from dark wood with a tone of class and distinction.

THE STORY BEHIND ALFRED

It's late in the evening, and Alfred Margotski is sitting down in the living room with Hilda and her four brothers. He's attentive to what they're saying about the political issues of the day. They continue drinking beer, even though all the guests have gone home.

Alfred tells his new friends that he was born in Warsaw, Poland, from a Jewish family. He has a younger brother who left for Chile, South

America, when he was very young. He says he's going there one day in the future to visit Richard, his brother. Alfred continues graciously narrating his life. His father and mother were Jewish, but his grandfather, Abraham, was Catholic.

Abraham had a prestigious grandfather clock shop in Warsaw. Alfred's talent is like that of his father. He has a concrete mind geared to working with wood. Upon his father's death, he decided to move to Munich, Germany, where he opened another grandfather clock shop. His father, Jakub, kept the business up to the time of his death. Alfred took over the business and expanded throughout other cities in Europe. Alfred loves to tell his story, and he has found a good audience, the Hardwicks. He says that he has been carving wood since he turned fifteen. He enjoys assembling the beautiful clocks that he advertises all over Europe.

Alfred returns to the topic of his younger brother. He says that one spring morning, Richard left his family for good. Nothing exciting was happening in Warsaw, and the boy was longing for excitement. He left without considering the anguish he caused his family. Richard left for Puerto Montt, Chile. The young man embarked on a huge cargo ship and, without knowing where he was going, he left for South America.

Several months later, the family received a letter. Richard was in Brazil. Eventually, he embarked to Puerto Montt. His letters continued to arrive with the good news of how prosperous he was becoming. Richard was working in the field of ship maintenance. He invited Alfred to join him in the letters he sent home. The invitation stood firm for several years as a part of Alfred's future.

Alfred is telling Hilda and his brothers that he's a widower. He was twenty-three years old when he married his first wife. She was a twenty-year-old Jewish girl whose voice was fragile and hard to hear for someone with average auditory capacity. His wife was the daughter of a distinguished member of the elite Jewish community in Munich. The couple got along very well and were married a few months after they met. Alfred and his wife had two daughters, Ruth and Abigail. Ever since their infancy, the girls had a devoted nanny, Esther. She was a single woman who had dedicated her entire life to the welfare of the girls.

Life was good for Alfred and his family. The girls learned to play the piano and did well in school. When their father's time allowed it, they went on trips around Europe. Unfortunately, when his wife became ill, the family's stability was interrupted. She began to lose a lot of weight, and her complexion became very pale. When Alfred finally took his wife to the doctor, they found out she had tumors in her left breast. She died a few months later.

HILDA AT THE CLOCK SHOP

Alfred stays in town for a few days since he's looking for a suitable place to open another shop. He wants to settle in Sternberk because he fears the political uneasiness in Germany and Poland. He often visits the Hardwicks, and he recently offered Hilda a job as a cashier in the shop. She delightedly accepts it, and her brothers approve her decision. Hilda has moved to town since she works in town at Alfred's shop. She wants to be closer since the farm is two kilometers away from downtown Sternberk. She's renting a room from a widow whom she met in the cathedral a while ago.

Alfred and Hilda are dating, and when they go into the countryside in his black Mercedes station wagon, she sits in front of the steering wheel as Alfred teaches her how to drive. To his amazement, she's learning fast. Alfred enjoys her innocence, excitement, and spontaneity. Her boyfriend helps her feel on top of the world.

Soon after, Alfred and Hilda realize they're madly in love. They know their relationship is complicated since Hilda is Catholic and Alfred is

Jewish. But they know they're destined to be together. They make each other the promise that they will break the barriers that separate them—age, ethnicity, religion, and status. The only way for their union to work will be a Catholic wedding. Patrick, being the oldest sibling, needs to approve of the marriage. He will if Alfred converts to Catholicism.

THE PRIEST AND THE PLANS

Hilda's brothers are not surprised about Hilda and Alfred's plan to get married, but are concerned since they don't share the same religion. When Alfred asks Patrick for his sister's hand, Patrick tells the couple they should think about the problems they will meet, primarily because of the unpleasant political climate in the region at this time related to Jewish ethnicity. Alfred states that his intentions are good, and he does not mind marrying Hilda in the Catholic Church and converting to Catholicism. Hilda already knows about Alfred's intentions of renouncing Judaism and adopting his new bride's religion since he has decided to adopt her last name as well. It would be easier for Alfred not to have a Jewish surname because of the oppression Jewish people are enduring.

The couple, along with Hilda's brothers Patrick and Henry, decide to go to the cathedral to talk to John, the priest, and set the wedding date.

The priest welcomes them with a big smile and a cordial welcome. Father John tries to shake Alfred's hand with a gesture that show he wants donations to help cover the church's financial needs. Alfred does not pay attention to it and continues talking, announcing that he wants to be baptized since he honors everything the parish is doing for people in need, including Jewish people.

At the end of the conversation, Alfred offers a generous donation to help the needy looking for aid from the church. The priest agrees to baptize Alfred and doesn't require that he learn anything about the dogma of the Catholic faith. At this point, Alfred extends his hand, and the two men shake hands as though sealing a business deal.

Two weeks later, Alfred and Hilda get married. Hilda has decided to have a private gathering: her brothers and Martha, her nanny.

I'M WATCHING IT ALL

It's about six months after their wedding, and my parents are happy honeymooners. They laugh, play, talk, and even cook together. However, when Hilda wakes up in the mornings, she runs to the bathroom to throw up. She feels nauseated. Nothing she eats agrees with her. Alfred is alarmed because he suspects the inevitable. It's not the first time he has seen a woman with these symptoms. The signs are that Hilda is pregnant, and Alfred has not told his daughters about his new wife yet. Hilda often thinks about this issue, and when she does, she cries. She feels that Alfred believes she doesn't deserve to be in his family.

WHERE AM I?

My mother thinks she's alone with her thoughts. But I know them. I sense her tears when she cries, and I see her when I go out of her womb just for curiosity. My soul has been planning to unite with Hilda's fetus. I have my reasons to be born from her. I know I need to be part of an awakening.

REMEMBERING MY MASTERS

While I'm in Hilda's womb, I remember my two Masters, Yahim and Tarboo. They're beautiful eternal beings who help me while I live lives. Yahim is going to be my voice of reason during the life I'm about to begin. He will carry the torch of wisdom for me to accept and surrender. Tarboo is going to guide me with endurance and divine knowledge.

Taboo tells me that my name will be Marlene, after Mary Magdalene, the woman who helped wash away human weakness and muddy energy during Christ's time. I want to increase my fortitude because that quality brought me closer to God during my past experiences. I'm aware that I will shed many tears while at the same time experiencing the love of my family toward me. My soul will learn lessons to help me grow in the life that I'm about to begin.

Hilda is going to be my new mother. I want her because she's part of my eternal family in the endless constellations of planes, and we have lived many lives hand in hand before. Any time we meet in life on Earth or in another dimension, we have fun.

My father is also an old soul. He's not actually a part of my beautiful eternal family. But I know him from other lives and from another cluster in the infinite plane, the place where people live when we drop the flesh. The name of this place is "life between lives." I feel sad for him because he chooses to create conflicts that don't serve him. Papa will need to discipline himself and learn the lessons for his soul's growth and endurance.

Hilda's womb is a comfortable place to reflect. Sometimes, I play the "in-and-out game." That is, I come out of my mama's body and check the outside, then return to her womb to rest and reflect. I'm in a bubble of warm water. I assume it's Hilda's "water bag" or womb.

MY NEW PARENTS

Mama is much younger than Papa. And, who cares? Where I come from, there is no such thing as limitations of time. Time is flexible, like an elastic band that stretches back and forth, from past to present and into the future. There is not any concept of time in that reality.

My soul is united with a little girl's body in Hilda's womb. My eternal personality will manifest according to the stories created by my earlier lives and the upbringing my new parents will give me. I will be mindful, and I will listen to their advice while growing physically and spiritually.

I'm tiny, as big as an adult toenail. I don't feel many sensations, except that I'm floating in a bubble of water. I feel protected in the warmth of my mother's womb.

It's fun to be inside Hilda because I'm aware of all the motions in her body. The sound of her heart palpitations makes a rhythmical vibration in my new being. I feel my soul being part of the little body. However, my soul is not in charge of the body, nor does my so-called fetus over-power my soul. I prefer calling it "baby" because it houses my soul, and the word "baby" dignifies it.

Hilda is making plans for my arrival and is trying to figure out how to help Alfred find the words to tell my older sisters about my mama and me. She worries too much, and I just want to say to her that all is fine. Unfortunately, she's unaware that I know what she thinks. Well, Papa will eventually learn how to utter the words he needs to use when he finally dares to tell them we exist in his life.

My father's DNA is very much part of my flesh. Hence, I also see and sense him when he's around me. I can hear him from Mama's womb, the sound of his station wagon approaching the house. Then, I quickly peek outside Mama, and I see the automobile arriving home. Alfred is a good man, but he keeps on returning to the school named "Earth" to learn how to be sensitive and more empathetic about other people's feelings. He doesn't know how to measure the consequences of his actions; he has failed to learn this task many times. Hence, he unintentionally hurts others.

LABOR TIME

Mama and I are in labor. The midwife is here with us. I hear my mother screaming, pushing, and feel her pain. I'm sad for both of us because we're suffering. She's in pain, and I'm breaking barriers through the birth canal. Papa is here too, and I feel love for both of my parents. My memories are not that clear. My trinity—soul, spirit, and body—is integrating. I'm tired, but I have to go on.

WHAT MOTHER DO I HAVE?

I'm confused. Hilda's womb was shaped differently from the one where I am now. I'm experiencing another kind of warmth from another mother. I listen to my mother while she sobs. What is happening here? Is she Hilda? But the smell in the womb is different. I'm in another womb, another mother, and she's sad and anxious. I have to peek out one more time. My mother is lying in a humble bed facing a narrow window covered with a shiny, burgundy-colored curtain. She's holding her stomach while crying. I look into her eyes, and suddenly I remember her. She was my mother before in another life, and she wishes me back in her arms. Her name was Darsha, and she was Pijush's mother, my mother. This woman wants to love me and protect me. But I want Hilda. What an ambivalent feeling! Her name in her current life is Donelia, and we are in Bogotá, Colombia. All is confusion in my tender existence.

I feel tired and need oxygen. Donelia is pushing hard. This mother is well trained and knows how to give birth to a child. Goodness, she has strength and wisdom. She is a very old soul who has learned a lot throughout the many lives she has lived. I like her knowledge and strength, and I feel very lucky because I am going to have a strong role model. She has given birth seven times before giving birth to me; hence, she knows how to manage the ordeal. I follow the rhythm of her breathing, and I'm not afraid anymore. My mother is going through labor without any help because the midwife hasn't arrived yet. She's breathing rhythmically, and I follow her motions. Finally, the labor process is over.

I look around and see an old sewing machine and a narrow window with a colorless curtain. I cannot distinguish colors with my human eyes because I am color-blind. It's five o'clock in the afternoon, and Donelia is holding my umbilical cord with her fingers because the midwife didn't show up on time; hence, Mama strives to keep me breathing. I have some clarity about the events. I remember my experiences when I was born from Hilda's womb while experiencing my birth from Donelia's uterus.

Donelia presses my delicate groin because of her effort to keep us alive, and it hurts so much. Yet, I still remember. I remember Hilda; I remember Alfred. I'm in the flesh, and the limitations of time will soon deprive me of remembering whatever happened to me while I was Marlene, Abraham, De Ros, Pijush, and other lives I have lived.

Mystical Notes: Remembering

Yahim is with me. He looks radiant and tells me that it's healthy to remember past lives for our peace of mind. At this moment, I am thinking about Abraham's poetry; I need the poet's fantasy to endure what is yet to come during this life.

As Yahim guides my soul to be nested in my spirit and physical body, I receive strength from my earlier life experiences. My Master Yahim tells me, "When we experience strong emotions, we may retrieve a past life. We humans should pay attention to our five senses and to the intangible sense called the sixth sense."

Yahim comes to me with a final comment, "Whatever we experience in any given life is sealed in eternity. We have to connect to our past lives to continue our efforts to enrich our souls. The written scrolls of our past experiences are available for us to read and use. The empty pages from it are for the Masters, to continue with the writing of our ongoing stories. And dear Marlene, what is the most important lesson you have learned up to now?"

Tarboo is ready to answer for me, "All the experiences we have in each life matter because the Masters write them in our scrolls for eternity. When we return to a new life, we bring memories that inspire us. I believe that the memories from Abraham are going to sustain me because they reinforce positivity, endurance, and imagination. These qualities will help me throughout the challenges you Masters have been predicting."

Tarboo reads a poem I have stored in my eternal memory files from the time I was Abraham.

SEALED IN ETERNITY

Oh, the enchanted soul of a true poet
Whose mysterious eyes your truth reveals
And your pen is turned into the magic instrument
That captivates the insight of many spirits.
Who needs hope and trust in their beings embedded?

Your melodious voice subjugates the listener
When you pour your thoughts in the form of lyrics
With the unique words that adorn your message
By transforming the intrigues into enchanting epics

Marlene and Me

I still can see your salt-and-pepper beard
And remember your long and gifted fingers
Then, I realize that you and I are one in soul and spirit
When I remember Ukraine's green meadows

And your feet are bare, and you don't care.
To feel the naked nature under your thick arches
At times, the snow you crunch with your walking
And other times, the heat your feet endure.

So much poetry you created
Telling the enchanted world's tales
Giving color to the ancestors' epics
And with their messages, the zest of living you have revealed

Oh, the poet in your childhood, I do remember
I feel the passion of your youth in fire
I close my eyes to think of all you've to endure
And as a symbol of your strength your poetry you revealed
And I confirmed, nested in my soul is your eternal poetic spirit

CHAPTER THREE

TIES

EUGENIA, 1950

HEALTHY FAMILY DYNAMICS

All happenings are for a reason
The purpose of suffering, to decipher is too hard
Many tough lessons are taught on demand
For unveiling the meaning of tribulations at hand
And the family is present for happiness to guard

CIELITO, MY NICKNAME

My mother Donelia calls me *Cielito* as she first holds me in her arms. (The word means "Little Heaven" in Spanish.) I feel very lucky because I have a strong mother who knows how to be a rock to her children. She loves her offspring more than her own life. She thinks I'm a heaven-sent little gift for her to nourish and love.

My new mother is beautiful. She has long black wavy hair, fair skin, and delicate features. Her dark brown eyes portray the suffering she has endured throughout her life. Her hands look overworked, dried and somewhat wrinkled. She is thirty-six years old. And I already love her. My eternal memory is telling me that she is a courageous woman who knows how to nourish and care for children, and I am her child now.

She has had a hard past and does not have the financial ability to support another child, but I know that being her child is my destiny because I will learn strength and determination from her. Those are two things that I am craving to learn during this life.

I hardly ever cry because I'm a good and happy baby. Mariela, Omaira, Sara, Lilian, Marie, Lucy, and my brother Hernando also call me as my mother does, *Cielito*. I like it because it goes with my tiny body. My mother hasn't baptized me yet; therefore, *Cielito* is not my official name. When my mother talks to the parish priest, he refuses to register me as "Cielo" because it's not a biblical name; instead, he baptizes me as Maria Eugenia, naming me after the daughter of Colombia's nineteenth president, Gustavo Rojas Pinilla.

THE TWO MASTERS ARE MY COMPANIONS

Yahim and Tarboo are with me again. They make me feel safe and protected. The family dynamics at Donelia's home make me feel the same way. I feel at ease, even though I sleep most of the time.

When I sleep, I travel to the other plane—"life between lives." We humans go there sometimes, and we are not even aware of that reality. I leave my little body, making sure that its vital organs are protected and functioning. Hence, I calmly breathe before departing. There is a flow of energy that is around and within my body that extends to the infinite. It takes me places in the universe in a split second and brings me back in the same fashion.

Today, Yahim is taking me to see other Masters in a remote constellation. I see them dancing and floating on a spacious galaxy. I see homes, trees, and narrow roads. My vision is limited to black and white. This state makes shapes look gray. I am color-blind as I was when I came out of Donelia's womb.

I am looking at the Masters now. They are very tall and have the keys that open the rooms that hold the scrolls that keep every person's stories created during their time on Earth.

THE VISITOR DOESN'T LIKE ME

I'm six months old, and someone special is coming to meet me for the first time. My mama dresses me in a white crocheted dress with matching socks. She adorns my head with a pink ribbon tied in a bow that ends up resting on my upper forehead. I have the smell of fresh mint mixed with chamomile. Mama sits me on a rectangular wooden table. I can almost sit down by myself; nevertheless, she places pillows around me to protect me from falling to the floor.

I hear an automobile arriving at the house. The sound connects me to an endearing noise of the past. Is that my papa, Alfred? Is he here? The man is near me, by the rectangular kitchen table. No, that man is not Papa. I cry; I don't feel safe and I know he doesn't like me. I let out a loud wail after he speaks. I'm too young to understand the language but not too young to understand his demeanor. His tone of voice is threatening, and his body language is scary. The man looks into my eyes with disdain, and I read his body language.

I see how he raises his right hand as disapproval of my presence. My soul language helps me understand the meaning of his words, "Take this child away from me. I cannot stand the color of her shiny hazel eyes."

I cry loudly again. My ten-year-old sister Lilian takes me away. I don't like that man. At the same time, I want Alfred, my papa. He's the one who always finds me sitting on the kitchen table when he comes home.

Lilian and I are in the bedroom, and I continue crying. The two of us peek out the window that faces the street. I see how that man with a white collar and a black cassock gets into a light gray Jeep, turns the ignition on, and disappears down the road. He and his vehicle fade away. I go to sleep, and I go into the plane where there are no time restrictions.

MY FIRST BATH

I'm eight months old, and I find myself inside a circular metal tub placed on top of a washing board on a patio. The sun is shining in Bogotá, which is rare. I have the sensation of being naked for the first time. I have a feeling of freedom, sensuality, and communion with Mother Earth. I feel the lukewarm water splashing on my head and running over my body, and I like its smell.

My mama prepares the water, boiling it first with mint and chamomile herbs. I enjoy it; therefore, I don't cry when she bathes me. She dries my body, dresses me, and places my little body in the inner corner of her bed. That is the place where I sleep. I go into a perfectly relaxed state of mind, and I dream with Yahim, my wise Master.

Tarboo shows up and is resting beside me in my mother's bed. He speaks for me. "The joy I feel when my mother bathes me in the metal tub comes from the purity of the water she uses; it's a channel to remember past lives. It feeds the soul when it touches the skin.

"When we shower or bathe, the largest organ of the body, the skin, receives stimuli. We reflect, relax, and bring back memories triggered by the alertness from the freedom of thought. The wonder of this experience is a miracle given to humanity by our Creator. Water is what keeps eternal memory alive and vibrant. For humans, water is also what breaks the barrier that exists between the flesh and the soul."

This experience helps me remember my other mother. It is Hilda who I want during these instances of my infancy. I'm also thinking about Donelia. She picks me up and consoles me while providing me with her fresh, delicious milk.

MY EARLY CHILDHOOD

I'm one year old, and I'm discovering my looks when I look at myself in my mother's magnified vanity mirror on her nightstand. I stand next to her bed, grab it, and look at my face. I have olive skin, cinnamon-colored hair, and hazel eyes. I make faces in front of the mirror, and I laugh.

My reflection is strange. I'm used to seeing myself with the soul's eyes. When I see myself with my soul's eyes, I mirror a brilliant aquamarine light that moves with speed faster than the sun's rays do on Earth. That is the reflection of my eternal soul.

THE PARTY

I move a lot and have lots of energy. I'm learning to walk, and at the same time, I'm learning to dance. I have the rhythm of music blended in my eternal DNA; hence, I move according to the sounds of Colombian music, Irish folklore music, and music from other countries I have experienced before.

My sisters are having a party at the house. I'm about fifteen months old, and I'm dancing already, moving around the people in the living room. I stand on a dark brown step stool, reaching the radio's volume control and turning the knob to its highest sound. I come down from the stool and dance for hours. As I dance, I'm recalling some memories from earlier lives.

MY FIRST FRIEND

My one and only playmate is my sister Lucy. I'm two and she's four. The young couple who live in the room closest to ours, in the big house where we're staying, gave Lucy a tiny toy armoire. And I like her favorite toy. The small rectangular box is the home of the Holy Trinity. The Father, Son, and Holy Spirit graciously stand in the cute make-believe armoire. What amazes me the most is that the little doors to the box have hinges.

When my sister allows me to hold it, I entertain myself with the squeaking noise the tiny doors make when I open them and close them. I pretend I'm finding an imaginary wardrobe in the depths of the rectangular box.

Lucy's mind is communicating with mine; hence, we share the same thought. She tells me that she sees how the arms of each one of the bodies that form the Holy Trinity hold our pretty imaginary dresses. I'm thinking about a friend from other times when she had my doll, and I had hers. That is a scene from my previous life.

AN ACCIDENT

It's early afternoon, and I'm playing with Lucy's favorite toy, and an accident happens at the big house. While older children play by the front door, a four-year-old girl steps on a glass bottle that someone left on the ground. Children scream, and there is confusion all over the place.

I'm staggered by the screams of alarm coming from the house's community. Lucy and I follow our sister, Marie, who is seven. We're curious about the havoc. I want to find out what is going on too. Since I'm so little, I can place myself right in front of the injured girl.

I see the blood streaming from her lacerated right foot and notice that a lady is sitting on a bench beside her. The woman carefully removes the large and small pieces of glass from the bottom of the child's foot. I don't have any emotions and reason in silence, *I've seen worse than this because I'm a child of the Holocaust.* Then, I disengage and see the commotion as if only my soul is present.

Marie pulls Lucy and me away from the scene. The three of us go back to the room. Marie is a smart little girl; hence, she describes what we witnessed in detail to our mother. I try to say the word "holocaust" but I don't have the language to express my thoughts.

My sister Sara takes me to the room, gives me the bottle, and I fall asleep.

BLISS AND SORROWS OF MY FAMILY

We're in another house, and I'm with my mama in a room with two beds. My mother and I are alone. She's lying on a bed next to a window with a set of pliers in her hand. I'm in the other bed next to the door drinking milk from my bottle. I observe how she inserts a pair of pliers in her mouth, and as she sobs, she pulls a tooth from her mouth. I walk near her, and she tells me to move away. She has a bloody tooth in her hand.

I feel sad and impotent because I cannot help her, a sensation I had before with another mom I had. She places a white towel bathed in blood on the floor next to her bed. I connect my reaction to something else I witnessed before. Another mother I had in another life had a bloody towel around her, but I cannot remember who.

Moving a lot

We move from house to house all the time as I continue growing up. It's evening time, and the breeze is cold. Donelia and I are outside on a street corner, waiting for something, and I'm still two years old. I feel the cool of the evening breeze on my arms and legs. I'm glad I'm wearing the white shawl Mama knitted for me a while ago. I sense how the wind is blowing. The shawl goes high, and it descends again onto my tiny arms.

Down the road comes an old truck. Mama is happy and tells me, "We are moving to a better place." The truck driver is robbing me of what I believe is mine once again, my home. I'm crying, and my mother consoles me by hugging me and kissing me. I don't know where we're going.

We're arriving at a big house and are in our new room. It's freezing in this place, and my little shawl is no longer doing the job of keeping me warm. There is a large patio in the middle of all the rooms. My mother will soon use its washing board to wash our clothes. Mama usually says she wants us to look as clean and dignified as she does.

Donelia must share the washing board with the other tenants. When it's her turn to wash, Mama takes me there, all bundled up in blankets, and I love it. I'm cold, but I don't mind because I'm with Mama, and it's easier for my mind to fly when I'm outside. My mind wants to fly away, but I'm losing that ability. Time and matter are taking over. My eternal mind is putting aside memories of other lives I have lived before.

BECOMING AWARE OF SOME OF MY SISTERS

I'm four years old, and my mama bought our first home. We're staying at a model house until our house is ready for us. I'm in the back-yard playing with tiny pebbles and marigolds.

Sara, my twenty-year-old sister, appears behind me and touches my shoulder. She asks me to follow her into the house because she bought a present for me. It's a beautiful light blue lace dress with matching gloves. I recognize the color in my subconscious mind because my analytical mind doesn't recognize the colors' names. For some strange reason, I feel I have worn a blue dress sometime in my past.

I put my dress on with her assistance, and I become distracted watching the front doorknob. Then, I ask her, "What does *buy* mean?" She responds with a smile, "To buy means you pay with money for what you want, and I wanted this dress and these gloves for you."

I'm in front of the doorknob again, and I cannot resist it anymore. I'm wearing short pants, and it's easier to swing on the door now. As I hang onto the doorknob, to swing from side to side, I remember something about the dress. I'm sure I wore a light blue organza dress before.

It's morning again; I wake up and have a vivid memory of the dream I just had last night wearing the blue dress and patterned black shoes. I was six years old, and lived in a pretty house, and I was seated at an oval table across from my two sisters. The table was covered with a fancy tablecloth. My oldest sister called me, and I walked toward her feeling shy. She had a present for me, but I did not see it in my dream. I remember wearing a blue organza dress with pretty patterned shoes.

We're moving to the new house. Sara is telling me, "We won't ever have to move again because we're buying that house." I like her remark, and I go ahead with the question four-year-olds use the most, "Why?" She's shaking her head and leaves the room. As she walks away from me, I ask her, "Does it have stairs?" She doesn't respond. The following morning as Sara goes to work, I meet her at the front door, open it, and after she leaves, I swing side to side by holding myself from its knob. I think about a house with stairs and with a room up above. I visualize an attic.

Today is the day we're moving to our own home. All the family members gather in the model home living room to walk to our permanent home. I have been asking my mother if our new house has any stairs. She always says, "Yes."

As we march to our new home, I ask the question again and again. I finally get an answer from my mama, and it's still "Yes." I ask her if the house has a room up above, and she replies, "Yes." I cannot be happier. Our new home has stairs and a place up there, near the roof. It's just like the one I have with another mother, another family. But I cannot recall anything.

We arrive at the house. It has the smell of fresh wood because it's new. The house is huge in my four-year-old eyes. Indeed, to the sight of an adult, it would have appeared as a tiny house. It has a living room/dining room and two bedrooms. There is a door to the patio where the wood stove and a small utility room are. It has a bathroom with a shower that sprays almost freezing water from some waterfall in the Andes Mountains. There is a washing board in the middle of the patio and gravel at the patio's corner. That is the home of the future flower bed, and the peach tree Mama will soon plant.

I like my house. But where are the steps? I want to go upstairs. I demand, "Where are the stairs?"

Mama says, "No, no stairs, *Cielito*."

I reply with loud crying, "But you told me, Sara told me, you all told me!"

I cry and stomp. I want those stairs.

Sara takes me by the shoulders and tells me, "I never told you the house had stairs, *Cielito*." She's right.

THE BLUE LIQUID

A lady comes to our house to wash our clothes and watch me while my mother works. The morning weather is freezing, and the clothing and sheets dry in the patio at a slow pace. I cannot even see the peach tree because all the clothes are blocking its view.

I imagine I'm in a place with many tiny rooms where people talk, cry, and sit on bunk beds. I remember a lady without any teeth talking to me. That woman tells me that dying is not that bad. She says there is a bottle with a blue liquid that will take me out of misery.

I look at a stand on the patio, and I see a bottle holding a blue liquid that looks like the one I saw before in my imagination. I take it and begin drinking from it. As I drink from the bottle, I reason that death is not that bad. I remember that someone from my past told me so.

When the washing lady sees what I'm doing, she drops the clothes on the washing board and runs to me. She scolds me while shaking my shoulders, "Are you crazy? You're poisoning yourself! You're going to die in an hour." I'm not afraid, neither am I crying.

When Mother comes home, she asks me, "Why did you drink from the mouthwash bottle? It could have been poisonous." She makes me promise not to drink or put anything in my mouth without her approval. Mama doesn't spank me, and I'm still not fearful of death.

THERESA, MY IMAGINARY FRIEND

I'm six years old with an imaginary friend. Theresa is slim and about my age, but a little taller. Her skin is white, and her hair is cinnamon color. I usually play in a squat position and talk to myself about the stories I create while playing. When Theresa comes to see me for the first time, she squats toward my right side and begins a conversation.

"I'm your old friend."

I nod. She talks about the many times we played together. I ask her if she might bring toys next time. She promises she will get the ones we shared before.

When she returns, she brings a rag doll and tells me her name is Ollie. Theresa also says I will receive a beautiful big doll when I turn eight. I'm happy about the doll news.

Theresa comes to see me any time I wish her presence. She tells me she will stay with me for as long as I need her.

FACING A CHILD'S TRANSITION

I'm still six, and I'm in a park on the same street as the schoolhouse. I wait for my sisters, Marie and Lucy, on a bench near their school. I become weary of waiting and instead, I walk around and I see the door to a house open.

I go in and see a coffin with four large candles at each corner. A woman comes over to me and tells me to go home.

I ask, "What is going on?"

She explains to me that her little boy is in the coffin.

I understand death a little better, run home, and return to that house with a loaf of bread. I'm giving the bread to a little girl who opens the door with the intention to console the family for their loss. Then, I run home thinking that I'm not afraid of dying because I know by intuition that people live many lives.

BEGINNING SCHOOL

It's 6:00 a.m. and my first day of school at Pilot Elementary School of Barrio Quiroga. I'm wearing my well-pressed white cotton uniform with ruffles on both sides of my chest and black mooring shoes with white knee-highs.

I don't have a book sack; therefore, I'm carrying my notebook and a set of colored pencils in my hands. I'm standing on storm drains, and my hands let go of the box of colored pencils. The pencils go down through the metal grate, and I sob.

I'm in my classroom now. There aren't empty seats in front of the row. I sit in the back and continue crying.

It's the second day of school, and a little girl who sits at the front row invites me to sit next to her. Everyone is drawing their families with colored pencils. The little girl lets me use hers. I don't know where to start.

She tells me, "Draw your father, your mother, your sisters, and your brothers." I have a mother and sisters. But who is a father? I don't have a clue. I'm drawing my mama and a couple of my sisters. All the other girls have a "father."

I'm seven years old, and I don't have a concept of what a father is.

MY DOCTOR AND THE MEDIUM

The teacher is giving us homework, and I'm taking it home. I have to draw a circle. What is that? No one at home tells me anything about the shape and its uniqueness. Mama is busy sewing, and my sisters aren't around. Even though I'm seven years old, I don't know anything but one-digit numbers. I don't know letters and their sounds. Forget about adding and subtracting. These words sound complicated when my sisters mention them in front of me.

I'm confused when it comes to learning. The family is alarmed because I'm not learning at the same pace as my age. Omaira suggests that my mother take me to the doctor, but it's impossible because Mama doesn't have any money. Omaira says she knows of a medium who channels Dr. Gregorio, a prestigious Venezuelan doctor who lived in the nineteenth century.

Mama is open to the idea. Mother, Omaira, and I are in a dark room. The deceased doctor is showing up through the medium.

Omaira tells the lady that I'm often absentminded, and I cannot retain any of the information my teacher gives me at school.

The medium replies after a short pause, "This child has an atrophic mind, and there is nothing I can do about it."

I know that the word "atrophic" is not pleasant; however, I memorize it to define my condition. I will never learn because my "atrophic mind" will never let me keep any information. My mother believes the medium, and without meaning to belittle me, goes around the house telling everyone that I have a "chicken brain" because I will never learn. I don't like it at all, but I never complain when she calls me the "chicken brain" of the family. I don't cry, nor do I suffer. But I feel different. I feel inferior to Lucy and Marie.

The medium's diagnosis is correct to my family; hence, they all believe I have an "atrophic brain." Regardless of the medium's diagnosis, I decide to continue making a solid effort to succeed at school.

I CAN LEARN, AFTER ALL

Ms. Teresa, my first-grade teacher, asks the class to draw a circle in the classroom notebook. I have carefully drawn a face applying the concept of the circled shape. It has little round eyes, nose, and mouth.

The teacher comes to my table and looks at it. She's puzzled by the perfection of the circles inside the large one. She asks me, "Whose face is it?" I look around and know that all my classmates have fathers. I have the answer, "My father."

Ms. Teresa replies, "You have a handsome-looking father." She's lifting the drawing so that everyone can see it as the sample of the activity.

I'm proud and happy. I may not be a "chicken brain."

I BURN MY SISTERS' CLOTHES

Donelia is a seamstress, and she works from home. While mother works diligently, sewing and mending clothes for her customers, I'm in the bedroom thinking about my diagnosis and trying to figure out what it means to have an "atrophic mind."

I ask myself why those phony thoughts come to my head, and why I remember things from other times. I concentrate, and I reason I have lived different lives.

I close my eyes tight, and I remember a scenario. I need to save people who live in a dark forest and who want to come to my house to be safe from bad people or furious animals.

I light the candle Mom has by her bed, go into the family closet, and start to self-talk, "I will save you; I will take you to my house where there is a bed for you all and food; please, follow me."

Mama comes to the room and screams, "Fire! You have started a fire!"

She brings a bucketful of water from the patio and puts the fire out. She scolds me, and I go under the bed and feel miserable because I burned both my and my sisters' clothes. Mama will have to figure out how to replace them.

It's the first time I feel guilty. When mother leaves the room, I stand in front of the Sacred Heart of Jesus portrait. It is hanging on the wall. I ask Jesus to please remove the eternal memory constantly haunting me.

New York, Where Is That Place?

Mother is usually glued to her sewing machine since she has the business of little clothing alterations. Someone is ringing the doorbell now. I see through the window that two visitors are arriving. I open the door, and there are two women on the doorstep. I go around the living room in circles while the ladies get comfortable in our new couch that Sara had just bought. They're selling Singer sewing machines. The ladies are from New York, and they look interesting.

I cannot resist my curiosity and ask them, "Where is it?"

The lady with the black bundle of hair placed on top of her head replies, "New York is in the United States, a country to the north of this country. There are plenty of cookies, lollipops, and chocolates there to eat. You should go to that city when you grow up."

I'm excited, and I want to go over there right away to try some of those goodies. I know at this moment that one day I will go there.

I turn my attention to Mama, who says what I'm thinking. She tells the ladies, "One day, I will go to New York and buy a Singer sewing machine, but for now, I must continue to use my mother's old sewing machine."

She shows the ladies her old machine, inherited in 1948 from her mother, Ana Rosa, after she died.

MY SAFE PLACE AND THE PLACE OF HIDING

I'm looking for a place to hide in the house, and it's hard because it's small and crowded. Six people live here, my mama and her girls. Mariela and Omaira are already married and in their own homes, as is the eldest, my only brother Hernando.

I use my ingenuity and figure out that I can create a safe place behind the sofa in the living room. It's my haven and the place from where I talk to the Masters when I need them. I stay here for hours, and no one questions me. While here, I imagine being in other places that I had been to before. I was someone else in the distant past.

I'm in front of my house, mesmerized as I watch people passing by; I observe how they stand on the corner at the bus stop. They get on the bus, and the ones who disembark disappear at the curve of the street.

Something is triggering my eternal memory, and I remember how I held my breath before. I was in a room without light or windows with other people.

I get up from my little chair and go behind my mother's bushes in the front yard. They're taller than me by now. I can hide here, and I create a new game. I imagine I cannot breathe because I fear the air is poisonous. I keep the air in my lungs for as long as I can stand it. I'm brave, and I can stay alive if I can keep myself from suffocating. Somehow the game empowers me and gives me a sense of control.

After I'm exhausted from playing the breathing game, I go inside the house, and there is a smell of fried meat that comes from the kitchen. I imagine dead people and officials placing the bodies in giant pits. I see many bodies piled up around it and how the ones already in the hole are burnt. The ashes go up to the sky in red and yellow flames.

I'm behind the sofa in the living room; I am in tears because all these thoughts are tormenting me.

I have my eyes closed, and Yahim shows up. He is telling me he is sad for me and has a few insights to reveal to me: "During infancy and childhood, the person remembers how a past life may have created a circle made out of wonders. The child plays, imagines, and remembers characters of past lives. When a baby smiles when sleeping, he is experiencing the realm of 'life between lives.' When the young child is quiet, and suddenly and without any reason smiles, it's because he's experiencing moments from the distant past, other lives, and other places.

"On the contrary, when the child breaks into a loud cry of desperation, it may be because the little one remembers traumatic memories from any given life from the past. The new child's mind doesn't have accountability for the frames of time or space. Hence, it bounces from there to here without the awareness of the limitations time imposes on the human being."

As I reason, I confirm and surrender to the fact that my thoughts are for real, and I must endure them for my soul's understanding and growth.

I don't like the smell of fried meat, even though it implies that my working sisters, Sara and Lilian, have brought their paychecks home. Mama buys meat only on paydays because beef is costly.

The flashbacks continue and take away my peace. The bodies in my imagination are very skinny. People fall into a hole without any clothes.

Mama notices my uneasiness and cannot figure out the reason for it. She finally asks me, "Why do you look so anxious?" I reveal my secret, and she tells me I need to do the sign of the cross on my forehead anytime I have these thoughts. She has holy water in a small bottle on a stand near the Sacred Heart icon hung on a bedroom wall.

Mother also tells me, "Have your thumb ready to do the sign of the cross, water your finger with some of the holy water I have on the stand, and ask Jesus to take away these crazy thoughts."

I have become disciplined enough to remember my salvation because thinking that way is a sin, so my mother tells me. I will do my best to prevent this from happening again. From now on, I will always hold my left thumb to have the right one prepared to do the sign of the cross; then, I will imagine that water pours from the sky and bathes me. The water will heal me from the horrific thoughts because water is an analogy for the purity of spirit.

THE BARRACKS

To make things worse, I keep on remembering some two-story buildings that house many people who are desperate to escape. There are feelings of sadness, rage, and frustration here.

I cannot keep my mind away from this scenario; hence, I get my mother's sewing basket to distract myself. I get a needle and red thread and begin sewing the palm of my left hand, creating the shape of the buildings that are tormenting me. The barracks of the place of torture.

I continue with this odd pastime until years later when we move out of our little house in El Barrio Quiroga in Bogotá.

MASTERS, SAINTS AND GUIDES MEAN HELPERS

I am eight years old, and I am having an aha moment. The saints, the guides, and the Masters are all a conjugation of the verb *help*. No matter what name I use, I get the same result: help and guidance when I invoke them.

I'm in second grade, and I have learned to read. I'm noticing there are more illustrated books about saints around the house. I bet they come from the Father, the priest who lives in Bucaramanga and seldom comes to visit my mother.

I read the stories of Saint Andrew, Saint Anthony, Saint Martin of Porres, and many others, and I'm trying to figure out how to strike myself with a whip.

Yahim came in a dream last night, and he said, "We don't need to imitate any saints' flagellations, a religious dogma that encourages self-corporal punishment. This is not the right thing to do, and never try it."

I'm listening to my Master, and I will never do that.

MY BROTHER'S VISIT

Hernando, my oldest sibling, is visiting us from Bucaramanga. He stays with us for a short while until the doctors manage to get his illness under control. He has severe sinusitis, and the ailment prevents him from breathing properly.

To my surprise, he brought a gift. It's the most beautiful doll I have ever imagined. She has brown hair, pink cheeks, and she looks like a little girl. The prediction of Theresa, my imaginary friend, has manifested.

Hernando is twenty-two years older than me; hence, I see him as a father figure, and that is a warm feeling that makes me vibrate in joy. I polish his shoes every day, and since I learn to prepare coffee, Hernando has his coffee every morning. I prepare it as I pretend he's my father.

The morning latte is easy to make. I boil water and add a teaspoon of Nescafe powdered coffee. I add cream and sugar, and the coffee is ready for him to drink. I'm preparing his coffee now, and I think I have mastered the art of preparing coffee.

The hot water I warmed on the gasoline stove falls on my upper right leg. It hurts, and as I feel the pain, I remember this happening before in some other place and time. While my throbbing pain continues, I see a snapshot of me as someone else in another place and time.

I'm in excruciating pain, but Mama doesn't have money to take me to the doctor. She tries to alleviate my suffering with an aloe vera juice she manages to extract from its leaf.

I'm not allowed to use the gasoline stove anymore.

WHAT AN UNPLEASANT SURPRISE

Things are peaceful at home, and two more of my sisters, Sara and Lilian, are engaged. I listen to their plans and the enthusiasm about the new life they both are yearning for, the married life. I'm melancholic and don't talk about my feelings to anyone. But I'm expecting their departure from our home, and that makes me sad.

I have also just finished second grade at Pilot Elementary. The teacher hands me the report card, and to my surprise, it's stamped with the word "RETAIN."

I'm crying inconsolably and am in fear of going home. How am I going to tell my mother and sisters about the terrible news? I know for sure I'm a "chicken brain."

I'm strolling home because I don't want to get there.

I hand the report card to my mama. She looks at me and doesn't say anything about it. We have oatmeal soup and fried green plantains for supper tonight, but nothing goes down my throat. I wait in silence for my sisters' arrival from work. I don't know how they're going to react to my failure. Lucy and Marie talk mischievously to each other. I have a feeling that I don't belong to their clique.

I hide in my safe place behind the living room sofa, and when my older sisters arrive home, Mama shows them the report card.

Lilian is not interested and goes into the bedroom to change clothes. Sara analyzes the report card, then speaks to our mother with an accusatory tone. "You kept her from going to school for twenty-five days. What do you expect? She's going to be a year behind in school."

I know I'm petite; I will not tell anyone my actual age. Sara is right. Any time I told my mama I didn't want to go to school, she would tell me to get back in bed, right at the inner corner where I always rest.

I feel a relief. My failure to pass on to third grade is not all my fault.

As I leave my safe place and run by my sister Sara, she doesn't say anything to me. Mama is in the kitchen, serving supper for my two working sisters.

I check my book sack under the dining-room table and get a pencil and a notebook from it. I will not be using it for a while since the break at the end of the year lasts three months. It's November, and I will be back at school in February.

I return to my safe place and discover that I can put my thoughts down. I begin writing rhyming poems today. I have not learned about rhyming words at school, but I'm figuring out that the verses in a poem sound better when the words at the end match.

MY UNCLE MANUEL IS VISITING US

My Uncle Manuel, my mama's brother, visits us with his wife, Nepomusena, and Miriam, their little girl. They live in a village near Socorro, Santander.

Their little girl is a year older than me and has never gone to school; therefore, she doesn't know how to read, write, or do numbers. I think I could teach her, even though I have just failed second grade. I get a notebook and a pencil from my backpack and diligently begin basic math and language lessons.

She's smart, and before I know it, she learns the letters and some of the one-digit numbers. Toward the second week of intense teaching, she's putting letters together and is reading syllables.

I'm pleased with our success because I'm her teacher, and her learning makes me proud.

It's Wednesday today. My Uncle Manuel and his family are leaving this afternoon. It has been a month since they arrived, and Miriam can read high-frequency words and can add and subtract up to number ten. I used beans as manipulatives when I taught her math. This experience has given me insight into being a teacher in a faraway land one day.

Mystical Notes: Family Ties

I'm ten years old today and am afraid and sad. I'm behind the sofa in the living room. I'm talking to my Masters, but I don't know if they're listening to me.

Finally, I sense Yahim and Tarboo roaming on top of my head; hence, I tell them my sorrows since they always have an open ear for me.

I tell them, "I don't understand why my father is never mentioned in the household. There is an instinct telling me that my father is not my mom's deceased husband. There are no clues, and no one has told me anything, but I have to ask my mother. Today I asked her, and Mama didn't respond."

I am deciding to go with the inquiry on my own. I climb on the tall dining-room chair and reach the wall shelf where mother hides her documents. The first thing that falls into my hand is her husband's death certificate. He died ten years before my birth.

I know life facts, such as that a woman is pregnant for nine months; hence her husband cannot be my father.

By the time I'm on the floor, she comes to the dining room and notices what I have in my hands. She slaps my face and tells me never to look into her documents or ask naughty questions again. I comply and run to the backyard to find comfort under the peach tree.

Yahim is sad and tells me, "Cielito is the name your mother gave you when you came to this world because you're a little heaven to her. Some children don't have a father, and you're one of them. Your father is someone who cannot recognize you; therefore, let it go. Enjoy your family ties, and don't suffer for not having a father in this life. It didn't fit with your self-growth plan."

I reason and feel the immense love I have for my mother and my sisters. We have family ties created with love, tenderness, and care. The difficult times we are enduring are serving to strengthen this family.

Yahim agrees with me about the fact that my family has strong family ties. If something happens to any of us, the other members of the family are ready to intervene. My wise Master smiles with kindness and asks me, "So, my dear Cielito, tell me what is the most important lesson you have learned up to now in your new life?"

Tarboo reads what he sees in my eternal mind. He says, "I learned that a father is as important as a mother for a child's well-being; hence, it is foolish to think that one parent can be wholly responsible for a job that was meant to be assigned to a mother and father together. However, one parent is capable of doing the job assigned for two. That is the reason I admire and honor Donelia. I also realize that fears are easier to confront with the support of our loved ones."

Tarboo reads the fears I am carrying in my subconscious mind from my previous life and reads a poem I have just composed.

FEARS

Loops of terror, circles of fear
I'm in anguish when the night is near
Yet each morning's warmth appears
Nothing is to dread; the sun is bright and clear
Living the moment is the key to defeat; forever, I'll cheer

Other lives of other times in thoughts appear
What to do when to remember
Those memories bring my eyes to tears
I need the Masters to come to me, near

I should be firm and find the spears
To help me defeat the fears
The pain and sorrows that my soul bears
The arduous task to carry in my childhood, its years

Marlene and Me

Memories are fresh from humans falling
A Jewish girl who was once tortured
From a boy in the distance who suffers a great deal
From a poet writing, from a villain smeared

I have asked God to free me from those memories
To allow my childhood to be endeared
Creating memories to sustain my walking
Through the roads of living without any fear

"Remember" is what the Masters are telling me
Because the best way to defeat this agony
Is confronting it with strength and courage
Because injuries of the past can be healed
With the strength of the ties that with others we have sealed

CHAPTER FOUR

LOYALTY

MARLENE, 1939

WEB OF LIFE

We live and learn—the old cliché
Masters with their guidance will help
And in the process, the ladder we'll ascend
Holding hands with people who help us our purpose meet
In reciprocity, we help them to follow their goals to reach

GETTING TO KNOW MY PARENTS

I'm about three months old, and I enjoy seeing my mother, Hilda, working in her garden. She wraps me in blankets, lifts me up, and puts her cheek next to mine. Her cheeks are rosy because she's light-complexioned. My skin is olive, and my hair is dark brown.

Mama is often working in the garden. She plants and harvests vegetables, roots, and fruits. She also milks the goats and cleans the house. Since she labors hard, she opts to wear dirndls instead of wearing the pretty dresses in fashion these days. Mama enjoys buying scarfs of solid colors. She wears them on her head with matching dirndls.

I'm only four months old, and I already miss my father, Alfred, when he goes to Munich. He goes there often. He's at our doorstep right now and tells us he brought us a fancy family antique, a grandfather clock. When he's at home, he sings to me and rocks me to sleep in his leather recliner next to the clock.

I like it when the clock chimes. It gives me a sense of belonging to the Margotski family since it witnessed my great-grandfather Abraham, my grandfather Jakub, and my father's stories unfold. It is witnessing mine now. Mother, father and I are home for now. But I know he will leave for Munich at any time.

FATHER'S DECISION

My father is back from Munich. He's happy, entering the house with a melody on his lips. My mother sits me on the light brown kitchen table. She always sits me there when she hears the thick keychain moving as he unlocks the front door.

She places her large hands around my waist to protect me from falling. The three of us know the routine. When he comes through the door he picks me up, bounces me up, and for a split second, I float in space. Then, I return to his arms, safe and sound.

I laugh because I enjoy the maneuver. His love and tenderness toward me are clear, and when we're in proximity, he looks deep into my eyes, and they hurt. But I'm joyful; then, with a sound of endearment, he tells me, "How beautiful your big brown eyes are." I let out an innocent laugh.

He tells me, "Marlene, you're going to meet your sisters; we're going to Munich."

Mama looks at him and repeats what she says every day when we're together. "Have you told your daughters about us?"

He answers with an endearing tone of voice, "No need to tell them now. They will find out when they meet the two of you. It will be a sweet surprise to them."

Mama loves my father and trusts his judgment. She reasons in silence that if that is the only way for the girls to find out about us, she will go for it. Hilda follows his wish to go to Munich.

ON OUR WAY TO MUNICH

It's early spring, and the landscape is beginning to look colorful and pretty. Hilda is pleased and enthusiastic about the trip and moving to Germany. The three of us are in the black Mercedes station wagon, and I notice some tension between my parents. It seems that they're not at ease. I'm not at ease either because I'm a reflection of their moods. They argue, and even though I don't understand language yet, I sense they're in discord.

Mama claims that there are dangers around us. Papa doesn't confirm her remarks. I'm on Mama's lap, and she wants to take the wheel. Papa doesn't want her to drive.

Papa drives along the road, and he seems tense. We seldom stop because Mama is afraid of the police. We finally stop somewhere, and she takes the steering wheel by force. Alfred and I go in the back of the station wagon, intending to hide. We're fortunate because no one stops us. My parents are afraid because sometimes the Gestapo police show up unexpectedly and stop cars that are going by. Those men don't like Jewish people. Papa and I look very much as such. Mama looks German; hence, the chance that the police will stop us is less since she's driving.

MEETING ALFRED'S FAMILY IN MUNICH

After being on the road for many hours, we have just arrived at my papa's home in Munich. He leaves us in the car, and I can see all that is going on.

Abigail opens the door, and I see a short fragile girl with long black hair. The young woman reaches to her father's face and kisses his forehead with tenderness and happiness. Next comes Ruth, a little taller than her sister, fragile looking, with a bundle of black hair on top of her head. She's not that affectionate. Ruth kisses him on both cheeks but keeps her distance. The three of them disappear into the house.

My mother is nervous, and all she knows to do is to hug me and talk to me. "My sweet Marlene, this is your father's house, and we will be fine here. We need to support your father on this."

Next, Alfred comes to the car to get us.

Alfred stays home the first week after our arrival. He has postponed his business engagements to stay with us. Nevertheless, the mood is tense. Abigail and Ruth are not helping to ease the situation because they're avoiding us. When my mother goes to the kitchen, she meets Esther, the girls' nanny, who gives her a forced smile. Esther tells my mother that she's cooking breakfast and asks Hilda to wait in the living room and to stay there until it's time to eat. Mother obeys and feels like an intruder.

My father is home, and I enjoy my parents being close because they enjoy each other. I'm on my mother's lap while she and my father eat breakfast. She's letting me go onto the floor, so I can crawl and discover my surroundings. I keep on pointing with my right-hand index finger to the back-patio door. My father reads my body language and opens it. The three of us go out there and sit on a swinging bench for a while. I fall asleep between my mama and my papa.

FAMILY DYNAMICS

When Esther talks to Mama, she does it factually. She wants to keep her distance from us out of loyalty to the girls since they have not spoken to us. When Hilda and I go outside to sit on the swing, Esther makes Mama dust off her shoes before coming back inside the house. She doesn't do that when my father is around.

Esther tells Mama that peasants don't know how to keep a home clean. Mama feels humiliated but doesn't respond to her derogatory remarks.

It has been four months since we arrived in Munich. We see Abigail and Ruth leaving the house early in the morning and returning in the evening, but they never look at or talk to Mama and me. They ignore our presence. I think the only place where I truly belong is in my mother's arms.

My father is around when he comes home from the shop in the evenings. I'm watching and see how frustrated Mama looks.

ACCEPTING THE UNACCEPTABLE

Winter has arrived, and the situation with my sisters has not changed. They don't speak to us. Esther doesn't like us either. We brought back the grandfather clock, and it's back to its old place, a corner in the large living room. It chimes with a rhythmical sound every hour, giving a sign of unity to the whole family. That is what I want, but we're far from being united.

It's Sunday afternoon. My papa and my two sisters are arguing in the living room. I'm in my nursery. The argument makes me afraid, and I cry at the top of my lungs. Mama is with me, trying to keep me quiet. After I finish crying, she thinks I'm asleep; but my soul is in the middle of the living room watching my sisters and father argue.

Papa says, "Stop asking why I married a non-Jewish woman. I fell in love, and that is that."

Ruth stares at Alfred while kneeling in front of him. He's seated on the old recliner. Abigail is sitting on the floor next to her sister. The embroidered doily that adorns the back of the seat's recliner falls to the floor. Their mother carefully crocheted it, and it has been there since long before her death. Neither of the girls picks it up. It seems like it's a sign that their mother's memories are fading away.

The feud continues, and Ruth asks our father with a broken voice because of her tears, "How dare you marry that peasant woman and keep the secret from us for months."

Abigail hurts as well; she reacts the same way as her sister, even though she's not speaking much. They know they cannot forgive our father at this time.

As the feud continues, Ruth makes eye contact with Alfred to connect with his soul. He cannot stand his guilt and disengages from her eyes. Ruth keeps trying to communicate with her father since she doesn't want to give up on her effort to reconnect.

She says, "Papa, I like the baby. She's adorable, and I don't mind Hilda. But you acted opposite to what you told us many times; that is, not to ever look at anyone who is not Jewish for marriage. That we should remain within our parameters because of our history, faith, and ethnicity as God intended for Jewish people. And you broke away from us. It's the most painful thing that has ever happened to me."

Abigail agrees with a facial gesture, and Alfred takes a deep breath; then, he replies, "God also intended with his fifth commandment for children to honor their parents, and he never said children should judge them. Besides, remember my grandfather Abraham was a Catholic and did the same thing. He married a Jewish woman. Remember, Marlene is your sister, and Hilda is my wife."

Abigail proceeds by asking him the most challenging question of all, "Papa, peasant girls from Czechoslovakia marry only within their faith. Did you marry Hilda in the Catholic Church?" Alfred looks surprised and puzzled, and without pausing, says, "How dare you ask me that? I'm a Jewish man, and I would not do that to you or my Jewish faith."

I need to see Yahim; I float like a feather above the living room and embark on to the other plane. Mama continues thinking I'm fast asleep. My Master is waiting for me as if he knows I need guidance and support. Yahim is talking about life and the joys and challenges of living.

SAFETY IS MISSING

The Jewish people's persecution is imminent in Europe, but it's worse in Germany. Jewish scholars who hold prestigious positions in various academic institutions are losing their jobs, and we're removed from our deserved influence at several workplaces. Professors at the university where Ruth works fail Jewish students regardless of how well they do on their tests; classmates mock the Jewish people. There are many put-downs and humiliations geared to undermine our ethnic group. Some Germans don't talk to us, behaving as if we don't exist. It's as if the Jewish voice is fading away.

Ruth works at the registrar's office. She has a stubborn personality that makes it hard for her; she cannot tolerate the ongoing injustices. Some of those demands include demeaning people like her with office jobs and cleaning assignments after working hours. My sister feels humiliated, and it infuriates her when her boss tells her that she has to do that work along with her regular office managerial responsibilities. Regardless of the mistreatment she has to endure, she decides to stay at her job because other young people want to unite to look for a way to liberate the Jewish people from such harsh marginalization.

Abigail is a teacher in a Jewish children's grade school where she feels safe and happy. Her passion is teaching Hebrew religion, history, and traditions to the little ones. Esther is her mother figure, and when she's sad, the girl goes to her nanny looking for moral support. Esther creates a nurturing home for the girls; for instance, she makes sure to bake lace cookies on weekends.

HANUKKAH WITH MY JEWISH FAMILY

It's Hanukkah time, and I'm just over a year old. I can walk on my own. My sisters are coming around, and they're playing with me. Sometimes Ruth appears to be very much into her thoughts; regardless of that demeanor, she likes me. We go on walks in the neighborhood, and she tells me that things will be fine for us, the Jewish people, by the time I grow up. I don't respond to her comments because I don't know how to speak yet.

Abigail enjoys reading children's books to me, and I pay attention to the readings. She reads the same book many times until I choose another one from her pile of books.

On another token, Mama still wants to go back home for the holidays. Father decides that we're spending Hanukkah in Munich and Christmas with my mama's family. The Jewish holidays are over on December 15th, then we will travel to Czechoslovakia.

The year 1929 is coming to its end. We're going to be a happy family, so I hope.

CHRISTMAS IN STERNBERK

We're leaving Munich this morning, and it's Wednesday, December 18th. Mama is excited about our trip to Sternberk. The girls stand at the door of the house as we're ready to depart. Papa has a sad face because my sisters are staying behind. Mama, on the contrary, is pleased and cannot hide her joy.

She's driving because my parents feel safer when she drives. Papa and I ride in the back of the station wagon. Thank goodness we're not being stopped on the road.

We have arrived, and my Uncle Mark is not that affectionate to us, but the shining in his blue eyes shows the joy we're bringing him with our presence. Uncle Maurice shows up with his red cheeks and a broad smile because he's receiving the best Christmas gift ever, our visit. Uncle Henry and Uncle Patrick are barbequing a goat and stop the task to come inside the house and embrace Mama and me with family warmth.

The giant Christmas tree is standing next to Uncle Henry's recliner and his grandfather clock. As I stand in front of it, I notice the transparent glass covering the front of the standing clock. I look at myself, and for the first time I'm aware of my reflection.

My hair is curly and brown, my skin is olive color, and I'm small. I play by making faces in front of the mirror and run back and forth as I entertain myself with my reflection.

After I admire the clock and my looks, I walk around the house, and my uncles take me to the field to see the goats, the cows, the hay house, and all that I can see and admire, including the white snow that covers the ground.

It's late in the evening, and Uncle Patrick, Uncle Henry, my papa, and my mama are walking to town to check on our house. All is in place, and there isn't dust on the furniture. Martha, my mother's nanny, has a family from church living in the house. They're taking good care of it; for instance, they keep it clean and attend to the garden and the goats.

Mama seems pleased and smiles. We stay here just for a little while, and now, we're walking to the farmhouse.

My mother is radiating happiness because she feels at home. She laughs, cooks, and spends lots of time with Martha. While we're at my uncles' house, Mama and I sleep in Martha's room. They talk for hours and often go to sleep late.

At times, while they speak, I go to the place where I usually see Yahim. I feel great when I'm with him because he always tells me words that make me feel better. When he says that my father's family issues will not resolve, I'm sad; however, his honesty proves that I can always trust him because he's truthful.

Tarboo is sometimes unavailable because he likes his quiet time to rest and reflect on his poems.

BACK HOME TO MUNICH AND
THE STAR OF DAVID

We're safely back home in Munich. My sisters and Esther are waiting for us. It's still Sunday. Soon after our arrival, everything goes back to the routine we had before going to Sternberk for the holidays. Mama is sad again, and Papa gets into feuds with my sisters when they talk. To make matters worse, Esther continues her unfriendly attitude toward Mama.

It's Saturday today, and it has been a week since we returned from Sternberk. We are all going to the synagogue, even Esther and Mama, as a happy family. I'm wearing a blue lace dress Papa got me at a store in Sternberk. Abigail cannot resist talking to us. She says she missed us. Mama and Papa smile, and Papa hugs her; to my mama's surprise, Abigail reaches over to my mama and hugs her too.

Once in the synagogue, my father introduces us as relatives from Czechoslovakia. My mother's eyes are full of tears. She doesn't say much, and no one notices her sadness but me. On the following day, Mama dresses me again in the same blue dress. When we go to the kitchen for breakfast, Abigail takes me in her arms. I'm a heavy fifteen-month-old baby, but she doesn't seem to mind carrying me.

Ruth asks all of us to join her at the round table in the kitchen. She has prepared a treat for the family. It's tea and baked challah. We sit down around it. The table has an expensive beige tablecloth that Papa and his deceased wife got as gifts at their wedding celebration. Papa looks happy. It's the first time the whole family sits together, and there is a positive flow of good energy around all of us. Esther joins us, and as always, Abigail sits by her. Mama still looks sad.

Five years have gone by since we returned from our holiday vacations at Sternberk. Papa is usually busy at work, and we don't go to the synagogue much. He has to use the bus to commute to his shop; however, he's terrified to ride it because Jewish people are in imminent danger. At one point, he decides not to leave the house anymore. Strangers oversee the business. They're not doing a good job managing it, and he's losing a lot of money. My father decides to let go of the clock shop and never returns to it. He also decides to abandon other shops he has established around Europe, except for the one in Sternberk.

Mama is slowly becoming friends with my sisters and Esther. It seems that the fear we share about losing our stability and safety somehow creates the magic that unites us. My mother is finally happy because her brother Henry is coming to Munich to visit us. He says he misses us a lot and wants to see us.

I'm six years old, and I have a new blue dress my sister Ruth bought for me. My wavy brown hair falls gracefully on my shoulders. It's Friday evening, and Esther has baked challah cookies at Abigail's request. Ruth calls all of us to the table. I sit opposite her, and she asks me to walk to her seat because she wants to tell me something. I timidly walk toward her, showing a slight hesitation. It seems unreal; deep in my heart, I have always wanted some attention from her, and it's happening now.

As I sit on her lap, she takes my little hands and enlaces them onto hers; then, she says, "Marlene, I love you very much, and I want you to be in my life. Please, remember this regardless of whatever may happen to us. I have always considered you a little jewel." As she talks to me, she takes a gold necklace with a Star of David pendant from her purse and tells me, "This is the Star of David. Treasure it. Any time you're stressed, touch it. It will calm you down."

I stay with her for a little while. Papa is crying, so is Hilda. The spell of discord in our family seems to be breaking. We have hoped for family unity for a long time, and it has been manifested.

CONSEQUENCES OF THE LIE

Today is Tuesday afternoon, and everyone is at home, except for Ruth. We're in an expectant mood because we know Uncle Henry is on his way to visit us. Henry knocks at the door; my mother opens it and cries for joy when she sees her brother. They hug effusively.

Henry lifts me as he did when I was younger, even though I'm much heavier. Abigail comes out of her room to greet him. Esther fixes a delicious meal for the company with pleasure and a good disposition. She bakes a lamb's leg to celebrate the visit. We're gathering in the living room, as Henry admires my father's house.

Papa serves beer from a barrel in the cellar. All is good until Henry announces he has a surprise for Alfred and Hilda. He reaches for his suitcase and takes out Mama and Papa's photograph from their wedding day. Henry took it in front of the Catholic cathedral at Sternberk. Abigail and Esther are speechless, and at that point, everyone stops eating.

Abigail is by her father's side at the round table. She at once stands up and goes around the table to sit down next to Esther. Her cheeks turn red, and her eyes are full of tears. Hilda looks at Alfred and sees how he brings his chin down as if he's ashamed of his lie. Abigail's resentment is back and worse than before because the little trust she had for her father is completely gone.

Abigail is waiting for her sister in the living room. Ruth arrives at midnight from her secret meeting to gather other youth to discuss possible solutions to our oppression. Abigail cannot wait to share the terrible news with her sister; hence she says to Ruth, "Ruth, Papa lied to us. Look at this photo. He converted to Catholicism to marry Hilda. He lied to us."

Ruth cannot tolerate such treason. It's Wednesday already, and Ruth is leaving the house for good. She feels humiliated, betrayed, and taken for a fool.

Months go by. Esther and Abigail seem to be more accepting of the situation because they still talk to us. Abigail finishes the rag doll she started to sew for me a long time ago. We have decided to call her Ollie. The name is all my idea because I like circles, and O is the first letter of Ollie. It gives me an insight into the sphere of life. My eternal memory finds affinities between the ring of life, the round frame of time, and the experiences we have to do over when we reincarnate because we didn't learn enough from them.

We're terrified for Ruth. Abigail and Esther are distraught and inquire at the university, the synagogue, and with her friends. No one knows about her because she's not working at the university anymore. But people say she's making good plans with the members of the liberation group that gather with the purpose of protecting the Jewish people.

LOOKING FOR HAPPINESS

Abigail looks sad most of the time. The only time she smiles is when I knock at her bedroom door because I want her to read a book to me. I like *Cinderella* and *Little Red Riding Hood*. My favorite one is *Good King Wenceslas*. The last person who read this story to me was my Uncle Maurice when we were at Sternberk for Christmas, and before that, my father used to sing it to me when I was an infant.

MY SISTER'S FATE

When I wear the blue dress with white knee-highs and the black-pattern shoes, I think about Ruth, and I look at the place where she used to sit at the dining-room table. The news we receive from the synagogue is that the Nazis banned secret meetings that advocated for Jewish rights. They took all the young people who were taking part in the secret meetings. Ruth was one of them. As the rabbi tells the news, we become desperate. Abigail, Papa, and Esther break into loud crying. Mama and I follow.

Parents of young Jewish students are terrified to send their children to school. Therefore, little Jewish children's desks are becoming empty at the private and public institutions. Another reason Jewish parents are afraid to send their children to public schools is that teachers and children bully Jewish children by making fun of their looks and demeanor.

Abigail is not teaching at the elementary school any longer; therefore, she holds classes from our home. My sister usually has about twenty-five students in the living room. She places long low tables and tiny chairs so kids can comfortably sit while they learn. I'm one of the students, and Hilda helps Abigail as a teacher's assistant. Mother teaches math to all of us.

There is a little girl who wants to be my friend. She's timid, and I'm not. Hence, I usually begin conversations with her, and she softly and gladly responds to my questions. She's the first friend I've ever had. Her name is Theresa, and she sits by me. When another kid takes her seat, she quietly sobs. Theresa is proud of her colored pencils and shares them with me. I share my crayons with her. Sometimes her mother allows her to stay after class so we can play. I have Ollie, and she has her rag doll. We pretend the dolls are our daughters. She finally feels comfortable with my company since I do much of the talking when we're together. She's asking me if we can be friends. We make a contract to remain friends forever.

LEAVING MUNICH

Papa makes up his mind. Munich is not a safe place for us anymore. He feels defeated, frustrated, guilty, and unsafe. He's upset because he has always been proud of his successes and status as a person of wealth. He has liked to have money and enjoys watching his business flourishing under his management. But now his shops are closed because of political uneasiness.

GOING BACK TO STERNBERK

I just turned eight years old; therefore, I can understand the uneasy ambiance around us. We have just returned from the synagogue, and as always, we have tea and challah bread.

Papa speaks as though he had prepared his speech before. My father tells us, "To begin with, I just want to ask forgiveness to the ones I have hurt around this table."

Abigail and Esther engage in eye contact.

My father proceeds, "We all suffer the pain of not knowing Ruth's whereabouts. I want to announce that we are all going to Czechoslovakia since it's there where I have my only source of income, the Sternberk Grandfather Clock Shop. Also, I don't know what is coming to us Jewish people. There, at least, we have Hilda's family."

Papa pauses to give Hilda a warm hug from the back.

"We will be leaving next Wednesday. Things are wrong in this town. The Nazis raided two homes in the neighborhood two days ago. There is a rumor that the people in those houses are now in detention camps."

We have begun to prepare for the move to Sternberk. The only piece of furniture we're taking is the grandfather clock from great-grandfather Abraham.

Mama and I stand by Alfred. We kiss and hug him while Abigail regresses to childhood and kneels by Esther's knees. Esther declares that she's not going anywhere and assumes the responsibility of refusing the offer. Abigail is bathed in tears and says, "If Esther doesn't go, I'm not going either."

Papa is torn and knows that if he stays, he will not have the means to support his family; he also knows that the persecution is coming like a storm at a fast pace. If he returns to Sternberk, he thinks he will be protecting part of his family, Mama and me.

Abigail and Esther hold hands, and Esther speaks in German, "Wir verlassen nicht." We're not going.

It's evening in Munich. Abigail and Esther are together in the kitchen. Mama, Papa, and I are in the bedroom.

The questions I have for Papa are, "Why is it that Nazis hate Jewish people? Why is it that they call us hooked noses, takers, and cheaters? Why is it that you had to give up your clock shops?" With his big brown eyes humid in tears, he responds, "There is an answer for everything you ask. It's all related to humanity at its worst."

My Uncle Richard, my father's brother, lives in Chile, a country far from ours. Alfred often says he misses his only sibling. If we go to Chile, we can avoid all these political problems.

I pop the question to my father. "Why don't we go to Chile? I want to meet Uncle Richard."

What he's saying is giving me hope. He tells me that he has thought about it, but it's not the right time. He also says to me that one day we might all go to Chile. I am enthusiastic that Papa is still considering the possibility of moving there.

ABIGAIL'S GOODBYES

Abigail knocks at my parents' bedroom door and tells me she wants me to be with her for a while. We go to the back patio, where we sit and rock on the swinging bench. She tells me she loves me very much and she's never going to forget me. She says I'm a brilliant little girl and learn faster than any other kid she has ever taught.

I ask her if she has changed her mind about going to Sternberk with us. She replies with a definite *no*. My sister tells me her place is in Munich with Esther and the people from the synagogue. She says she has a boyfriend and wants to be married very soon. I wonder why she has not told Papa about her boyfriend, but before I can think of the answer, she tells me she loves our father, but she doesn't trust him anymore.

We go to the kitchen and prepare lace cookies to take for the trip back to Sternberk. After the baking time, we part from each other. I go to my parents' bedroom, and she goes to Esther's kitchen.

It's Monday again, and right after dinner, Papa asks us all to go to the living room. He's straightforward when he asks Esther first if she has reconsidered coming with us to Sternberk.

She says, "I won't go anywhere. My place is here, and I will remain here. I told you, I will assume the responsibility; therefore, if I must die, I will die with my people."

Abigail speaks next and says, "I'm not going, Papa. I'm staying home too. I'm in solidarity with our community. You take Marlene and Hilda to a safe place. Esther and I will watch out for each other. So don't fear, Papa; we will be fine, and I have forgiven you."

Alfred is devastated and cannot keep from crying. He continues sobbing for the next two nights.

The three of us, Papa, Mama, and I, are in the bedroom packing the basics because we want to believe we will soon return. Abigail enters the bedroom abruptly as we're closing the suitcases. She tells my papa not to forget to take great-grandfather Abraham's chiming clock with us, "It would be safer in Sternberk, and one day I will probably visit you there."

ON THE ROAD AGAIN

The SS officials stop us before we leave German territory. Hilda takes out the lace cookies Abigail and I baked for the trip. They eat them with delight in front of us. One of the officials gives us the pass to go ahead since a long line of cars is waiting behind us. We continue the journey to our hometown and avoid stopping because we're afraid of the Gestapo police.

The good news is that we will arrive home late on Thursday. I cannot wait to visit my uncles' house. Ollie, my doll, is with me because she will remind me of Abigail from now on. I have the Star of David on my necklace, and that will always remind me of Ruth. The Star of David on my chest will also be a constant reminder of my life in Munich.

WELCOME-BACK PARTY

We're at my uncles' farm, and they have a welcoming party for us. Many people are celebrating our return. I'm missing my front teeth; therefore, I don't smile much.

Papa seems distracted, drinking beer, and listening to his brother-in-laws' jokes and humor. He's smiling. Mama talks to people, but she's glued to Martha. Hilda is experiencing a sense of belonging in her brothers' house.

I'm getting tired, but people are still eating, drinking, and even dancing. My mother takes me to her old room. I fall asleep and go to the other plane. I'm not fearful as I dream, but I perceive hard days are coming our way.

RETURNING TO OLD ROUTINES

We are at our home at last. Papa is already gone to see the shop. Mama is cooking a delicious breakfast, bacon, eggs, and potatoes with cornbread. Father eats all the goodies on his plate, but puts aside the bacon. Mama sings and dances in the kitchen because she has the freedom to be in her own home.

After breakfast, Mama takes me on a walk around the house. We go to the attic, where there are several trunks full of clothes and other things. I am intrigued by the little window that faces the ceiling. The attic has a small bed, a rocking chair, and some photo albums. Mama tells me, "Marlene, this is our safe place to reflect and meditate. We will come here anytime we need to feel better." I smile, and we both run to the ground floor. We find ourselves in the big kitchen. It's rudimentary and never as fancy as the one in Munich. But I like the rectangular table. It brings back good memories from Papa and me; I remember with my eternal mind when I was tiny, and he used to suspend me in the air for a second, and I returned in safety to the warmth of his strong arms.

We're outside, and we see two healthy goats. My mother explains that Uncle Patrick replaces them every two years. There is a vegetable garden, and the gardeners have managed to keep it healthy during the years we lived in Germany. She shows me the potatoes, cabbage, and radishes. We return to the house, and down to the cellar we go. There is one tiny bed and many barrels. Some have wine, some others have beer, and others are empty. I'm not too fond of this place because it's too dark. Mama says it's a place of hiding just in case the Gestapo police ever raid our home. We go upstairs, and I play with Ollie. I close my eyes, and I think about Abigail, Esther, and Ruth. They seem so far away.

Mystical Notes: Loyalty

I'm in a dream and I'm feeling as if I'm in another reality.

Yahim is repeating a word over and over again. He is saying, "Loyalty, loyalty, loyalty…"

He wants to talk, and I have an open ear for him. He is calling me "Cielito," and goes on with a message. "One of the qualities that would help you endure the calamities that you are soon to face is loyalty. Yes, the loyalty you perceive from your parents and uncles would be your support. The trust you have that your Uncle Henry will never fail you, will keep you from giving up your hope. Humanity needs to practice loyalty."

I am smiling, but I am a little confused.

He continues talking. "Just remember the word loyalty. Remember it because lessons to come will help you to understand this concept."

He looks at me while rubbing his hands. "Little girl, what have you learned up to now in the life you are currently living?" I am giggling, and then burst into laughter because I am nervous. He is going to tell me something that is going to make me afraid.

Tarboo shows up, laughing uncontrollably. He is also afraid, and my laughter is contagious.

He takes charge and speaks for me after he manages to control his laughter. "Loyalty, loyalty, loyalty. It is the zest of harmony and the strength of relationships. It should be among family members, friends, neighbors, nations, and the world. If loyalty is not present among members of society, the world comes apart."

Tarboo talks for himself. "Betraying people in your life is an act of selfishness. You are lucky, Marlene, because you are among your loved ones, and they will always be loyal to you as you are to them."

Yahim invites me to travel through planes in the avenues of the infinite universe. He talks to me while we fly all over the skies.

Tarboo prefers to stay behind and meditates on his poetry. He sits on a stratocumulus cloud and waits for our return.

Yahim is telling me as we fly away, "There is energy all over, and all began with the stars. Humans are sparkles of the stars. I can attest to it since I have been a person from time to time throughout the long history of humankind. When God sends me to Earth to carry out a given task to help humanity, I do it gracefully. I'm delighted to be chosen because I like aiding humans to find the light that helps them develop their sixth sense. It helps them solve their conflicts, accept what they cannot change, and find a way to change what they can."

Yahim continues, "The universe has two essential identities. There is light energy, and there is muddy energy. These two powers balance the galaxies. When humans allow themselves to be guided by the rays of light (the good, benevolent) energy, they find harmony and peace from within. On the contrary, when we're guided by muddy energy, we feel anxious and unhappy. Muddy energy prompts humans to react in confusion, hate, and feelings that weigh heavily on people's shoulders, bringing the person down."

Yahim's teachings will help me to find balance for the rest of this life.

Yahim and I are seated by the bank of a river. I tell him that Hilda's energy and mine are paired together in the soul and the flesh. My Master asks me to be more specific.

I say, "I feel her sorrows and happiness."

Yahim looks at me with a sweet demeanor. He says, "Marlene, you are an empath and have been one ever since you were De Ros, back in the twelfth century. It awoke in your spirit at the end of De Ros's life. Your empathic energy manifested within, while you departed this plane."

I remember that I repented at the time of that death, and compassion took ahold of me. I notice that Yahim is looking very sad; hence I ask him the reasons he has to be unhappy. He wants me to be prepared for difficult times of tribulation.

He tells me, "You're just about to begin a sad journey with the purpose of soul purification. God is in control, and He loves His chosen people, the Jewish children of Israel. Since you're part of the chosen ones, your flesh is going to suffer a great deal. You will grow in grace while helping other people who are and will be present in your life."

I'm afraid, but I continue listening to Yahim's words, "Family members have an innate need to assist each other during troubled times. Good, intended actions strengthen the family ties, and caring for our loved ones is engraved in the soul's DNA." He addresses me directly and says, "Little Marlene, what is another important lesson you have learned about life by now?"

Tarboo suddenly joins us. He rushes to extract words from my mind and begins talking for me. "Each one of us gives a great deal of support to those in our lives who need it from us. We should treasure the moments with our loved ones, parents, family, friends, and others who may cross our path. Be loyal to your loved ones because that loyalty unites family members. If we fail the people who chose to hold hands during each life, we break the web of energy and love that unites us with our family members. If the web is broken, there is pain and sorrow that eventually creates a forced silence that causes self-isolation. Think about this: we may be holding hands with someone very dear to us who was once very close to us in a past life or past lives. The mutual healing goes on."

Tarboo stops talking for me and begins telling us what he is thinking. "Loyalty is a quality that gives humanity peace of mind and a clear conscience. Deceiving people provokes feuds and resentments. Our eternal family in the afterlife is waiting for us in the place found among a constellation of stars. Now, allow me to recite a poem that I wrote about life a long time ago. It's about the concept of life observed from a Master's point of view."

MASTERS

Masters have the mysteries of happiness
They live in bliss using all the talents
That long ago they perfected
While walking on Earth and among many challenges

Tarboo is talking and his wisdom is admirable
"I am the writer of the secrets of Masterhood, its status
Not an easy task, but the reward is knowledge
Of how to live and triumph

"I reflect, the pen has told me with its subtle sound.
What I wrote with an extract of a rose, its petal
On the pulp of old scrolls and in Heaven, it's stored
Life is in the flesh, brief, short, and intangible

"While in the body, life encounters thorns on its path
Its walk goes on unpaved, harsh rocks that lacerate its arch
And humans, at times, don't understand
The reason for agonies, dissolutions, and gasps

"There is an imprint of an infinite tear
That's attached to the soul, and at times it sheds
Appearing in the eyes, it flows
To let out its anguish, to relieve its sorrows

"It's the reality that we live as we're dying
While hopes and dreams are left on hold
It's the fading away of the flower, its petals
It's just the decline of the flesh, once vibrant

"At the end of life's pathway, people vanish
Final goodbyes to those who joined our traveling
As we depart, we fly away with calmness
To reunite with our eternal families
And we'll be back for the pending business's closure"

CHAPTER FIVE

STRENGTH

EUGENIA, 1962

HOPING FOR A NEW BEGINNING

The challenges are many; the sources are few
Determined is my essence the tasks to perform
For the long-awaited achievement
that will reward my soul

SMALL SHOES ON MY FEET

I'm in fifth grade. Sara and Lilian want to indulge me because I'm doing well at school. It's a beautiful pair of white and blue Oxford shoes. They hand them to me as soon as they walk into the house to visit us.

I'm trying the shoes on, and they look great; however, they're small for my feet. I don't tell my sisters how uncomfortable I am because I don't want to sound like an ingrate. Besides, I need the strength to endure oppression since it is a way of living for me. They have spent money on me, and that is all that counts.

A knot in my throat deprives me of speaking. I remember something I heard before. "I need to keep my laments to myself to save my people." I feel obliged to feel gratitude to the people who help me survive because it's up to them if I make it or not.

I know that these feelings were created in another life and another place.

I wear the shoes only when I go to church with my mama and when my sisters come to visit. The only thing that keeps me from suffering is my poetry. When my toes and navicular hurt because of the oppression of the shoes, I distract myself from the pain with thoughts about poems I could write.

Poetry is my best friend. I also wear my pair of new shoes after I write a poem. The words of the sad poems stick in my head, and I don't feel much of my imaginary oppression.

I continue growing and wearing the shoes regardless of how painful it is to walk in them.

GLIMPSES OF PAST LIVES

When I meditate behind the sofa in my home in Bogotá, I often think about a land named Ukraine. I don't have any reason to know about that country. I have never heard the word before from my teachers at school, my family, or anyone else, and we don't have a television to watch the news. The radio only plays "radionovelas" from Mexico, but the word "Ukraine" pops into my mind all the time.

Another thing that is happening to me is that I often wake up crying because I'm trapped in a huge library. I like to sit between books, but I move a lot. I don't have a body or a form; I'm just here, on a shelf with the books. The thing is that I try to open them, but I fail every time.

I often have sleep paralysis when I try to return from my dream, and I scream to get out of it. My mother gently wakes me up; after her nurturing, I go back to my peaceful sleep.

CHILDREN ARE GETTING SICK

Mama usually tells me not to talk to boys because that is dangerous. I mind her; hence, I never speak to Ricardo, my ten-year-old neighbor. He goes to school with the boys in the afternoons, and girls go in the morning. We often cross paths on the way home. I go home, and he goes to school.

The boy tries to talk to me, and I want to talk to him, but I don't want to make my mother upset; hence, he speaks, and I don't respond.

It's Monday, and there are several students absent in my classroom. Some of my classmates are at home. The teacher says they are sick with mumps, measles, and even polio. I hate the thought they may end up in their living room with four large candles surrounding them. I have received the shots against those illnesses; therefore, I don't worry about getting sick. Mama tells me I will not get sick like my classmates because the Red Cross nurse who often knocks at the door has vaccinated me.

Mother is wrong on that issue because I'm very sick. My mother keeps me home in bed. I'm burning with fever. Mama doesn't have any money to take me to the doctor.

While having a high fever, I fall into a deep sleep, and I see my next-door neighbor. Ricardo is on top of his front porch tree. He often goes there to talk to me from up there. He looks down and smiles at me as he says, "It's okay to talk to me since I'm in-between lives. Tell Mama I'm happy."

After a week of being very ill, the fever has stopped. I have lost a lot of weight, and I even feel taller. When I go out to the front porch, Ricardo's brother tells me Ricardo died because he had leukemia. He died while I was having that dream.

It's the first time I have had such an experience with the mystical world. I'm shy, and I will not tell Ricardo's mother the message he sent her while I was very sick.

THE VISITOR

My mother and we girls expect the visitor at our house; therefore, there is uneasiness among us.

Mama makes sure I look presentable. I'm wearing my new shoes and a light pink organza dress.

It's the Father who is coming to visit. I run to the bus stop to meet him since he's not driving the Jeep anymore.

Father Perico is not that tall. His skin is dark, and he has a mischievous expression on his face. I greet him at the bus stop. While we walk from the bus stop to the house, he looks at me and says, "You're a natural child."

I don't respond to his comment, but I'm intrigued by the meaning of his words.

We go to the house, and he sits on the sofa in the living room. I look at his hands, and he and my mother look at mine. His hands and mine look just alike.

He tells my mama with a mischievous smile, "This girl is naughty. You better watch her." Mama sends me away, and I go to hide in the bushes where the peach tree is fully grown and bearing little fruits now.

ROUTINES AT HOME

I'm a compliant child who conforms with little resistance and seldom asks any questions. Nobody is home to greet me when I arrive home from school. I'm making good grades in fifth grade. To everyone's surprise, I have received the best fifth-grade student's ribbon award. I take it home, and Mama is proud of my success.

It's time to take the entry exam to be admitted to a government-subsidized institution. I need to pass the test with an excellent grade. If I fail the test, I will not be able to continue furthering my education. Only students capable of passing the federal exam can attend public high schools.

I keep my fingers crossed and ask Master Yahim to make it happen. I have a Sacred Heart candle burning in the kitchen. I have the confidence that God is listening to my prayers.

I have just received a letter from a school funded by the Red Cross. The letter says that I passed the entry exam, and I have been admitted to Red Cross High School. I'm very excited, and I need to learn to commute to north Bogotá, where the school is located.

It didn't take me that long to learn to ride from home in south Bogotá to my high school in the north. Passing that exam and being admitted to that high school have boosted my self-esteem. I think one day I will be a professional woman, so I hope.

MAMA GOES AWAY

My mother is finally getting her dream come true. An employment agency found a job for Donelia in New York, of all places, just like she told the women who came to our house selling Singer sewing machines.

It's April 4th of 1964, and my mother, Marie, Lucy, and I spent the night at Lilian's house because my mother is leaving tomorrow.

It's very early in the morning, and we are heading to the airport. My other sisters are waiting for us there. I feel an emptiness in my chest. I feel abandoned, but I don't have the words in my vocabulary to label my abandonment feelings.

My two sisters Marie and Lucy are going to live in a nuns' residence. I'm staying with my sister Sara in her farmhouse. It's about an hour and a half from my school. Hence, I have to commute each day on a country bus. The problem is that I arrive late for my first class at school every day. Sometimes, when the bus is late, I miss the first period altogether.

I'm in the position of feeling different in the school. It is my second year at the Red Cross High School, and I have been doing well. But I don't have a home anymore since my mother is gone.

Kids at school bully me a lot because I'm the girl who is late to school every day. I feel I don't belong, and I don't talk with anyone.

My older sisters, Sara and Lilian, notice my stress and have decided to move me to the nuns' residency, a place where young girls come to from other states to go to college in Bogotá. My sister Lucy is going to live with Lilian. There is no money to pay for both of us at the nuns' residency.

All girls at this home are in college, and sometimes they drink liquor they've hidden in their dorms. They talk about boyfriends and dates.

Some of the girls in residency ask me what I'm studying. I go from nursing to philosophy.

It doesn't take them long to understand that I'm just a fourteen-year-old girl. When they discover my age, they ignore me and treat me differently. When I go into the lounge to talk to them, they get quiet.

POETRY IS MY BEST FRIEND

I'm in seventh grade; hence I begin learning about European countries and all the abominations against Jewish people during Hitler's government.

I read the textbook, and it feels as if I have lived in those years. I find out that there is a country in Europe with the name "Ukraine." There is also a country named "Czechoslovakia" that has a province named Olomouc. I notice that my poem coincides with the landscape of those countries.

I keep the information to myself. I don't want people at the residency to think I'm odd. I continue with my thoughts and with the poems that I create from the memories of earlier lives I have lived.

MISSING HAVING A HOME

I miss my mama, since no one is nurturing me like she did. I try my hardest to please my older sisters by helping them with the house chores when I visit during holidays. Their time is limited with their husbands and children; hence, they do not notice my isolation. I don't feel their love or appreciation for my offers. The bottom line is that the only person in the world who ever gave me tenderness and nurtured me was Mama, and she's gone.

My sister Sara's housekeeper says that I look as if I'm smelling cow manure all the time. I don't like her remarks; hence, I become quieter.

I don't speak to anyone at home anymore.

It's September 1964, and Marie is leaving for New York. My sister Lucy follows her in April of the following year. Neither of my sisters said goodbye upon their departure, and their gesture of not saying goodbye makes it harder on me.

I feel like an intruder, and I want to be invisible, so I don't bother my other two sisters, Sara and Lilian. Even when I'm visiting I keep my distance as much as I can. I babysit their children a lot, but my mind is usually far away from my body, and I do a poor job because the kids often fall while under my care.

My sisters stop asking me to babysit.

BAD NEWS FOR MY SISTERS

The year is over, and I'm turning fifteen years old. There is not going to be a celebration for me since Lilian's children have the measles. That is okay, and I'm not sad about that. But how am I going to tell them that I'm not promoted to eighth grade?

I just got the report card, and it says in big bold letters "RETAIN."

I'm aware that since my teachers didn't promote me to eighth grade in a government school, I will not be admitted to any other government school in the country. I cry my eyes out, and I keep on repeating to myself, "You dumb, chicken brain, atrophic mind, you failed again."

I stroll the short distance from school to the nuns' residence, then on to Lilian's house. As I walk, I look at the trees and children playing in the street and feel mesmerized and away from reality. At Lilian's house I hand her the report card. She notices the big letters stating "RETAIN." It's as if we're reliving the day I brought the report card when I was retained in second grade. She's looking at me with disdain.

She says, "We're not paying any more money for you to live at the nuns' residence."

I remain quiet.

The boarding schools

My sister, Sara, and her husband, Mario, find a boarding school run by the Sisters of the Presentation in a small town outside Bogotá. From here on, I will live in Chipaque and go to Bogotá only when my sisters can have me.

It's freezing in Chipaque, and we have to take cold showers early in the morning with icy water from the Andes Mountains. My eyelids are irritated and dried out from the cold, dry weather, and from crying.

When it's time to have lunch, the meat smells, and it appalls me because the nuns assume that the cold weather is enough to keep the meat edible. But obviously, this is not the case. I won't ever tell the nuns or my sisters, but I'm never going to eat that meat.

When I go to Bogotá on weekends, my sisters notice I'm unhappy. I'm listening to what they're saying. They're talking about the possibility of moving me to Zipaquirá, another nuns' boarding school.

I don't ask nor question what they're planning or why. I'm invisible.

I'm in Zipaquirá now, and life is better here. I still keep to myself and write poems when I'm sad. I feel awkward and inferior to my classmates because they are all younger than me.

I like this school better because the food is better, and the showers are warmer. Besides, I have made some friends.

Going to the United States

It's the end of 1966, and Marie is in Colombia for Christmas.

We learn that she's officially a keypunch operator at Dean Witter Company in the Wall Street area; she speaks English and has credit cards. Marie is thriving and prettier than ever.

My sister is my sponsor at the American Embassy to get residency status in the United States. My appointment at the American Embassy is on January 6th, 1967. We have all the papers.

The ambassador approves my permanent visa. Marie and I are going to New York in a few days.

IS THE FATHER MY FATHER?

The Father has found out that I'm soon going to leave the country. He shows up at Lilian's house in Bogotá. I notice he's constantly looking at me with a spark of curiosity. That makes me uncomfortable.

He doesn't talk or ask anything about my life or my plans. All he says to me is, "You have pretty teeth."

He leaves me puzzled. Who is this man to me?

I'm spending the weekend at Omaira's house, and I'm taking the opportunity to have a serious talk with her; therefore, I have asked her for a private meeting.

It's Sunday evening, and she's asking me to go to her house studio. We close and lock the door. Then, I simply pop the question. "Why does the priest try to be in my life? Is he my father?"

She responds that she doesn't know for sure but thinks he is.

She doesn't give me a definite answer, and that's what I want.

NEW YORK AT LAST

I'm leaving Colombia for good, and my four sisters are in El Dorado Airport saying goodbye to Marie and me.

I'm leaving my native country forever. I'm thankful because I'm taking along my culture, language, and the essence of who I am, a Colombian girl, to the country with limitless opportunities.

I'm on the plane now. I close my eyes, and Yahim appears in my imagination, smiling as if he knows what I'm thinking.

He says, "Eugenia, there is a reason you were born in Colombia. That land gave you your culture, your language, your faith, and your strength. Roll up your sleeves, because you will use all these attributes in your new country."

MY NEW HOME

Mama and Lucy are waiting at La Guardia Airport for Marie and me. We take a taxi to go to my new home in Manhattan. As we ride in the cab, I'm admiring the breathtaking architecture and infrastructure throughout uptown Manhattan as we go across the phenomenal bridges.

The apartment building's address is 317 West 98th Street, Apartment C on the eighth floor. The building is near Riverside Drive, and it's about a hundred years old.

It's a small apartment with two bedrooms, a small kitchen, and a living room. The windows face the back alley and the dumpster. There are no windows facing the street. I open the window in my mother's bedroom, and I hear loud Caribbean music coming from another apartment.

I'm at peace because I feel I belong in my mother's home.

My mother and sisters just left to work, and it's Monday morning. I'm getting ready to go out to find my dreamed-for high school. I ask pedestrians for directions in Spanish and finally find my destination.

I arrive at Brandeis High School on 85th Street and Columbus Avenue. I have the report card from the school in Zipaquirá in a small purse that my sister Lucy is letting me use. The school's male principal talks to me for less than a minute and at once admits me to the school.

Right now, I'm walking home on Broadway. I look around and see people, buildings, roads around me, and I feel blessed.

MY MAMA HAS A COMPANION

It's Saturday morning, and the phone is ringing. I answer the call. It is the man that my mother is dating.

From what I know, he's a Jewish man who is a schoolteacher. His name is Eric Gaster. He's tall, well-built, and handsome. Eric is very much involved with the family and is often in the apartment.

My sisters like him very much, and he has their approval. My mother's friend will eventually have mine.

CULTURE SHOCK

It's Monday already, and I'm taking the bus from 98th Street to 85th Street on Broadway. I'm getting acquainted with the neighborhood.

As I enter the school, it seems to me that I'm in a mansion, not a school. I feel out of place, as the kid who just has left a nun's boarding school in Zipaquirá. I'm a timid girl who is constantly struggling to survive.

I'm afraid of what may be ahead in my life as an immigrant. However, I'm managing to portray bravery and strength.

Being a teenager in New York is not easy. I have left behind my roots, those traditions that are the support of people's formative years.

No longer is the cumbia or the tropical music on the radio or television; instead, there's Elvis, The Beatles, The Monkees, and the too-skinny body of Twiggy, the role model of young girls of the time.

I love American music, especially Elvis Presley's music. But Latino music is part of my DNA.

I'm discovering the diversity among Latino cultures at school from my classmates. People from the Caribbean are transparent. They use their words without sugarcoating. They like music and dance to the rhythm of merengue and salsa.

I think about how Latin American people portray different behaviors.

Argentineans speak Spanish with an Italian language intonation, and some use the two languages to communicate.

Mexicans are sentimental, and their songs are usually on themes of romantic love involving deception and suffering.

Colombian people are absent from Brandeis High School, but I know my culture and I will never forget it. Colombian culture is very similar to elite Spanish society. People from Bogotá are proper and reflect the noblemen who once went there in search of El Dorado, the abundance of gold.

I'm a happy student, and I look forward to going to school every day; I'm making male friends for the first time in my life. But it's a revelation. I go from praying the rosary and guarding my virginity to seeing marijuana cigarettes passing under the desks in the classrooms; from not being allowed to talk about boys to listening to my female classmates talk about sex acts.

I ask Yahim how I can manage these situations, and he tells me, "These are trivial things in life. Concentrate on your goals and the eternal lessons you need to learn. Sex is a gift of God, and it should be treated as a treasure, not as trash."

SUCCEEDING AT SCHOOL

I'm in my second semester at Brandeis High School after the summer break. During the summer, I worked in a clothes factory with my mother.

I'm now a proud eleventh-grade student, and I finally begin to trust myself and believe I can learn. I'm breaking the chains that have kept me lagging behind in my academics for years. I consider the classes easier and the teachers friendlier in the United States. At times, I want some attention, and I act like a bit of a clown. My homeroom teacher has a way to redirect me to proper behavior.

Sometimes, when we have presentations at school, I recite my poems, and the audience likes my performance.

I dream of going to college at Columbia University. It's close to home; hence, I walk up along Broadway from 98th Street to 114th Street, usually on Saturday afternoons. I go on campus and see young people walking around with books under their arms and sitting on the lawn.

I hope one day I'll become a student here.

MY COLLEGE DREAM IS IN MY MIND

It's December 1967, and I finished the semester with straight A's.

I'm under the shower and daydream about my academic future. I'm enthusiastic because I'm going to graduate from high school in three semesters. I will then enroll at Columbia University, and eventually, I will become a teacher, a poet, and a writer.

The Father recently wrote a letter to my mama, where he said he's planning to get me a scholarship to study in Spain. Spain is the best choice for me since my native language is Spanish, and I would pursue a career in literature with the goal of eventually becoming a writer.

On the other hand, I could attend Columbia University, learn the English language, and become an English writer.

I have a dilemma because I love to read Pablo Neruda, Ruben Dario, and Gabriela Mistral's short stories and poems. When I was ten, I read *La Vorágine*, a Colombian novel written by José Eustasio Rivera.

But the reality is that I'm in the United States, and I don't plan to go back to Colombia.

I strive to understand the tragic tales of Edgar Allan Poe and the deep sentimental poems written by Emily Dickinson. My English is in its infancy, and all I have is the rhythm of its sounds and a minimal vocabulary. However, I have proved to myself that I can learn, and one day, I will be fluent in the English language if I continue trying to learn the language.

My mind switches gears, and I'm thinking about going to the movies the following Saturday to watch *Romeo and Juliet*. I have a fascination for Shakespeare's writings, even though I don't understand much old English.

THE DREAM WORLD IS OVER

Mama and Marie are calling me to the kitchen. They need to speak to me. I put my robe on and place a towel on my head while walking to the kitchen to meet them.

Mama speaks first. "You have an interview for a job at the Dean Witter Company tomorrow morning. That is a good job for you, and you will do well there."

I'm surprised about the announcement and ask Mama and Marie, "And school, how about the school? I'm doing well there."

Marie makes eye contact with me, and I'm back to my harsh reality. "It's time for you contribute financially to the household since you are eighteen now."

My dreaming has to stop. I swallow my tears once again because there is no place in the apartment to call my own or my safe place.

It's Monday morning again. Instead of going to Brandeis High School, I go with Marie to Two Broadway and take the elevator to the seventeenth floor.

My new boss is a good man. Mr. Ritz doesn't ask any questions because he knows my English is limited. He hires me on the spot to work as a file clerk for the stock market participants.

In the meantime, Mama goes to the school to withdraw me regardless of my teachers complaining. They beg her to reconsider it. I'm doing so well, and they think I have a future if I can graduate from high school. Mama cries, but she doesn't reconsider it.

I have become a high school dropout today.

It's tough to fit in at my new job. I speak very limited, broken English, and other young workers make fun of my accent. I develop a defense mechanism and laugh at all they say, accepting their derogatory remarks and their put-downs. My behavior gives them space to make jokes about the way I look, talk, and walk. I have a pronounced bust, and they make fun of that too. I laugh because it's the only thing I can do to defend myself.

There is a guy I like. He's about twenty years old, and his name is Tony. He also makes fun of me. I go along with the jokes, but I suffer intensely. As far as the job I perform, I do very well.

A few months have gone by, and I am doing well at my filing clerk position. Mr. Ritz is sending me to another company on

Wall Street to be trained in the skill of keypunch operation. Soon after, I'm typing cards at the keypunch machine.

Despite the fact that I'm making good money at the job and am paying for the apartment rent and my personal needs and wants, I feel sad and lonesome.

My two sisters, Marie and Lucy, are married now, and they have moved to California; hence, the apartment is very quiet. I work all the time, and when I go home, I'm usually tired. I like to work hard because that helps me with my loneliness.

Mama is busy dating Eric, and I'm busy at work or home writing poems. I have a couple of friends, and I talk to them a couple of days a week, but I hardly see them. I cannot go anywhere because my mother is afraid that something bad may happen to me if I leave the house without her.

Eric, my mother's friend, is recommending that I pursue my goal to earn my high school diploma. Eric has given me information about an adult school near Wall Street, where evening high school classes are being offered. I will give it a try, even though working for the stock market implies working overtime in the evenings.

I enroll and present myself at class on a Tuesday evening. I feel inept when it comes to learning high school subjects. I return on Wednesday, and the teacher is going over algebraic equations. All that I know about the subject freezes in my mind. I cannot even do basic math.

It's Tuesday again, and I'm in class for the third time. The teacher gives us a quiz, which I fail. I'm ashamed and want to disappear.

A man seated by me notices my demeanor and glances at the low grade on my paper. He tells me, "This is not a place for you. You're wasting your time and the time of your classmates because you're never going to learn."

The teacher is a tall man with a soft demeanor. He hears the derogatory comment about my school performance. He tells us he's a Jewish man who came to America from Poland with his parents when he was a little boy escaping the Holocaust.

He is a good man and tells me, "Don't believe him. You can learn and succeed. Believe in yourself; if you doubt yourself, read the story of the Holocaust."

I look at him, and I read compassion in his eyes. Since I know all the recent history of the Jewish people, I feel his pain and the pain of his people as if I'm one of them. When I connect with his eyes, I know he was someone I knew in my earlier life. Nevertheless, I decide that I will not return to that school because I feel incapable of learning.

I'm going home now and taking the first train that goes by at the subway station. I exit from the station, and I think I can transfer at another stop to take the train that for sure will take me home. Leaving the train station, I begin walking without any destination. I'm feeling a tremendous sadness. There is a Catholic church on the way. It's open; hence, I go in, sit on a bench, and cry inconsolably. I kneel, and my sobbing continues.

A man comes from behind the altar. He tries to console me, but I don't understand what he's saying. I run out the door, leaving the man puzzled.

As I find the train that will finally take me home, I reason, "Getting a high school diploma is not for me. I should conform and accept the fact that I don't have the financial means nor the intelligence to accomplish it."

I arrive home, and Mama doesn't question why I'm coming home at 10:00 p.m.

CIRCLE OF LATIN AMERICAN WRITERS AND POETS

Mama goes to church on Sundays at Notre Dame Cathedral, a Catholic church next to Columbia University. She knows how much I like to write poetry and strikes up a conversation at church with Dr. Cepedo, a scholar from Mexico City who teaches Spanish at Columbia University.

Mama shares with that professor that her eighteen-year-old daughter loves to write poetry. He suggests that I attend the Circle of Latin American Writers and Poets (CEPI) meetings to have the opportunity to meet other Hispanic poets.

When Mama tells me about it, I become excited about going to the meetings. It will be nice to share my poetry with other poets.

Going to the CEPI meetings becomes my hobby. I plan what poems to take with me to share with other writers. Dr. Cepedo and other CEPI members are giving me a title. I'm named "La emperatriz del CEPI." *The Empress of CEPI.*

Today is a special Sunday because I have the good news that some of us have been selected by Dr. Cepedo to appear in *El Tiempo*, the Spanish newspaper, with a photo and a short biography.

I'm astonished. Even though I joined just a few weeks back, my name, biography, and poem will be published. At this point and with the members' consensus, I'm formally named "La emperatriz del CEPI." It's an honor.

The enigma for the audience is why a young girl's poetry is pessimistic and sad. I know it has to do with the sorrows of my earlier lives.

Mystical Notes: Strengths

I'm in deep meditation in my bedroom at our apartment near Riverside Drive in New York. I'm thinking about the mysteries of life and why I'm usually sad and troubled. I am happy I have the strength to overcome loneliness and my sad feelings.

I ask Yahim to come and talk to me because he may have an answer for me. He shows up looking brilliant and beautiful.

He says to me, "Your eternal soul is alert and has remembered painful lives where you have been oppressed, or people who you cared about have been victimized. Someone you knew in your previous life wore small shoes to escape from oppression, and that was painful. You captured some of her pain; hence, wearing small shoes has become a symbol of oppression to you."

Yahim continues, "You are growing in strength and tolerance. My dear Eugenia, you have lived many lives before. Some of those lives have been of bliss and happiness. Some others have been of sadness and sorrows, and others a mixture. Tell me, my dear Eugenia, what lesson has affected you the most up to now?"

I'm thinking about the question. I cannot express all I want to say.

Tarboo takes the task of being my voice. "It's a healthy process to remember past lives to process virtues, qualities, and feelings that come along with our being. By recalling past-life scenarios, conflicts, and even happy events, an individual understands and accepts his or her idiosyncrasies, failures, talents, barriers to success, and the strength needed to understand ways to self-growth. I have learned that all happens for a reason, and challenging tasks are necessary to nurture the soul, to find peace, balance, and happiness.

"I have also learned that we are in the largest school ever created, the school of Mother Earth. We learn from our parents, siblings, friends, and people of the world. We even learn while we sleep, when the Masters help us recollect memories of other lives in dreams or insights that clarify our ongoing dilemmas."

Tarboo has written a poem about what I'm thinking right now and is ready to recite it for Yahim and me. Thank you, Tarboo.

LIVING

I have dreamed of an ample plane
Where it's possible to start anew
With the ones who were once
Your partners in the adventure in this world
And I have felt the love of God when I need to see His light

Who am I, and where did I start?
It's the enormous mystery of life
My eternal mind is telling me to consider what I think
That I'm an immortal soul, being fed by an enormous star

Since my early days, someplace afar
I have known that I have a very long past
Many lives I have lived on Earth and in some other planes
But my reasoning and the human mind keep me from accepting that.

We are on the move coming and returning to the other side
To the issues we left pending in this land
Soon we have to rush back to our eternal home
With the ones who are forever waiting for us
In a home that gives us bliss that no human can understand

CHAPTER SIX

PREDICTIONS

MARLENE, 1939

OLD IS NEW; NEW IS OLD!

Time is ageless.
Framed in months and framed in years
Life is time, and time won't stop
Enjoy your moments; soon, they'll go
To the forever space, time will run

INSTABILITY IN CZECHOSLOVAKIA

The tick-tock of the grandfather clock is the only sound present in the austere ambiance in my parents' house in Sternberk. I'm sitting near the clock, with my doll Ollie on my lap. I imagine stories of the past and predictions for the future while becoming mesmerized by the enchanting sound of the clock chiming.

The tall walls of the spacious living room welcome the short rays of sun that filter through the narrow windows. It's March 15th in the spring of 1939, and I'm ten years old.

I still carry my rag doll with golden braids. Its pale complexion resembles a fading lily. It reminds me of the times I played house with Theresa, my friend from school, in the backyard at home in Munich. My Ollie and my Star of David pendant are the only tangible memories I have from my two sisters, Ruth and Abigail. I miss them very much, and I know my father does too, even though he is always absentminded.

My uncles have taken over the clock shop because they need a place to sell the produce and dairy from the farm. The clocks are not selling. They just stand there displaying their class and elegance. The store's name has changed from *Margotski's Clock Shop* to *Hardwick's Apron Food Store*. My father has consented to the deal because the family needs a stable income. Everyone who enters the shop wants the clocks, but they need to eat first.

When I'm in my bedroom, I make believe we're a carefree family, and I hold my Ollie because she helps me imagine that I can fly far away to many places around the world. My imagination goes to places where I know deep in my heart I have been before. I also imagine savoring delicious foods since we don't have much to eat at home.

Papa is still going to Munich and is bringing me German chocolates. I hide them in the attic. But if they're not available, I still imagine I have them at my disposal.

THE FOOD IS TASTELESS

I know it's 5:00 p.m. because the clock has chimed seventeen times. It's freezing, and the sun is not shining today.

I'm kneeling by my bed, trying to refuse Mama's call to the kitchen for supper. I try to eat the boiled cabbage and potatoes. That food is tough to swallow, and it's tasteless. I seldom complain because my job is to keep my mama happy. I think I can eat it with pleasure by imagining the food Mama serves me is delicious, much tastier than the food Esther used to cook in Munich.

Hilda wants me to eat it because I'm too skinny, and my collarbones are visible. My arms and legs show how hunger has taken its toll on my little body. Mama worries about me and strives to keep me healthy and warm. She knitted a blanket for me to keep me warm.

DEVASTATING NEWS

Alfred is in Munich. Hilda and I fear that Abigail is in imminent danger. It's morning time; we hear Papa coming home. He comes into the bedroom where Mama and I are still sleeping.

Papa wakes us up and bursts into tears. "They took Abigail and Esther. They raided the house, and they took them to Dachau, the detention camp in Munich. I want to die; I don't deserve to live. I betrayed my daughters, my faith, my ethnicity, and I abandoned my daughters."

Papa is sobbing, and Mama consoles him.

I get up from my parents' bed and go to my room to cry alone. Yahim's prediction is manifesting.

I'm afraid.

WHERE DOES PAPA GO?

Papa seems confused and moves his hands all the time in front of his belly. He's trying to find clarity of mind and a grasp of reality. What worries Mama and me the most is that Papa often disappears for days. We know he's not going to Munich anymore because Abigail is no longer in his house, and the shop in Sternberk is, by now, *Hardwick's Apron Food Store.* He doesn't have a job there anymore.

Mama speaks to Henry in private, and he promises her he will help her figure out where my father goes when he's not with us. When I'm with Papa, I try to look into his eyes and make eye contact, but he refuses it. I think he's hiding something.

There are rumors in town that there is a secret place where people go to gamble. Uncle Henry says that it's a house owned by Romani people. Men are coming and going all night long to that place. It seems to be a site used for conducting illegal activities. We know that Papa is up to no good.

Alfred used to have lots of money saved in a safety box in his bedroom, but not anymore. There is absolutely nothing in there since its door is wide open. I figure he doesn't have money at the bank because the Germans closed them for good. The only income we have is the money my uncles give Mama for groceries and the money Mama makes by selling some of her vegetables from our garden. But what does Papa do with all his well-earned money? Henry decides to unveil the mystery, and so he goes on that mission.

Papa and Uncle Henry arrive at 2:00 a.m. and Alfred looks angry, and so does Henry. Mama is asking Henry what is going on with Papa. He says, "Look at your husband; he was gambling with dice in the company of lowlifes. That is where all his money goes. Now, he's penniless. He's putting all of us in danger. The SS officials have already labeled him as the next Jewish man they need to arrest."

Mama looks at Uncle Henry as if she doesn't understand what he's saying, so he repeats himself. "He's gambling away his money, your money, and the money we give him."

Papa breaks down in tears. He annoys me when he cries. Alfred explains to us he lost everything before he started to go to the gambling place.

Martha steps into our home at Sternberk. Papa, Mama, and I are talking in the living room. She's bringing news about new detention camps in our area.

She declares, "The Germans are building a new detention camp near here, in Poland, and its name is Auschwitz."

I'm seated by Papa's feet. I notice his demeanor changing in a split second; I know his mood change is due to his memories of my sisters, Ruth and Abigail. I stare at him just the way his other two daughters used to fixate on him while he told stories about his ancestors. I know that his mind is gone; however, I also know that he understands what Martha is saying.

I turn my eyes to the grandfather clock with an intent to become disconnected from the information we received from Martha. Then, I'm becoming mesmerized as I look at its hands, pointing to every second, every minute. I watch its hands slowly moving in a clockwise motion.

At this moment, I remember how Alfred used to tell me great-grandfather Abraham's fables and how much those stories enriched my imagination.

MAURICE SHARES HIS HAPPINESS

It's a Friday afternoon, and Uncle Maurice comes to visit us. We seldom sit on the porch, and I'm cold. However, we are enjoying his company. Maurice tells us he has found the love of his life, and he's getting married soon.

Mama doesn't seem that surprised. I am because I have never seen him with a girl before. He says that Margarette is seventeen years old, and once they get married, they plan to leave for New York.

MARRIAGE ON THE HORIZON

A week has gone by. Maurice and Margarette come to visit us. The whole family is here, even Alfred. Margarette looks much younger than her real age. Maurice shares with us that they will leave for America, and her parents are joining them.

Margarette speaks with her fragile voice and says she will take advantage of her childhood looks and is going to wear her First Communion shoes that still fit her feet, even though they're very tight. Maurice says that is a terrific idea, because if her feet get bruised, she can show them to the ship captain before she embarks for the new country to appeal for compassion.

I feel very sad for Margarette, and I am already feeling the pain she will endure on her feet. It's a pain of oppression that has been imposed on the Jewish people and other peoples who are controlled by the Third Reich. No wonder Maurice and Margarette are willing to do anything to leave this oppressed society.

We're all happy for them, and Patrick brings some wine from the cellar. They drink and toast for the young couple. Margarette and I don't drink.

A few weeks have gone by, and my Uncle Henry has found out from an informant in England that Maurice, Margarette, and her parents made it to the ship. His source said that indeed the plan of Margarette wearing small shoes worked. The bruises and the spots of blood on her feet made the captain of the ship feel sorry for her; hence, all the family went aboard.

HENRY, MY LITERATE UNCLE

My Uncle Henry is diligent at performing tasks at the farm, but he stays with us most of the time. He only goes to the farm a couple of days each week to pick up whatever vegetables the Jewish people have harvested for us to sell at Hardwick's Apron Food Store.

I see my uncle reading most of the time. I ask where the books come from. Henry tells me the priest and some Jewish people give them to him. He also has books from before the political uneasiness occurred.

Henry is clever and uses his imagination to protect the books. He hides them in a long aluminum box he built. It's in the corner of the garden, along with some expensive gardening tools. Uncle Henry also has an identical box with the same kind of gardening tools in our garden. I sometimes think that my uncle can perfectly fit in either of the two boxes. He makes sure the books are well wrapped in plastic before storing them at the farm and our home.

PATRICK AND THE FARM

Uncle Patrick is in his mid-thirties, and the demands of life, including the role he assumed of being the father figure for his siblings, have taken their toll. He has some gray hair and is a little overweight in the belly.

However, there is something else in Patrick's life besides his family that keeps him motivated. It's a woman. She's a tall, skinny Jewish woman with big sad brown eyes and long eyelashes. I notice they're in love because they look funnily at each other.

MY UNCLE MARK ISN'T HAPPY

Ever since my Uncle Maurice left for America, Mark looks very sad. He sits on the porch most of the time. The only thing that Mark finds appealing is drinking from the wine that is in the cellar. When he goes out, he comes back home very late and is usually drunk. When I ask him anything about his life, he stares at me and doesn't answer.

My room has an extra bed, and my father and Uncle Mark sleep there. I have moved to my mother's room permanently.

THE PROTECTORS

The year is 1942, and everyone is worried about the uncertainty of the government and our future.

I'm thirteen years old now and I feel a knot in my chest all the time, as if I'm about to burst into tears. I want to be happy, and I can't. My only escape is to let my imagination float.

I can feel the desperation of Jewish people who swing by our house before going into hiding in sympathetic people's homes. They have managed to arrive at Olomouc from all over Germany and Europe.

The demand for shelters is high. We have two spare rooms: one in the attic and the other in the cellar. Therefore, we should share our home.

It's Tuesday, about 2:00 a.m. My Uncle Henry is coming home with five people. He's saying he found them hiding near the road. They're cold and hungry. He says we need to keep them in our home because if we don't, the authorities will take them, and they will be doomed.

Henry introduces us to two little orphan girls who are twins. Their names are Matilda and Margola. Also, there are three other people: father, mother, and daughter. Their names are Marco, Johana, and Elsa. She's about sixteen.

Mama decides the twin girls will go to the attic because they're only eight, and she will be able to care for them better that way. The family of three will go to the cellar.

Mystical Notes: Predictions

As I rest on my bed, I'm reflecting on the uncertainty of what is coming to me, my family, and the world.

Then I see Yahim as he sometimes presents himself, radiant in his purple tunic and a sweet smile on his lips.

Tarboo follows as always, looking pensive and inspiring and ready to use his gift with words. His green tunic has a gray tone today.

Tarboo looks at me and reads what I have in my thoughts. He, as always, utters my thoughts in profound flowery words: "I'm thankful because my two Masters are here. I feel lonesome, even though I have a family that loves me and nurtures me."

Yahim notices my sadness and asks me what is the most important lesson I have learned from my sorrows.

I respond through Tarboo's voice, "I'm overwhelmed with the predictions of my final doom that I so strongly sense. But I'm learning to surrender to the uncertainty. This issue is forcing me to mature way beyond my years. I think a lot about great-grandfather Abraham and his poetry. When I close my eyes, I see him, just the way Papa used to describe him to me. When I'm sad, I think that I can find wisdom in the thorn of the rose that stands for my life. I am the petals, and I can turn the thorns into wisdom as I let go of what I cannot change."

Yahim takes over and tells me, "You have been brave, my dear. Always remember that this shall also pass."

Tarboo is ready to recite the poem he extracted from my melancholic spirit. He recites it to Yahim and me, and we're attentive.

UNCERTAINTY

Uncertainty is torture, and we're trapped
As birds in nests without wings, banned from flying high
Because the beasts of prey are waiting for our flesh to have
And take us by force in torture as they tear us apart
Hiding? The solution for now, but they will soon devour us

Oh! God, for my people, I fear, and I'm also your child
Please tell me how and tell me why
People who hate us and our dead want
What have we done; how did we fail to act?

Please, my dear Lord, come and rescue us
I know you're listening and helping us you want

Some monsters are thirsty and our blood they crave
God, in your tears, I want to blend mine

Little children, do they need the sacrifice?
All the Jewish people, young and old alike?
Give me some light; I need to understand
I know you're listening and the strength you will let me have

The heavens are waiting for us, and I should know that
After the storm, the sun always shines
With music and angels, the homecoming will start
Your omnipotence will guide us to surrender in your arms
The bells of tranquility up there will chime

CHAPTER SEVEN

REASONING

EUGENIA, 1968

ENIGMA

The mysteries are many, realities are few
I'm anxious to discover
What is there awaiting on my path
Joys and sorrows are surprises
That the end of each journey seems ephemeral on the eternal path

IS ROMANCE POSSIBLE?

I'm eighteen years old, and I'm financially independent. I'm responsible for the rent at Mama's apartment, and I pay other household bills without any difficulties. Mama buys groceries, and she saves money for her trips to Colombia.

I'm content most of the time; however, I become melancholic when I hear the other girls at work have boyfriends. I see couples kissing in the parks or on television programs, and I want the experience too.

The possibilities of finding a boyfriend are few because many boys my age are in Vietnam, and there are not many young men around who I would consider dating. There are former armed forces young men at work who have just returned from the Vietnam War. Some of them smoke pot, and others are addicted to acid and other drugs.

Besides, I'm a girl without their language. My culture is opposite to theirs, and there are not Latino boys in the office.

I think I will never find a date that will agree to take my mother along as a chaperone.

Mama continues going on her dates on Fridays and Saturdays. I'm alone on weekends.

Today is Friday, and I decide to get some wine on my way home. There is a liquor store on 97th Street and Broadway. I'm stopping at that liquor store. The clerk is not asking me for my ID because I'm hiding my face behind my long hair. I'm walking through the aisles, looking for an inexpensive bottle of wine. I have seen my mother purchase Manischewitz wine, so that is what I want.

No one is home because Mama and Eric are on a date. I have the apartment for myself and my wine. I go to my room, close the door, and drink two-thirds of the bottle. I have never drunk wine before. It tastes sweet and soft.

I'm sleeping. Master Yahim is by my bed, and he looks sad.

Suddenly, I feel a flash of wind going through the closed window at a tremendous speed. I think he's not happy because I'm drunk. I am reasoning that getting drunk does not help me to enrich my soul.

WILL I FIND LOVE?

I hope to find a wonderful man who will make me happy for the rest of my life. He will marry me in the Catholic church, and he will be the father of my three daughters. I keep on dreaming of finding the love of my life.

It feels like it's time because most of my sisters married at eighteen, and I don't want to be an "old maid." That is what I heard when I was younger, "Marry young, or you will end up being an old maid."

Even my two sisters, Marie, and Lucy, are already married and living happily in Los Angeles. My mother has a boyfriend, and I'm alone. But my prince charming is going to bring along so much suffering.

MEETING ANDREAS

It's Wednesday evening, and I'm leaving the office and am on my way home; I stop at the ladies room before exiting the seventeenth floor where the Dean Witter offices are.

It's empty, and I feel good about it because I can send a prayer to God, "Dear God, I know I have a new lesson to learn with a man I'm going to meet soon. Let it be tonight because I feel lonesome, and I'm ready for the upcoming adventure of understanding what it is to have a boyfriend."

I walk down Wall Street on my way to the subway station, and I'm embedded in my thoughts. The train ride is smooth, maybe because it's not the express train. The in-out of passengers at each stop entertains me. Soon, I find myself at 96th Street and Broadway.

As I ascend the steps at the subway station, I notice a man looking at me. I'm not afraid but delighted. He has intense blue eyes, and he's good-looking. I walk fast, but he walks at my same pace. When we arrive at the corner of 98th Street and Broadway, we both stop walking.

I feel curious and excited at the same time. I'm pleased because deep in the core of my soul, I know that meeting this man will help me deal with unfinished business I left pending in the past and another life. We have deep eye contact. His shining eyes reflect freedom and carelessness.

I experience empathy toward him. Why do I feel sorry for someone I just met? This is insane.

We continue walking together and arrive at my apartment building at 317 W. 98th Street.

I look at him and say goodbye as if I have done it before. He asks for my phone number, and I look in my purse for a pen or paper to write on.

I know that giving my phone number to a strange man is not right, but I do it anyway. I see a piece of paper in my purse, but no pen. I decide my lipstick can serve as a writing tool, and I write my phone number down. We say our goodbyes as I go inside the building, and he goes his way.

IS IT WISE TO DATE ANDREAS?

While Mama serves my supper, I sit at the kitchen table. She asks me how my day was.

I tell her, "I met the most interesting man just a few minutes ago. He has the most beautiful blue eyes, and there is more to it. I know him from a previous life."

Mama is looking at me as if I'm crazy. She doesn't enjoy my comment and leaves the kitchen.

I'm in my bedroom now, and I'm having second thoughts about this guy. I don't feel comfortable dating him. It's as if Yahim is trying to send me a message, that dating him will mean many tears for me.

Andreas is persistent because he calls me every evening, and I don't know if I want to talk to him. I like him a lot, but I suspect that dating him will cause many problems; honestly, I don't want to put myself in this position. Nevertheless, I feel a tremendous force pushing me toward that man.

I know I have had my share of strikes; hence, I should protect myself from difficult situations. But the pushing force is powerful. This force is, in my essence, pushing me to abide by some old contract I agreed to a long time ago.

I have suffered tremendously from what I have lived in this life—feelings of abandonment. Hence, I have the dilemma of giving Andreas a chance or not.

I told my mama that if he calls me, to tell him that I'm not home. She did so, but he's calling me again, and Mama answers the phone. I'm telling Mama not to let him know I'm here. She passes the phone receiver to me and says, "You tell him."

Before I can tell him anything, Andreas tells me that he will throw away the flowers and champagne he bought for me. I decide to let him come upstairs because if he insists so much, I should let him in; besides, Mama just signaled to me that she is okay with him visiting me at the apartment.

The Greek man is charming, but my mama is staring at the watch on his wrist. It's missing its hands. I'm wondering what good it is to wear a watch without its hands.

Andreas just arrived from Greece; hence, he speaks broken English. Mama approves of him because the young man speaks some Spanish. He talks to us about his worldwide traveling experiences. Andreas opens the bottle of champagne, and the three of us drink from it.

Towards the end of the evening, my mother asks Andreas what he does for a living. Without hesitation, he says, "I'm a cook. I started as a dishwasher. I did a good job, so I became a busboy in no time. Now I cook, and my boss is pleased with me. I never steal, and I work hard."

Mama tells him and me that the only way he may continue visiting me in our apartment is if he introduces us to some people who know him. He smiles with charm and tells us we're going to his friend's house the following day. His Greek friend is married to a woman from Nicaragua.

It's Sunday noon. Mama and I are just returning from church. Andreas is already waiting for us at the front door of the apartment building. He's ready to take us to see his Greek friend and Nicaraguan wife. The couple greets us with kindness, and the lady offers us a delicious Greek meal.

We're having a conversation with the lady. Andreas is talking to his Greek friend. Before we leave, my mother makes sure to ask the Nicaraguan lady for her phone number.

REASONING WITH MOTHER

Once back home after Andreas has left our apartment, Mama tells me that she wants me to find a husband because matrimony is the way for a girl to keep her status and dignity. Being single and going out with different boys is dangerous and unhealthy.

She also tells me that Andreas is not the man for me. I'm sad about her comments, but I'm aware that she's right.

I'm in bed now, and my thoughts are going all over the place. I want to get married because it's what young women do back home in Colombia. I'm over eighteen, and if I wait any longer, I will become a childless and unhappy old maid.

It's Monday, and I just returned home from work. It's not that late since the stock market closed earlier this evening. As I'm eating my supper—white rice, beef stew, and fried plantains—Mama is telling me she spoke with the Nicaraguan lady earlier today, and she said that Andreas likes to gamble heavily. That he previously had a serious girlfriend who broke up with him because of his gambling habits.

My mother is telling me to let him go. I should not get involved with him, and I know it. If I continue seeing him, I'm setting myself up for great suffering and deception. I am listening to the voice of reason. I will let go of my impulses, and I will put a stop to our romance before we start dating.

It's Tuesday evening, and Andreas is waiting for me in front of Two Broadway. He invites me to have coffee at a coffee shop near Wall Street because he says he has to tell me something serious about him. I also want to convey to him that I cannot be with him, and that we have to let go of each other.

I reason within myself that we're different because we come from opposite backgrounds. For instance, I speak Spanish and broken English. He speaks Greek, a little Spanish, and very limited English. How are we going to communicate on a deeper level? Also, his parents are across the sea, and I would like to know about the family of the man I may begin dating. I don't know anything about Greek culture and the concept of gambling in his country.

We have arrived at the coffee shop, but I ask him to take me to Riverside Drive and 98th Street instead since I want to be closer to my apartment. I figure I need to go home soon after our conversation, and I don't know how to react. He agrees, and we take the train that will take us there. We're at Wall Street train station and en route to 96th Street and Broadway on the express train.

We're at Riverside Drive Park, standing below a large tree with thick roots. He looks straight into my eyes and tells me he's happy because we're together; Andreas reaches into his pocket and takes out a ten-cent coin. "I'm broke, and I don't have anyone who loves me near me. They all are in Greece: my mama, my papa, my brother, my sister. You're my only hope."

Before I have the chance to tell him my prepared speech, he takes me into his arms and kisses me with frenzied passion.

This is the first time a boy has ever kissed me. The flesh at work has managed to set aside my reasoning, my logical thinking. My mother's advice and my common sense vanish. My instincts have taken over my reasoning.

EMPATHY OR EMPATH

A few days have passed since I did not break up with Andreas. We meet every evening at Battery Park, by Two Broadway, the building where I work. Then, we take the subway to 96th Street to go to Riverside Drive by my apartment building.

There is strong chemistry between us, but there is also a unique sense of hopelessness on my part. I have a strange need to help him, as if he stands for unfinished business from the past. It's as though he needs my help to heal old injuries, and the only one who can help him is me.

126

We're at Riverside Drive Park now, and Andreas proposes matrimony to me. I accept him as my fiancé because he wants to marry me.

I'm taken by surprise since we have not dated much. What is up with this man that he wants to marry me so fast? I'm confused.

He's telling me that I make him feel as if he has family in this country. As he pants, he says he misses his family a lot and wants to go back to Greece. My boyfriend explains that he wanted to stay in Athens when he left the Greek Armed Forces but he could not do so because there were no jobs there.

THE MAKE-BELIEVE HAS BEGUN

Andreas is waiting for me at the subway exit at 96th Street and Broadway. I'm returning home from work, and he wants us to go to the park and sit on a bench. I agree. We talk about our wedding plans. I tell him I want to get married in the Catholic Church. He agrees. I ask him if we can marry in the Greek Orthodox Church as well, and he says that is possible.

Andreas dreams about having a rug business. He will import Persian carpets, and we will have a lucrative income, and eventually, we will be rich.

What I'm hearing are the words of a man who has big dreams. He sounds like he wants to be the right provider for his future family. I like what I'm hearing, and I believe in his dreams.

After a long pause and a flaming kiss, he proceeds with the conversation and tells me something that shocks me. He's undocumented in this country. When he arrived in New York, he jumped from a ship and swam to shore. Andreas ended up in The Village in Manhattan and is working for a Greek man in a restaurant.

My feelings of empathy for Andreas are beyond reality. I think about ways to make him feel better. And the worst of all is that I'm falling in love. When I sit on a bench at the park, I feel safe near him. His masculinity, his vibration, his essence are endearing to me.

It's the first time in my life that I'm close to a man. My subconscious mind announces that I have met him before, and I'm back with him for a particular reason.

MAMA DESPERATELY ATTEMPTS TO PROTECT ME

It's early afternoon on a Saturday, and the apartment is quiet since neither Andreas nor Eric is visiting. Mama uses this quiet time to advise me again about my relationship with Andreas. She's telling me that she likes my boyfriend but doesn't want me to marry him. She's telling me the gambling is an addiction, and I will have to suffer the consequences for not listening to her.

I think about it, but it's too late because I'm crazy in love with him. My saga is about to begin.

MY ENGAGEMENT RING

My relationship with Andreas continues regardless of my mother's advice.

As time goes on, I take on the role of Andreas's caregiver, and he loves it. I buy him shirts, vitamins, and remind him to stay in contact with his family in Greece. He wants to marry me, but he doesn't have any money to buy me a ring.

It's Saturday evening. Andreas and I are visiting in the living room of the apartment. He tells me he wants to buy me an engagement ring but doesn't have any money to buy one.

Mama overhears Andreas's comment and joins us in the living room. I'm surprised when she tells us she wants to help with the purchase of the ring. She has a jewelry box in her hands and opens it for us to see what she has in it. There is an engagement ring with a tiny white topaz. I get up from the sofa and stand by her to admire the pretty white gold ring.

Donelia tells us she's selling jewelry for a co-worker from the factory. If Andreas buys it, he can pay for it in installments. My mother tells us there is not a profit for her if we decide to buy it.

Thanks to my mother, I'm finally getting the engagement ring. I know deep in my soul that this is not right. He should be the one shopping for the ring, not my mother.

It has been about four months since I started dating Andreas, and my obsession to help him with all his difficulties continues growing. For instance, he cannot get a better job because he's undocumented. Once we marry, I can sponsor him to get his legal residency in this country. He will stop gambling, and we can have a prosperous and happy life together. We will have three children, if not more. The firstborn may be a boy, and Andreas will name him Spiros, as he has told me many times. But that is him, because what I want is a baby girl.

A WEIRD DREAM

I have a very vivid dream. I know I'm sleeping, yet I'm aware that my mother and boyfriend are in the living room. I think I'm in another dimension. I'm hiding with other people because we're afraid to be caught by men wearing black uniforms.

I feel suffocated by being confined among other people in a small room. The phone wakes me up. I'm in my mother's bedroom. It's Andreas calling me. My boyfriend's voice sounds agitated as he says, "Eugenia, I've been chased by immigration officials. These men invaded the restaurant, and I think they're following me. I don't know if I will ever see you again. You're a nice girl, and I'm happy I have met you. I'm calling from a phone booth to say goodbye."

I'm crying, and my mama comes to the bedroom in alarm because of my crying. Eric follows and tells me I should not tolerate him calling me to upset me.

Mama says that it's time for me to break off my relationship with Andreas.

A few minutes have gone by, and Andreas calls again to tell me he's in a friend's apartment on 28th Street and Broadway and that he's safe. Mama and Eric are upset at him, but I'm happy because he evaded the immigration authorities.

THE WEDDING PLANS

Christmas season of 1969 is coming to its end. And we want to get married soon. We have set a date for May. It's Saturday morning, and I'm at Riverside Drive Park by myself.

I'm cold here, but I am trying to distract myself from my doubts about marrying Andreas. I'm delegating to the Virgin Mary the enormous task of keeping my upcoming marriage healthy for a long time.

As I reflect on what I'm asking of the heavens, I realize that no one manages my decision, and I will have to face the results if it doesn't go my way. I have peace of mind.

THE MARRIAGE IS IMMINENT

It's Saturday evening, and as usual, Andreas is visiting me at the apartment. We're telling my mama about our plans to have a church wedding at Notre Dame Church. Mama feels uncomfortable and just leaves the living room, obviously because she's unhappy about our plans. Andy says he needs to go home. As I go to the kitchen to grab a cookie, my mother approaches me and tells me, "For the last time, my child, stop this nonsense. This man is very charming, but he's not for you. You will shed tears of sorrow with him. He's a gambler."

I did not dare ask why, if she did not approve, she provided us with the engagement ring. I have learned to be prudent with her ever since I was ten years old and found her husband's death certificate in our home in Bogotá.

PLANNING THE WEDDING

Having the sensibility of a poet is not easy during the time of romantic decision-making. In my view, poets see the world through different lenses. I refuse to see reality as it is during this time of my life.

Andreas is giving me two hundred dollars every week to put aside for the wedding, and I have just finished paying for the engagement ring. Counting his and my savings, I can pay for all the wedding expenses and a honeymoon trip.

I made it happen my way, and we're getting married at Notre Dame Catholic Church. The reception will take place at a penthouse near Columbia University.

It's an April evening, and the weather is mild. Andreas and I are walking along the road toward Notre Dame Church to talk with the priest about the marriage approval. Suddenly, he stops walking and tells me he's scared. I tell him there's still time to change his mind. He explains that he wants to marry me but doesn't want a double church wedding; he doesn't want the Greek priest to be present. I don't object, but it gives me doubts about the love he has confessed to me many times.

We leave the church with a date in mind. We will get married on May 30th. I will wear my sister Lucy's wedding dress, and she and Marie will come from Los Angeles to be my bridesmaids. Andreas's Greek friends from the restaurant will be the groomsmen.

The maid of honor is an acquaintance from work, a timid American lady who feels honored because I ask her to fulfill this role at my wedding. Eric Gaster will walk me up to the altar, and he's proud of it. Most of the guests are friends from CEPI, and a few friends from my mama's place of work are also invited.

I have a special German friend from work who is attending the wedding. Her name is Margot. I invited her because we have coffee breaks in the lounge every morning. She's in her early fifties and was a child when World War II was going on. She likes to talk about how she never married because all the men around her age went to war and came back to her town in plastic bags. That figures.

Ironically, the pain of World War II pertained to all people on the European continent. It was not only the Jewish people who suffered. The Germans also had their share of sadness and despair. Well, enough of those thoughts, because this will be my special day, and those thoughts make me feel unhappy.

The wedding day has arrived, and all seems in order. Mother is shedding a few tears, but I feel on top of the world. We're at the reception now. The poets from CEPI have asked me to recite some of my poems. I agree, and all is wonderful. All the attendees seem to be having a good time. It's dark before we know it, and I think I have it all, even a make-believe father for the celebration, Eric Gaster.

I planned it all with a little help from my mother, and all turned out great.

THE HONEYMOON

We're in a taxi on our way from our apartment to Manhattan Grand Central Station. Andreas and I want to catch a Greyhound bus. Without planning anything, we end up in Atlantic City and stay at a Holiday Inn. We sit in the hotel room. Andreas says he wants to smoke a cigarette. It has been two hours since he left, and he just returned. It's our honeymoon night, and I feel puzzled. My saga begins on my honeymoon.

It's morning time. Andreas and I are going sightseeing. We're riding in a minibus and visiting historic buildings. After touring Atlantic City, we have decided to go farther south. Hence, we're taking another Greyhound bus. That will take us to Norfolk, Virginia.

It's dark, and we're at a hotel near the beach. My new husband leaves the room and returns after a few hours. He does the same thing he did a few days ago. I wish I knew where he goes when he leaves me in the room.

After a couple of days of beach, sun, and sightseeing, we're ready to return home. We're on the bus again, on our way back to New

York City. I notice he's not as sweet and loving as he was when we were dating. Andreas snaps at me a couple of times.

For instance, when we stopped in some town, at a convenience store to stretch and such, I told him that I was hungry. He responded, "So what do you want me to do about it?" I'm hurt, and I don't know what to do but swallow my pride. I manage not to show my frustration and sadness.

I let go of my thoughts, and while I look at two little African American girls playing with their Barbie dolls, I become mesmerized. The girls move the dolls up and down, from right to left, making motions with excellent mastery. They pretend their dolls can fly away, and my mind flies away as it composes a poem.

NOSTALGIA

I want to go back in time. I do
To feel safe and protected too
to dream of a future, beautiful and full
Without fear of an ineffable doom

I want to jump rope or play with toys
Skip on the path of a game of hopscotch
Pick up flowers hidden in large rocks
And hold them in my hands as I witness them pass

I want to be a little girl again
Without noticing that a child I'm not
The times of playing long ago passed
And my tears are hidden, and strength I must have

This little girl, a woman has become
My hair has turned from cinnamon to black
My youthful dreams were erased by time
Hence, I'm not dreaming; innocence no longer is mine
Endearment is absent; solitude is what I have

I remember episodes of my life from when I was a child. I reasoned, "Children use their imagination to escape the cruel realities of humankind." I open my eyes and notice we're arriving in New York. I will work tomorrow, but Andreas will have to look for a job now since he didn't ask for time off for our honeymoon. His boss has fired him.

We return to my mother's apartment. There are nights when I stay awake all through the night waiting for his return, but he doesn't show up. I cry until I don't have any more tears to shed. Every minute that goes by becomes more sadness trapped in my body. I wish I could look through a window facing the street to watch when he is coming home, but there are no windows facing the street at the apartment.

I fear for him because if the immigration authorities arrest him, I will never see him again. Also, there is a possibility he may be mugged or hurt in another way.

PREGNANT?

I need to go to the doctor to get a pregnancy test because I suspect I'm pregnant. Andreas takes me to Dr. Farcerotis, an obstetrician. He confirms my pregnancy.

Andreas seems optimistic and thinks all will be fine. He's finally getting a well-paid position at Maxwell's Plum Restaurant as a waiter. It's an elite restaurant in Upper East Manhattan; hence, he brings home rolls of dollars in his pocket every night from tips he receives from his customers.

It's a sad thing to admit, but my husband is living a single life. He comes and goes without thinking about me and how much I want and need to be near him.

Mama often reminds me that she told me not to marry the man. "He's a gambler, and he's going to continue with his vice."

She repeats these words all the time, and they're becoming cliché.

Mystical Notes: Reasoning

It's Saturday night. Even though I'm almost sure Andreas is not coming home tonight, I'm still hoping for his arrival. I have my eyes fixed on the window facing the other building and the dirty alley below.

I'm in a state of mesmerism and see Yahim at the window smiling at me. He talks to me about reasoning when making decisions.

"My dear Eugenia, you made a contract to save Alfred a long time ago. You don't have to sacrifice your new life with Andreas because you have the intuition that he's Alfred. Obviously, he is set in his ways, and you can avoid the contract you once made to save him from his torments."

My soul is sad because even Yahim is telling me I did wrong in marrying Andreas. Of course, my Master knows how to read my mind and opts to clarify himself.

"We all make decisions that sometimes make us suffer and live in a state of anguish. However, as we go through life, we learn from the impulses that rush us into choices that have negative outcomes. It may be the time for you to learn to reflect and reason before acting on choices.

"Before you fell in love with Andreas, you thought about letting him go. You were aware that you didn't have much in common with this Greek man. But that is then, and this is now. All lessons lived are important lessons. Now, Eugenia, what is the most important lesson you have learned from your experience of deception from Andreas?"

Tarboo always abides by his promise of being my voice when I talk to Yahim, and he says, "I'm aware that rushing into decision-making and being guided by the impulses of the flesh is an unwise approach. I own my actions, and I should learn to live with the consequences. It's not easy because those impulses may come from contracts we made with people who shared our lives in past lives. However, I'm not obliged to save the person in the agreement. I may want to help if he wants to change and asks for aid. The eternal being handles his/her doings throughout the lives he has lived. Also, the untamed desires of the flesh may create great havoc for the reward of short-lived physical pleasure."

I thank the Masters for their concern about my self-growth and terrestrial happiness, and Tarboo has a poem I composed when I wanted to stop my romantic relationship with Andreas.

REASONING

Before I know who you are and who you're not
I will let go of the hope that you might be mine
We're different, made from two different kinds
Our union is doomed; with time, it will dissolve
Tomorrow, at sunset, you from my life will depart

My darling, my man, the idea should fade
Your wife will be another who knows what you are like

Marlene and Me

I want many things that are as big as the stars
Unable you are to shine on my path

Don't try to stop me; the saying is hard
With the glance of your eyes, deep memories hide
I'm aware, I knew you, since some other life
My dear, my darling, this is not our time

It is sad to depart before firm love has struck
But it is what it is, different we are
No pains and no sorrow from any man I want
Lacerated is my spirit; please understand
Tomorrow, at sunset, our togetherness will fall apart

CHAPTER EIGHT

HONORING

MARLENE, 1942

FAMILY SUPPORT, DIVINE GIFT

Intangible is life; I'm not pretending
Soon my flesh in gray ashes will disperse
And my mission, my efforts will quietly ascend
My purity of spirit with harmony, my legacy will be
And my soul will rest in peace and bliss

INCLEMENT WEATHER

It's early December 1942, and I'm sad because I'm afraid for what is yet to come to our family and many other people in Europe. I see how the inclement weather is affecting our region through the big kitchen window at my parents' house.

The orphaned twins, Matilda and Margola, are no longer in the attic because they cannot bear the cold since the walls allow freezing weather to filter into them. The girls are sleeping on a bare mattress in Mama's bedroom, and we have accommodated them with an old blanket we had in the trunk in the attic. I sleep in my mother's bed.

My papa has moved to the attic because he could not stand sharing the room with Mark anymore. Mark snored very loudly. The family of three is still in the cellar. I don't know how they manage to stay there because it's cold in that place.

MARTHA HAS TRANSITIONED

Mama and I are going to the farmhouse because Martha, her nanny, is sick in bed. She looks pale and sad. I try to go closer to her, but my mother tells me I can't because she has the same illness her parents had when they died. It's typhoid fever again attacking our family.

I wave at her from the bedroom door, and she waves back with tears in her eyes. I want to hug Martha, but all I can do is send my love to her from where I stand. I look into my mother's eyes, and I notice an infinite sadness on her face. Martha has been the mother figure ever since she was eight years old when her parents died.

Martha says her goodbyes to my Uncle Patrick. I think he's brave because he goes into the room and stands next to her bed. He kisses her forehead.

Uncle Mark and Uncle Henry also go into the bedroom and stand by her bed for a few minutes. It's the first time I have seen my Uncle Henry cry. Uncle Mark cries too, but it doesn't affect me since he cries a lot, mostly when he's drunk.

It's Tuesday morning, and we just buried Martha. We are all in the farmhouse living room. Patrick's Jewish girlfriend has cooked some porridge made from barley and potatoes. It's warm; hence, it's soothing for the cold weather of an early April morning. Mark, Henry, Papa, Mama, and I are going home before it gets dark. Patrick stays behind with his girlfriend.

As we begin walking, the sun starts to go down. I am almost fourteen years old. I am still growing and I feel comfortable wearing the new dress, coat, and boots Uncle Henry got for me not long ago. Going to Sternberk and returning home to the farm is a routine for us. I remember, from my subconscious mind, how my feet crunched the snow on that narrow road when I was a little girl and when I was Abraham on some street in Ireland.

CALAMITIES

Mama and I worry because there are rumors in town that the SS officials are building a detention camp near us. Its name is Theresienstadt. My Uncle Henry tells me all he hears from his friends in town. They have lots of information about new detention camps that are being built and about the ongoing war.

Talking about another reality, my father is in the house all the time. He gets up in the morning, goes around the house singing Jewish hymns, and calls my sisters as if they're with us. He keeps his head shaved all the time and says he does it to honor my sisters and reconcile with his guilt. He still thinks he's a traitor to his ethnicity, family, and the Jewish community.

FORBIDDEN TO GO OUTSIDE

The winter has returned in full blast, and I hope the upcoming Christmas will bring joy to our desolation. I'm continually talking to Uncle Henry because I want to know what is happening in politics. He reads the London press, which he manages to get twice a week from the priest at the church. We have found out about the bombing of Pearl Harbor and the presence of the United States in Europe. The war is progressing, and according to Henry, things will get worse before they get better.

My mama and uncles have forbidden Papa and me to go outside; hence, we never do. Besides, I'm terrified of the SS officials. My uncles only go out when it's imperative to do so. The Hardwick's Apron is temporarily closed because my uncles are intimidated by the Nazis. When the shop is open, the SS officials are in there, watching with vigilance as if they're up to no good.

My Uncle Henry is reading me a column from the British newspaper. It says that besides the strange disappearance of some Jewish people, others are also disappearing, including some Romani, and people who are different in looks and behavior, such as gamblers, drunks, and gay people. I'm wondering what happened to the shoemaker who lives with his male friend. Henry says they are suddenly banished from town, and no one knows where they are. He believes they're now prisoners at Theresienstadt.

It's the end of February, and the mailman has brought a letter sealed with a note on the envelope that reads, "URGENT, READ IMMEDIATELY." It comes from the Nazi government, and that terrorizes us.

My Uncle Henry reads it out. My three uncles have to appear in the police station on March 19th, 1943, at SS headquarters. Mama,

Papa, and I are not included in the letter. What an irony. Papa and I are the Jewish ones, and Mama is the wife of a Jewish man. I know they made a mistake when they left our names off the list of people they want to question.

GUESTS AT THE FARMHOUSE

It's Friday, March 19th, early in the morning, and we plan to place the Jewish guests in safe places. The guests at the farmhouse are kept in the cellar like sardines. The guests at our house are either in the basement or the attic. The little girls look frantic; hence I give them my Ollie to keep them protected. Each of the girls grabs the rag doll by her arms.

My uncles went to police headquarters. Mama manages our well-being and is giving us instructions. All the guests and I are going to hide down in the cellar. We know how to move and find our stations next to the barrels. I'm begging my mother to let me stay with her in the living room. She finally allows me to be with her during this scary morning.

It's seven o'clock in the morning, and the clock is chiming. My uncles just left for the meeting with the authorities. We're hiding in our assigned places because my mother has the suspicion that the SS officials are going to return for us.

It's eleven in the morning, and Mama and I hear the loud roars of the SS motorcycles. They're arriving at our house. Mama stands in front of the clock, and I hide behind my father's recliner. I'm so petite that I can roll up my body into a snail position.

MY UNCLES' FATE AT THE SS HEADQUARTERS

My mother's brothers are waiting in a room without windows. The light in there is dim. It comes from a single light bulb on the ceiling. My uncles are tired, hungry, and afraid. They realize how dangerous their situation is and sit side by side in a row of chairs.

The officer addresses the three brothers while looking at Patrick as if he knows he's the head of the household. He says, "You aren't Jewish, but you shelter them, and you know that this is a crime. Are you aware that what you have been doing could send you to a detention camp? You're in deep trouble, my friends."

Mark seems disoriented, as if trying to understand the situation. He feels threatened, and all the preparation his brothers gave him for the interview goes down the drain. He speaks to the officer and tells him, "I'm not a Jewish person, and you cannot blame me because my sister married a Jewish man."

The officer fixes his attention on Mark, "Oh, that is not on the records. So, you're affiliated with Jewish people by marriage? And who is your brother-in-law?"

Mark goes quiet, and Henry picks up the explanation. "That happened a long time ago, and he doesn't live in Sternberk anymore."

The official says, "And what about your sister? Where does she live?" Henry answers with a firm voice, "I don't know. She lives in Munich."

The interrogation continues. The official asks, "Do they have any children?" Henry responds with a loud NO, as if he's trying to protect me.

The definite no Henry utters prompts suspicion in the officer. The official shakes his head and commands the jailer to take them away to a cell. He says, "I'm wasting my time with these liars."

He releases the brothers early the following morning and tells them to go home and not go anywhere because they're under house arrest.

The brothers' feelings are conflicted. On one side, they're happy because they're going back home. At the same time, they feel tremendously anxious since they don't know if a terrible fate is waiting for them.

MAMA IS NOT SMILING ANYMORE

Six SS officials arrive at our house wearing black uniforms. They are embedded in arrogance. One of the men asks Hilda, "Where are the Jewish people you hide, you traitor? Where are you hiding them?"

Mama is not intimidated by those men, because she's as tall as they are. Hilda declares with a firm voice, "I'm not hiding anyone. I'm just a law-abiding citizen. What do you want from me? What is going on?"

One of the men pushes Mama, but she keeps her balance. Hence, she doesn't fall; instead, she steps in front of the aggressive man and dares him, "What do you want to do? Tell me. Kill me?" The man takes a revolver out of his holster. "Yes, woman. If you don't cooperate, I'll kill you right now."

Mama has never lost her temper before, and I have never seen her that upset. The man pushes her again, and Mama knees him in the groin. He targets her with his gun and shoots her.

I hear one shot, two shots, three, four.

Oh, my God, he killed her. I listen to their steps going toward the cellar. Twelve feet are stepping down the narrow stairs to the basement. I pray to God for them; unfortunately, it's too late because they have all the guests.

I hear the voices of the twins screaming in desperation. I remember when my mother instructed Johana and Elsa to protect the girls if something went wrong. As I hear their steps coming up the stairs, I visualize Johana holding Margola and Elsa holding Matilda. I want to see how Mama is doing, but I cannot even move. I'm afraid because those men are still there.

The clock chimes thirteen times, and I'm sensing my father touching my right arm. He takes me into his arms with the same tenderness he gave me when I was a little girl. He covers my eyes with the palms of his hands, but I peek through his fingers. My mother's blood is all around her; she's immobile, dead.

I cry with all my strength while my father hugs me. He gets a thick white towel he found in the bathroom and covers her body with it. Then, he softly and smoothly holds my hand, and we both walk to the garden.

Papa asks me for gardening tools. I know precisely where to find them. They're in the tall aluminum box where my Uncle Henry hides his books. I also know where to look for the key to it. It's under the rock that holds the tomato pot. He gets the shovel and begins digging the hole.

It has taken Papa four hours without any breaks to dig the hole to bury my mother. He is finding the tools he needs to perform the task. Papa doesn't want me to help him because he doesn't want me to bury my mother. He's not speaking much, but his mind is present.

When we go inside the house, Papa asks for water to drink and tells me to sit and wait. I watch how Alfred drags my mother's body, all wrapped in white sheets, from her bed. He's leaving a trace of her blood as her body reaches the garden, where he will bury his wife.

I look through the kitchen window and see how Alfred places her body in the toolbox where Uncle Henry hides his books and keeps his gardening tools. He carefully puts my mama's body in it and closes it. Next, my father pushes the box to the hole using his arms, hands, legs, and feet. He succeeds in his effort.

I bring my head down and let it rest on the kitchen table.

By the time he finishes the exhausting job, it's 6:00 p.m. We sit down in the living room and rest. My father is acting normal again. He's making eye contact when he speaks to me. He tells me that we have to leave because they're coming back for us at any moment.

I'm tired, and I want to go with my mama to that plane where Masters wait for us when we leave this world. I'm closing my eyes with all my strength, and I can imagine her beautiful transparent smile.

Father and I leave the house in the station wagon.

MY UNCLES RETURNED HOME IN ANGUISH

It's late at night when my uncles slowly walk toward the house as if they're afraid to arrive and find out what happened at home while they were gone.

The front door is ajar. Once in the house, Henry calls out my name. Then, he calls for Hilda, to no avail. There is no electricity because the SS officials turned it off before leaving, but he finds the oil lamp beside the woodstove. He lights it with a match he found on the kitchen counter and yells, "Is anyone home? Marlene, Hilda, Alfred, the guests?"

No one answers.

When he looks at the floor in the living room, he sees Mama's blood. He steps on some of it. He screams, "Oh, no, blood! Whose blood is it?"

The brothers unite in a common lament and sob. It's very dark because it's nighttime. They cannot continue looking for whatever happened in the house earlier that day. Mark and Patrick decide to sit on the couch. Henry is taking Alfred's recliner. They listen to the grandfather clock chiming as if it's telling them to hold on until the sun shows up with its light. They need the morning to see the whole picture of the tragedy.

It's morning, and the brothers realize Hilda is the one who was killed. The three brothers go down to the cellar and sob because no one is there. Still having a glimmer of hope, they go to the attic, and it's also empty. They notice there is no blood in either place; hence, they hope that there is only one death.

The brothers cry in desperation, but they have not seen the worst. Giving each other courage, they go to the garden, following the trace of blood on the floor. Henry notices his long aluminum toolbox, where he had his books and gardening tools, is missing. The books and the tools are scattered close by.

There is a piece of Hilda's light brown dirndl, the one she wore yesterday morning. It's sticking up through a section of freshly turned earth. "Her body is there. Hilda is gone." The men kneel and pray for her soul while reciting "Our Father."

MARLENE AND ALFRED'S ODYSSEY

My papa Alfred is driving his car with confidence and taking control of the situation. I'm amazed by his change of demeanor. Papa goes from being an almost insane man to a loving father who is doing everything he can to keep me safe.

I'm numb, and my eyes are fixed on the road. I wish another car would come by and kill us. All I'm remembering is my mother's curled body upon receiving the bullets to her stomach. I put my hands on my face, and I think of my great-grandfather and the tales Papa used to tell me about him and his adventures. That keeps me from losing my mind.

Papa still has the key to *Hardwick's Apron Food Store* in his pocket. We arrive at the store, and he diligently walks ahead of me. I wish I had my Ollie because she used to give me strength during stressful situations. Ollie belongs to the twins now. I gave it to them because they're fragile and needed a doll to make them feel better. I still have the Star of David pendant Ruth gave me long ago. I touch it and rub it as I often do to calm my stress.

We're inside the shop, and he asks me to hide behind a large grandfather clock. Papa looks frustrated and speaks to me, something he has not done for a long time, "You're too tall now, and this is not a good hiding place for you anymore."

I'm exhausted, and all I want to believe is that everything that is happening is nothing but a terrible nightmare. I think to myself, *The Masters' predictions are manifesting.*

We sit on a bench at the store, and I place my head on my father's shoulder. We both cry until it's morning.

THE PAINFUL SUSPENSE CONTINUES

It's Sunday, March 21st, about 6:00 a.m., two days after my uncles returned from the meeting with the SS officials. The officials have come in an automobile and on motorcycles and they're raiding the house again. They're looking for my father and me. Patrick tells them we're not there; nevertheless, they continue with their search.

One of the officers looks at Patrick with disdain and asks him for the people he's hiding. Patrick tells the official he doesn't know anything about anyone who might be hiding from the authorities.

The officer pushes my uncle against the wall and spits on him. Not even the humiliation breaks Patrick. He keeps his control, stands up, and wipes his face with his shirt sleeve.

The SS officers check every room, every corner inside and around the house.

They go to the backyard, step on my mama's grave, and go to the stable where we keep the goats. One of them shoots the animals. Two of them carry their bodies to the automobile. They laugh and scream as they disappear down the road.

The SS officials are leaving disappointed because they didn't find us. They're aware of a mistake someone made by leaving our names off the list of Jewish people who live in town.

It's about 9:00 p.m., and the Gestapo are breaking down the door to the shop. I cling to my father's body, but it's inevitable; they have found us. They have lanterns with bright lights. We humbly surrender.

The SS officials guide us to the automobile that takes us to headquarters. The first thing they do is give us the Star of David emblem to wear from now on. After we sign the acknowledgment letter, the officials let us go home to pick up two bags for each of us—one for our garments and hygiene goods, the other for food. They tell us we need to come back to the address they're giving us in a letter. We must surrender in two days, and they recommend that we comply, or we will have to pay horrifying consequences.

We arrive home at dawn, and to our pleasant surprise, my three uncles are there. Uncle Henry opens the door and says, "Marlene, whatever happened? Where have you been?" I explain to my uncles that we're supposed to show up at SS headquarters in two days. I narrate to them all that happened.

Papa is not talking again and goes on singing Jewish songs. Henry and Patrick tell us all about their painful ordeal. We're afraid to be apart from each other.

It's morning again. I gather a few garments for Papa and me, some soap and some bread, fruits, and raw vegetables. I include items such as the goat soap Mama made last week.

It's terrible to know we're leaving my mama's body behind. My father is wearing his Swiss wristwatch, and I'm wearing the gold pendant with the Star of David. I'm sewing the Jewish star on the front of my dress. Papa attaches the emblem on his upper right sleeve.

We're at the assigned place, and many other Jewish people are already lining up with their two suitcases. They are all wearing the Star of David, even the little children.

The suffering is very intense, and I have great anguish. I look at my father's eyes, and I feel his presence because he has shown me he still has his mind.

Mystical Notes: Honoring

Yahim is listening to my words and is appearing in my dreams every night when I'm in a deep sleep, to console me and give me strength. He's predicting that more challenging times are on the way.

I know his warning is for real because I see the Gestapo policemen all over the place. I know those men are after my father and me because we are Jewish people.

When my thoughts torment me, I reach for the magic in my imagination to fly away. I pretend I'm going to the tall Andes Mountains in Chile, where Uncle Richard lives. I also go to some forest where I can be safe with my family.

This make-believe happens under my maroon blanket. I no longer have my beloved Ollie, but the necklace is still with me. My fingers touch it, and that gives me comfort.

Yahim and Tarboo are with me this morning. Tarboo wants to tell Yahim the way I'm feeling. He's using his voice to describe my feelings and emotions.

"This morning I woke up with a terrible sadness because I have the horrible feeling trapped in my heart that our end is near. In my dream I saw people dying all over the place."

Tarboo stops talking because he's pensive. He's saying, "There are no goodbyes!"

Yahim is talking now. "The infinite pain caused when someone we love transitions to another plane leaves us in a state of misunderstanding, frustration, guilt, anger, and sadness. The truth is that we will see the person who is no longer physically with us in the memories he/she leaves behind, and then, we will meet again on Earth or in another plane, in another dimension. Humanity needs to learn about the importance of leaving a transparent legacy for themselves for the sake of loved ones, for the sake of the world itself. Sound vibrations from the loved ones who have left stick to the living and attract synchronicity and balance. So, my dear Marlene, what is the lesson that you have mastered up to now?"

I'm thinking about it, knowing that Tarboo is behind me, reading my thoughts.

He says, "I learned the importance of honoring our loved ones as companions in our life journey. The support of family members is essential. Blood is vital because it can be thicker than water. Members of any given family continue returning to the same nuclear group because there is a secret code that unites people throughout generations and from life to life. We walk through each life holding hands, falling, standing, stopping, and continuing our paths together until the circumstances of life break us apart. We should learn to embrace our families because we're together to achieve a common goal, learning to love and accept each other. At the same time, we should set healthy boundaries to keep the family unit healthy. Healthy family ties help us overcome great trials and don't dissolve with death; they continue forever."

Tarboo is ready to read a poem he composed while standing behind me, about the anxiety he found in my soul.

PERSECUTION

Oh, the destiny of my origin, so I'm proud
To be in this form and shape, I scream aloud
So, I'm Jewish, and I was once chosen
Since old times, I began this journey
To offer the world my martyrdom, my sorrow

Oh, destiny, my origin, it's a blessing
To be present right here and now
I will suffer, I know, my blood will be shed
For those people who conscious are in darkness

Oh, I'm Jewish, and I'm so proud!
My legend and my story would be forever vibrant
In the new souls descending onto flesh
To prevent hate, to stand for rightness

Oh, Holocaust, forgetting, not a chance
I will die leaving my mark
On a stable and transparent ground
To prevent this history from happening again

I will be the one who in soul and body suffers
The horrific assault against my people
And in the flesh, I will be condemned by hatred
And in soul and spirit, my virtue will prevail forever
In the eyes of God and His eternal figure

CHAPTER NINE

TOLERANCE

EUGENIA, 1970

UNREAL LOVE

He comes late. I just wait
Loving husband, "Darling, that's fine"
"Another woman, do you have?"
"Never, my dear. You're the one"

IT TAKES TWO TO MAKE A MARRIAGE WORK

Being married to Andreas is a disaster. I'm hoping that when the baby arrives, he will change for the better.

The sad part is that I depend entirely on him. I resign from my job because I don't have anyone to keep the baby after its birth; hence, I will become a stay-at-home mom, regardless of my pain and sorrows. I must be tolerant and wait for him to change because I know he loves us.

The time to give birth to my first child has arrived. I'm in labor and, of course, Andreas is nowhere to be found. Thank God I have my mom and sister Lucy who just returned with her husband from Buenos Aires and is settling in New York.

I had a beautiful daughter, and we named her Violetta, like Andreas's mother. I'm essentially a single mother. He's usually gone or sleeping when he comes home.

I don't go anywhere because it's challenging to leave home with the baby. Besides, I don't have the desire to do so. It's wintertime, and the only coat I want to wear is the one Mama got me when I arrived in the States three years ago. It has a hood, and it's warm. I have better coats in my closet, but the dark gray jacket is more than a garment. I sense the same nurturing and protection, especially the hood that another coat gave in another life, another time.

I feel awkward, and my self-esteem hurts. I cannot find a way to feel better. I'm lazy and without any desire to communicate with anyone. I'm a failure because I cannot figure out how to help Andreas become sensitive to my needs.

The only thought that makes me feel better is the repetition of words in my mind, "I don't deserve any better."

I'M A YOUNG AND DEPRESSED MOTHER

Sadness is a feeling of impotence and a lack of hope that is hard to describe. Days go on very slowly, and I don't have the initiative to do anything.

My baby girl is beautiful, and she's the only one who makes me smile. If I cannot get up from bed, she's there, pulling my blanket.

I'm forcing myself to go out today. As I push the purple stroller, I pass a bookstore and spot a book titled *I Will Cry Tomorrow* by Lillian Roth, a famous singer from the fifties. I have the fifty cents, the book's price. The words of the book and its title inspire me.

From now on, anytime I want to cry and feel sorry for myself and my abandonment, I will tell myself, "I will cry tomorrow."

I make sure to keep this message in my mind for the rest of my life.

GOING TO GREECE

Since Andreas cannot leave the country because of his residence status, I'm going with the baby to pick up documents from the Immigration Department. These are the documents he needs to begin his application to remain in this country legally.

His mother has other papers we need to start the application. I must travel to pick them up. I'm brave because I don't know the Greek language or the culture, but I have to help him. He needs to legalize his residence, and I have a strong desire to help him.

RETURNING HOME

The plane just landed, and I'm excited to return home because I'm bringing the papers needed for his legalization. I learned some Greek, and I want to speak to Andreas in his native language. But he's not at the airport because "he has to work." Lucy is waiting for me at La Guardia International Airport.

It's evening now, and my husband just opened the door, and I try to greet him. But he's absentminded and indifferent to me. His eyes look tired, and he refuses eye contact. He's not impressed with how much Greek I have learned while staying in Greece with his parents.

His attitude saddens me. I feel humiliated, and my self-esteem is going down the drain again.

THE SAGA CONTINUES

Ever since I married Andreas, I have tried hard to help him, but my efforts are not paying off. I'm deciding today that I'm a mother and, as such, I should behave. I'm promising to give all the attention to my new child.

Surprisingly, I'm managing to keep my childlike personality alive. I make my mother and sister laugh. I talk to people I perceive as amicable in the streets of New York City. I sit on benches at the parks while my young daughter plays in sandboxes. If I want to cry when Andreas disappears, I tell myself, "I will cry tomorrow."

I don't talk to Yahim or Tarboo because I don't think about them, and they don't manifest either. But there is unique positive energy in my demeanor. I can almost say that I'm happy, and I'm continuing to do whatever is necessary to help him obtain legal status in the United States.

GAMBLERS ANONYMOUS

I'm still obsessed with finding a way to help Andreas realize that gambling destroys him, his dreams, and his family. He continues neglecting us. I'm going to try something new, Gamblers Anonymous (GA).

He has just returned from a gambling spree in some poker house in New York. My husband initially agrees to go to a meeting at Gamblers Anonymous because he has returned home penniless. I have been waiting for him to go to the meeting. But now he's telling me he's not going anywhere. Andreas believes he doesn't need to change anything.

I'm sad and want to cry; instead, I'm going anyway. He can stay home with the baby.

I'm fascinated when the group members recite the twelve steps, but he is not here to take part in the ritual. After the opening of the meeting, I join the women, but they don't notice my arrival. One lady, however, is aware of my presence here. She has a bitter look on her face while asking me if my husband has the two problems.

I ask, "What are the two problems?"

She replies, "Gambling and mistresses."

I say, "Oh, no, my husband is loyal. The only problem he has is gambling. Overall, he's a good man."

The woman laughs sarcastically and tells me, "You fool child, go home and open your eyes. We will talk next time, and you'll tell me if I'm right or wrong."

A new thought is tormenting me: *What if Andreas is having affairs?* I return home in a taxi with a thick knot in my throat. Andreas is waiting for me and doesn't ask any questions. I kiss the baby, hoping against all the odds that our marriage survives. I know I have to make it work because I'm almost sure I'm expecting my second baby.

It's Monday morning, and I'm going to the doctor because I think I'm pregnant again. I'm afraid about having a new baby, but I'm joyful because being a mother again means that Violetta will have a sister or brother. Besides, I learned from the Catholic faith that women should respect and celebrate a new baby no matter what.

LIFE IS NOT EASY

Things in my home are going from bad to worse, and I need to do something drastic to save my marriage. I have decided to move my family to another city, and the only place I can move to without any money is Chicago because my sister Marie lives there. She and her husband are happy to have us in their home until we can get situated in our own place.

The hardest part of the move is telling my mother that I will move to another city. Mother is sad, worried, and confused about such a crazy decision. But I continue hoping. I just don't want to give up the possibility that Andreas will eventually change and become a devoted husband and father.

LIFE IN CHICAGO

Chicago is my second daughter's place of birth.

Andreas never ceases gambling; for instance, he dares to ask my brother-in-law to borrow his car so that he can go to the racetrack. His behavior is causing problems for the whole family. Nevertheless, last night he gave me five hundred dollars to rent an apartment. Tomorrow I will go apartment hunting with my sister, and I know I will find one.

I'm a lonesome wife with two little children in a city I don't know, and I'm far away from my mother. Among all the obstacles, I'm enjoying my new baby. We name her Sophia.

MOVING AWAY AGAIN

The girls and I are always alone in the old apartment where neighbors smoke pot all the time. I know that because it smells like the back street of the apartment building on 98th Street and Riverside Drive.

It's Sunday morning, and he didn't make it home last night. While I rest on the bed with my children beside me, I remember the dream I had last night. I saw myself in the same library I often see in my dreams. Yahim was there telling me to go to the library because something important was waiting for me there.

It's Monday morning, and I just left Violetta at school since she's already in kindergarten. I'm pushing the stroller to the library, and it's open. I go around, and something is coming to my mind.

I'm standing in front of the bookshelf that holds books on tourism in southern states. A book falls from a shelf to the floor. I pick it up. A strong voice in my head resonates, telling me, "Go to Texas. That is the place for you to move."

I take the book home, read it, and discover that gambling is illegal in Texas.

SHARING MY NEW IDEA WITH ANDREAS

I spend days thinking about ways to introduce my self-made plans to Andreas. It will be on one of those mornings when he shows up at home not having money.

Today is Sunday morning, and Andreas is depressed upon his arrival home because he has gambled away all his money at some poker table or racetrack.

I tell him about my findings of a city in Texas that suits our needs. It's Houston where we should move, because he likes to fish, and I like the beach. Andreas doesn't frown at the idea and bluntly tells me he's in with the plan. I will strive to manifest our move to Texas in the coming summer. The word is out among his Greek friends. He tells me he knows people who live in Texas.

My mama and sister Lucy are visiting us. Mama brought along a beautiful prosperity plant she grew at her apartment with a seed she brought from Colombia not long ago. She has told me to nurture it because if it flourishes, it will bring me good luck.

Two weeks have gone by, my mother and sister are gone, and my new plant is green and firm. I will take it to Houston because it will bring me good luck and I need it.

Moving to Houston is an obsession. Andreas wants to go there too. I keep on telling him how much better our lives would be if we were to move there. Chicago is cold, and I need sunshine to keep myself optimistic.

Today, I'm waiting for him by the window in the living room that faces the street. I see how Andreas is arriving home. As soon as he opens the door, he tells me that a Greek restaurant owner contacted him from Pasadena, Texas, and wants him to show up to work the following Monday. I have packed a suitcase with a few clothing items, and he says he's ready for the trip. I'm staying behind to take care of the furniture, return the keys to the apartment, and wait for him to become situated for us to go there.

After selling some of the home items and sending the furniture to Texas, he sent me the money for the plane tickets. I make sure to take a branch of the prosperity plant in my purse to plant it in my new home.

Mystical Notes: Tolerance

Master Yahim and I have interesting conversations while I'm physically alone with my children in this old apartment.

He says to me, "It's hard for Andreas to find inner peace since he cannot remember the issues from his distant pasts. The lack of memories confuses his soul. He cannot find the means to achieve synchronicity of thought. Muddy energies from the negative karma he carries keep him from seeing the light of reason. He lives in an obscure state of stagnation. I commend you for your incredible tolerance. Even though you live with a constant struggle, you tolerate his indifference and lack of care. You are trying, and the mere act of trying makes you a better person; hence, your spirit is growing in wisdom." I tell Yahim that from what I have seen, my husband is trapped in his current existence and cannot see beyond it.

Yahim nods in agreement with me. He proceeds with words of eloquence, "I put the idea of finding out about Texas in your head because that is the place where you need to be. Continue with your mission and find your true home. There is no gambling there, but he will continue with his vice; nevertheless, you will find your freedom with a new life journey."

At this moment, I remember the words in the book about Texas that I had picked up from the library in Chicago: "Texas, take it or leave it. If you ever take it, the chances are that you'll never leave it."

Yahim is looking at me with love and compassion, and he's asking me, "Tell me, my dear Eugenia, what is the most important lesson that you have learned up to now?"

I smile at him and have an answer for him.

Tarboo suddenly shows up and says he will use his voice to express my thoughts, "I learn tolerance is the mother of endurance. When we tolerate other people's wrongdoings, at the same time we need to learn to identify our own boundaries, so tolerance does not become an avenue to abuse. Remember, we can always offer help to others, but we need to know that we are only responsible for our own actions. It is wise to let others learn from their own mistakes to enrich their eternal soul with the wealth of wisdom."

I know that if Andreas never becomes a family man, my efforts to keep the family together right now are giving me endurance and perseverance to conduct great things in life that will serve my children and me. We humans should learn that perseverance is a behavior that becomes engraved in our conscious mind.

It is important to differentiate between tolerance and perseverance. Tolerance may open the door to abuse, while perseverance is a tool that we can use for self-improvement. Hence, tolerance is a quality that can be used with discretion, while perseverance can be used to reach our dreams and goals.

It's time for Tarboo because he's ready to recite a poem he found in the depth of my eternal memory. He recites it now.

DECEPTION

Oh, my husband, a promise you made
Of honor and loyalty, you pledge just to me
And now I have doubts that faithful you're not
The pain of your gambling is tormenting me
But you, having a mistress, unspeakable, that, I can't conceive

Is it that the other is just a woman with no flesh?
Who doesn't care for you, just for her?
Is her name perhaps spelled "Gambling"?
Who takes all your own, and dignity too?

You promise and promise day after day
That gambling you'll stop the upcoming weekend
But it never happens. The gambling is there, always in your head
And me with my tears, I bathe all the pain

Sometimes I do fear that you will disappear
That some of your lenders will hurt you because of your debts
But please, with honesty, tell me that the other is not a woman
It's gambling you cannot tame
My Masters and me, your vice want to defeat

CHAPTER TEN

MARTYRDOM

MARLENE, 1942

MARTYRDOM

Predicted doom from the storm that's coming
Tears of blood will soon be shed
From the Jewish eyes, without a doubt
Our martyrdom will be redemption
For the souls who exist in darkness

THE DAY OF THE TRANSPORT

We wait in line for a long time. I notice my father is making funny clown faces. I ask him why he's doing that. He tells me he doesn't want to think about what is going on at this moment.

I ask him to stop it, or they may label us as crazy people. He listens to me and stands by his suitcases. He's touching his bald head now.

I ask him, "Papa, why are you touching your bald head? What is wrong?"

He responds with a smile on his lips, "I won't have to shave my head anymore; the Nazis will do it for me."

Soon after, the train engineer addresses the crowd, "Our first stop will be in Pilsen."

We have departed, and the train goes on for hours and hours. I sleep while resting my head on my father's right shoulder. He takes some bread out of the suitcase and eats it. The SS official passes out a jar of water. We don't want to drink any of it because we try to avoid an urge to go to the bathroom.

TEREZIN, OUR NEW HOME

The SS officials are welcoming us in a large hall. We left our suitcases behind because they wanted to make sure we didn't have any weapons or contraband. We're receiving passes to go to the shower room and to go to a large cafeteria to eat. The man checking my father and me took my father's expensive watch and my gold pendant with the Star of David. The tangible reminders of our family in Munich are forever gone.

I'm clinging to my father's arm, and I cry.

It's early in the morning, and I see long wooden tables lined up horizontally with a tiny space between them. The few female SS officials are offering us black coffee and hard bread. I'm drinking coffee for the first time in my life, and it's bitter to my taste buds. I find it soothing because it is deliciously warm. I'm soaking the bread in it, which makes it softer.

Now, we're standing and waiting for orders. We talk to other people and share some of our personal stories.

Most of us are standing at the sidewalk curb now. The SS officials are calling us back to the cafeteria for lunch. There is noodle soup in big pots and bread left over from breakfast. The food is putting people's conversations on hold.

We're patiently waiting for the next orders.

THE CHECKING IN

The waiting line is long, and I cannot see where it ends. The elders, older Jewish men who help maintain discipline in the premises, are handing out thin blankets to each of us.

The process is taking a long time; hence, I decide to count numbers to kill time.

My father is whispering Jewish songs to distract himself. It's about eleven at night, and we continue inside the barrack where the dormitories are.

Each of us stands in front of the mattress assigned to each person; they were white at one time. However, after heavy use from earlier prisoners, they have turned almost black. The SS officials tell us that everyone in our group will spend the night with their relatives for the last time. I feel safe because I'm going to be next to my papa.

Father is sitting on his mattress and tells me that they're filled with shaved wood. I take possession of a bed next to him.

A girl wearing a brown coat is standing to my left. She sits on her mattress, looking very scared. She appears to be a little older than me. I keep my coat on as I lie down on the bed. My father tells me to guard my boots by putting them beside me and under the blanket. I don't have to worry about my coat with the hood because I will wear it all night long.

I'm uncomfortable because fleas are crawling over me. I'm itching. I sit down to scratch myself. The little girl beside me tells me not to scratch because the bites may get infected. The girl introduces herself to me. Her name is Isabella.

I only see the first rays of sun coming through the bottom of the large door because the room doesn't have any windows. When an SS woman opens the door wide, the light fills the room.

Isabella smiles at me and says, "Guten morgen." Good morning.

Isabella is from Terezin, the town where we're staying. Isabella tells me that she lived in a house with a window in her room facing the railroad track. From that window she saw the trains arriving in town with passengers on their way to the Terezin detention camp.

We're leaving the dormitory, and we cannot stand the itching caused by the flea bites; hence, as we walk to the cafeteria for breakfast, Isabella and I pick up chunks of frozen snow and put them on our affected areas. That alleviates a bit of the discomfort caused by flea bites.

MY UNCLES ARE AT THE CAMP

Papa sits on the sidewalk by the cafeteria after finishing breakfast. Isabella and I are going for a short walk down the street. We cross arms together and stand beside the new arrivals line.

There are about three hundred new arrivals in the line, men, women, and little children as it was in our group. They look as disoriented as we were when we arrived.

We're counting people, and when I say "fifty," I see a man who looks like Uncle Henry with Uncle Patrick and Uncle Mark. I jump with happiness, not realizing that their presence at the detention camp implies their doom.

I look behind them, and I don't see anyone else I know; my mind takes my eyes to the people in front of my uncles. I see the familiar faces of Jewish people who were at the farm. My heart is breaking for the twins again. Where are they? I have to cry.

We're back with my father, who is still seated where we left him. I'm telling my new friend all about my family, my beloved mama, and how a tall SS man killed her. I'm crying again, and I cannot stop. My eyelids are smarting, and I don't know if I can continue living without Mama. Isabella hugs me. That makes me feel a little better because I now have a friend who consoles me.

MEETING WITH MY FAMILY AND FRIENDS

It is lunchtime, and the SS kitchen officials are serving chicken broth and bread. I look around table by table, trying to find my uncles. Suddenly, I see my Ollie on the floor about four tables from ours. I see Johana and Elsa sitting next to Margola and Matilda. I jump as an expression of mixed feelings. It's a good thing they're with us and a bad thing because they share our fate.

I ask one of the elders in Hebrew if he will let me sit by the little girls because I know them. He allows me to do so. The girls look comfortable with their caregivers. I pick up Ollie from the floor and give the doll to Johana; then, Matilda grabs one of its legs. I feel a big knot in my throat, but I don't cry.

I go back to my seat, and after we finish eating, we go outside. Isabella and I play hide-and-seek with the girls.

It's 8:00 p.m. My father and I know the time is short because the whistle from the elder will go off by 9:00 p.m. I watch the clock on the tall white wall to distract my mind from worrying about our doomed future.

I spot Henry walking toward me. He's in front of me, hugs me, and kisses me on my forehead. "I cannot fail you, my dear Marlene. I'm here." Patrick and Mark are here too and also kiss me and hug me. The three of them hug my papa as well. We're not crying, but our eyes hold tears of uncertainty.

I'm lying down on the dirty mattress. The thin blanket doesn't keep me warm, so I'm wearing my coat. I have my old socks on, and they smell terrible, but I'm leaving them on my feet because I'm freezing. The hood on my coat helps me keep my head warm. I still have my father near me, and that makes me feel good. I cannot go to sleep because I keep thinking about Mama.

AUSCHWITZ

We have just left for Auschwitz, and the worst of our tragedy is about to manifest. People of all ages and genders travel like sardines in trains. The worst thing for me is that I cannot be with my father and uncles any longer. The SS officials separated us by gender before we began our terrible journey.

The smell of the sweat of my fellow prisoners is very unpleasant, and I don't have my father's shoulder to support my head anymore. So, I hold Isabella's hand tightly and notice how her tears are rolling down her beautiful, alabaster-colored face. I understand her sorrow because she doesn't have kin anywhere in the world. I still have a father and uncles, even though we're separated. I whisper in her ear and ask her if she wants to be my sister. Isabella presses my hand hard, and we connect at a spiritual level.

I feel the motion of the train going down the train track. It has been a long ride, and it's still moving. The SS officials are watching us and threatening us with their defiant eyes. They're carrying nightsticks to intimidate us. I'm taking my head into my hands and sobbing.

The train is stopping abruptly, and we all sway to its motion. We departed at dawn, and it's still going. The SS officials point at our faces with their lanterns, and one of them is saying, "Hurry, all of you. The other train is waiting. We're moving all of you to a cattle train."

The SS officials hit some of us with their nightsticks. They missed Isabella and me because we were fast and ducked. But two little boys, shorter than us, are getting the strikes as well as their mother.

We're locked in the boxcar and don't have any windows. I feel desperate; hence, I'm invoking my mother. I beg her to remove me from so much misery. I don't want to live under those conditions any longer.

All is silent, and I cannot hear anyone anymore. The only sound I hear is the chugging sound as the train moves. Isabella and I are lucky because we got a corner spot in the car and sat down here. Mothers with their babies also took corner spots to sit or lie down. Our corner spot places us away from the rest of the people bumping into each other. Other people have to stand in the middle of the car, holding hands with strangers.

THE END IS NEAR

We have arrived at our destination, and we're walking in a hurry because the SS officials are directing us as if we're stubborn cattle. I see two-story barracks on both sides of the road. They're not that tall—the bricks from the outside look new because they were built a short time ago for German soldiers.

I'm trying to fool myself by thinking that all is fine and better days are on the horizon. The SS officials are taking us to dormitories to be comfortable with soft beds and a radio. I want to listen to the news and become informed of what is happening in Europe and the war.

A couple of SS women guide Isabella, other women, and me to barrack two, room 23. We're going upstairs because that room number is on the second floor. There, the women in charge align us in front of wooden bunk beds in a large dormitory.

The SS women wake us up abruptly at dawn with the sound of a loud whistle. We're rushed from the dorms as if there is something significant awaiting us. The two female SS officials line us up as we arrive; hence, Isabella is behind me, and what a relief for us.

Upon our arrival to the barracks, a male SS official orders us to roll up our sleeves. He's tattooing us. I'm number 8, and Isabella is number 9. I feel a burning sensation on my skin, and I look at the number eight, my identity now. No longer am I going to be called Marlene. I'm "Number 8 from barrack number 23."

Another female official lines us up again, woman after woman, girl after girl in a straight line. They're directing us to another place. My black curly hair is long, and I constantly have an urge to scratch my head. I have lice, and my whole body has flea bites. Isabella is telling me she has the same problem.

We have arrived at an open square, and I smell something in putrefaction. It comes from a hole that I spot in the distance. There is decomposed human flesh in it. I see some men who look lame. The SS officials are directing them to walk faster. They struggle, but they comply. They stand next to the hole. The officials shoot them, one by one. Next, they push their bodies into the pit; I wonder if they're all dead when they fall inside it.

I hate seeing such an atrocity; hence, I hide my head in my shoulders. That is the only thing I can do to escape such brutal reality. Next, I look up at the sky and see how the morning sky is bathed with red smoke. I smell the intense repugnant odor of burning flesh as it turns into ashes that melt with the atmosphere.

I'm in a large room where SS women are working as barbers. They order us to sit at assigned stools. Women barbers shave our heads.

Isabella goes first. I observe how each one of her golden curls is falling to the floor. I'm next, and in a way, I'm relieved from the awful itching on my head. Lice have invaded my curly black hair, and as it falls to the floor, a female SS official who is passing by tells me, "Get a grip, kid. You look better without any hair."

I look around and notice that we all look the same. We're one ethnicity melting in the name *Juden*. Our identities have been dissolved in a common experience of suffering: Jewish people in the Nazi occupation site.

We're entering the shower room. It's a large shared shower room where there is no place for discretion. An SS woman orders us to take off all our clothes in front of everyone else. I find this order worse than murder because only my mother has ever seen me naked, and she taught me prudence and self-respect. I want to disappear because my shame is too painful. One of the SS women comes closer to me and strikes me with her nightstick. No one has ever hit me before. I'm humiliated, and the pain is unbearable. I have opted to obey the order, take my clothes off, one garment at a time, as I avert my eyes in shame. The woman strikes me again. The top of the nightstick strikes my right calf. That hurts too much, and I cry. She tells me, "Little pig, good for nothing; there is no room for prudence over here. You're not a human being; you're just a number." I finish getting undressed, walk limping to the shower room. Isabella obeys; therefore, none of the officials hurt her with their nightstick.

Goodness, that water is hot. It's good at the beginning because it offsets the cold weather from the outside. I'm holding a soap bar given to me by a woman showering next to me. The soap smells different from the soap Mama used to make from goat fat.

The woman says, "That soap is made from our flesh. Those horrible people use the little fat they can find in us after they kill us and recycle it by letting us use it on our skin."

I throw the soap to the floor, and she picks it up almost at once.

She says, "Don't do that. If they see you throwing it to the floor, they'll strike you again."

She introduces herself as Imelda and tells me she's not Jewish but Romani.

The water is too hot, and the SS women make us stay under the hot shower for a long time. Isabella tries to leave her place to escape the heat of the water. The SS woman comes around and delivers a blow to her back with her nightstick.

She rushes back to be under the hot shower and tells me, "I cannot stand this anymore. I'm going to go to my parents in Heaven very soon."

I want to be with my mother as well, but being the optimistic girl I am, I refuse to give up. I will continue living this horrific saga while hoping that all shall pass soon.

Finally, after an hour or so, someone turns the water off. Again, two mean ladies make us form a straight line of obedience. They tell us we need to purify even more with another shower. One of these women says, "You're disgusting pigs. No number of showers will free you from your dirtiness."

We stroll to the cold showers to repeat the torture once more, and the only difference is that it's a freezing shower. My eyes are red, not from crying, but from the extremes of temperatures in the hot and cold shower rooms that I have to endure.

We line up again. I'm hoping to get into my warm dress, coat, and ankle boots. I left them in a bundle of clothing when they ordered me to undress. The clothes are not there anymore. Instead, the SS woman gives me a uniform that looks too big for me. It's a two-piece white garment with dark blue stripes. I have no choice; hence, I put the suit on. I look around for my boots, and they're gone. I take a pair that fits me.

The Nazis are taking away all that I own: my star pendant, coat, dress, boots, socks, and underwear.

I look at Isabella, and her funny uniform looks much too large for her also. She looks at me and, with unspoken words, tells me the same thing I'm thinking about her. We're doomed, and we want to go home to Heaven.

We march in obedience along the camp streets. We don't know our next stopping point.

As we walk along, I notice flames from a fire ascending to the sky, and again, the smell of burning flesh is overpowering; it comes from our siblings in the depths of the hole.

Imelda is walking beside me, and she murmurs, "There are five holes like this one. The SS officials fill them with new corpses every day; then, the man in charge lights the fire to burn the bodies. That is what you see in the sky, the flesh giving freedom to the souls in captivity."

We're now in a large cafeteria, and I smell fresh brewing coffee. There is bread by the coffeemakers. It seems like a delicatessen to the other prisoners and me. The SS women walk back and forth, looking at us with disdain. One of them is making fun of me because I have trouble keeping my pants up since they're so big on me. I'm a small, skinny teenager.

It's lunchtime, and the official is guiding us to the cafeteria. There are large pots of noodle soup and empty mugs next to them, ready to be used. The soup doesn't taste that bad, and it's warm. We repeat the same story after lunch. We stand in the street, and SS women watch us as if we're criminals. Time goes by slowly, and I don't remember what day it is. I don't care.

I look at the open sky while surrendering to my fate.

THE BARRACKS

In the evening, I look around and I see Imelda right behind me. She's short like me and very skinny. She looks sixty, but she's only forty-four.

The SS lady watching the dorm of eighty-five women is distracted reading the newspaper, as she does every night. We're gathered in the dormitory and are getting ready to lie down for the night.

Imelda sleeps in a bed next to me at the bottom of a double bunk. I also sleep on the bottom bunk. I whisper while asking her if she knows today's date. According to her counting, she tells me that today is the last day of August of 1942.

I touch my bald head like my father used to do, and I feel naked and abandoned. Naked because nothing that I'm wearing is mine, and they have robbed me of my hair. Abandoned because the Nazis have succeeded.

I have surrendered my identity, the beloved Marlene, whom many cared for and loved before, to the brutal criminals who have managed to destroy us.

Imelda looks at me with compassion and asks me about my life and how I ended up in the detention camp. I softly narrate how the Third Reich official killed my mama and how my uncles, father, and I ended up in Auschwitz. She ducks as she tells me, "Do you want to end it all? Do you want to take something I have in a bottle, and if you drink it, you will go straight to Heaven to your mama?"

I don't want to die because I believe in my Uncle Henry's promise. My family will reunite again.

As if she were reading my mind, Imelda tells me, "Girl, your family is doomed. We're all doomed. You need to take the blue liquid and join your mama. This stuff is valuable around here because many of us want to go before they burn us."

I look at her, right into her light brown eyes. I'm aware that the SS woman who oversees the dorm will check us once she reads the paper. But I have to ask, "Why haven't you killed yourself yet if you have the fatal liquid?"

As she sobs, she tells me, "My daughter is in another dorm right now, and I'm waiting to be with her so we can go to the afterlife together."

It's time to get up, as usual, at 5:00 a.m. The whistle sound wakes us up, and we shake our infected uniforms to get rid of the fleas. We don't have to change clothes since we sleep in the uniforms. We go to the washroom to use the bathroom and wash our faces.

We just finished breakfast, and the SS officials are taking us to a large hall. They're assigning jobs to young people. Isabella goes to the infirmary, and I'm going to work at the cafeteria.

We're looking at each other with sorrow and desperation.

Isabella whispers in my ear, "My dear sister, if I don't see you on Earth again, I promise I will look for you in Heaven."

It's lunchtime, and everyone standing on the streets walks humbly into the cafeteria in a straight line toward the soup stockpots. The soup is okay, and there are bread leftovers from breakfast this morning. I manage to sit by Imelda, and she's playfully smiling at me. I think she's thinking about the poison in the blue bottle.

She whispers in my ear and tells me, "You're right, my child. The blue bottle is in the dormitory."

We have just finished eating, and the SS woman who has been making fun of me because my uniform is too big for me commands me to follow her. We go to the laundry room.

She hands me a two-piece pantsuit that looks clean and much smaller. "Here, wear this one. It's much smaller, and it's clean. You need to look presentable because you're going to be working in the cafeteria from now on. Do a good job, or you will be doomed before your assigned time."

I'm obediently changing clothes and feel clean for the first time in a long time. The uniform fits me perfectly. *Well, at least that nice woman found an outfit closer to my size. The SS women are not so bad.* Or so I'm thinking at this moment.

I have to keep the coffee brewers clean and full of water while in service during breakfast. If time allows it, and if the other girls need my help, I help clean the cafeteria's floor. I have an idea of how to sweep and mop because I saw Mama doing it at home, but I have never done it before.

WORKING HARD FOR NOTHING

It's six in the morning and the first day at the job. I'm paying attention to my duties and try my best to do a good job. I pour water into the coffeemaker as she has instructed me. I put a tiny bit of coffee into the brewer at times since she told me to ration it. When I'm not pouring water, I wipe the counters and make sure there are still pieces of bread out on the table.

When breakfast time is over, I have to deal with these big coffee brewers. I thoroughly empty the water from the containers. Since I'm short, barely five feet tall, the task is hard for me.

Today is the second day at my new job in the cafeteria. The counters are too tall for me. I have to stand on a stool to reach the coffee containers.

I'm maneuvering right now to reach the coffeemaker. God, I'm losing my equilibrium, and I'm falling onto the floor with the coffee container in my hand. The hot water has burned my right forearm and my right thigh. The SS woman is coming toward me as she lifts her billy club. I rapidly stand up and apologize. I'm getting a couple of blows on my back. The strikes add pain to the already intense burning sensation on my arm and leg.

I cannot say anything; hence, I go about my duties, suffering severe pain from the burns on my skin.

It's dark already, and I'm returning to my dorm; I'm happy to see my new friend Imelda. There she is, sitting in isolation, on her bed. She asks me about my day; I show her the blister on my arm and pull my pants down to show her my leg. It has a huge blister and a smaller one. I want to pop them, but she tells me to leave them alone.

She's asking me if I have considered her offer. I tell her that I'm still thinking about it. I know I'm going to see my family again, and our departure from Earth to Heaven should occur with all of us at the same time.

Imelda laughs as she covers her mouth so no one can hear her laughter. I ask her what is funny.

She replies, "Your innocence, kid, your innocence. If your family has not died yet, it's coming to them. You will never see them again."

I asked her for three days, but she responds, "I will give you up until tomorrow night, and that is it. After that, I will not be able to help you because I will be turning into the red flames that are ascending to Heaven from this horrible place."

I ask Imelda, "How in the world do you know that that is going to happen?" She smiles as she displays her toothless upper gums, "Because I'm Romani and I know a lot you don't know, my child. Don't lose your opportunity, because the pain yet to come is unbearable. Your father and your uncles may be gone already. Take the liquid, and you will be able to meet them soon in Heaven."

I don't respond to her suggestions, but I'm feeling miserable. My back hurts from all the blows I endured from the SS lady, and I can hardly walk. My arm and leg look inflamed because of the accident with the hot water. If my family is gone, taking the poison would be the thing to do.

I feel so lonesome and in despair. I don't even see the Masters anymore, and my best and only friend, Isabella, is assigned to work in the infirmary. She sleeps someplace else. I feel lost in my disgrace and at the mercy of those who hate my people and me.

THE TORMENT CONTINUES

It has been three days since I burnt myself, and I'm not healing. My injuries from the burn are getting worse, and I feel cornered. I notice I'm becoming less diligent at my job because of my aches and pains. I feel like an old lady. Those health issues are keeping me from performing the perfect labor they demand from me.

THE LIQUID DOESN'T TASTE THAT BAD

I'm in my bunk bed again and ready to rest; however, my body hurts. The SS lady struck me on my back today because I'm not diligent enough. I have a feeling she broke a rib on my skinny back.

Imelda is the only person who listens to my complaints. Hence, as usual, I whisper my lamentations to her as the SS lady reads the newspaper.

I softly ask her, "What is going on, Imelda? Why are you not smiling at me?" She looks at me with infinite sadness and tells me that one of the ladies told her earlier that her day will be the following morning. She's scheduled to go for the infamous shower with some fellow inmates.

Imelda knows very well that the "shower" is the gas chamber.

I see tears in Imelda's eyes, even though she's trying hard to keep them from falling. She looks at me and says, "I'm going to die without knowing my daughter's fate. That is what hurts the most."

I make eye contact as if I were trying to consolidate my feelings with hers and confirm that I'm ready for the blue liquid. She hands me the little bottle and tells me, "I was going to drink it, but you deserve to have it because you're still just a girl, and you shouldn't have to endure any more torments. I know that tomorrow will be my departure. In your case, you don't know how much longer they're going to continue abusing you."

Once back in my bed, I go under the flea-ridden blanket and drink from the bottle that contains the blue liquid. It has a sweet and sour taste. It doesn't taste too bad.

I softly tell Imelda that I did it.

She responds, "You will be dead within an hour."

I'M STILL ALIVE IN THE INFIRMARY

I'm waking up in a long white room, and everyone around is wearing white uniforms. Most of the people here are Jewish, like me. I feel safer here and know that the ones who are taking care of me are my people.

Isabella is here, and I'm not surprised to see her. She smiles at me and tells me she has the job of sweeping the floors. I don't know if I'm on Earth or another plane. A nice lady comes near the bed and tells me that I almost died, but since they brought me here in time, they could pump my stomach and save me. She gives me the bad news that it will be a long while before my stomach heals, if ever. From then on, I'm going to suffer from sporadic diarrhea. She's also telling me that my burn injuries are infected. I'm going to be in the infirmary for a while.

I lie quietly in the cot, aware there is nothing I can say or do that will change the timing of my end. At this time, I reason, *Why do they want to keep me alive, to turn around and kill me?*

Things in the infirmary aren't that terrible. The food is not that bad and much better than what I ate at the cafeteria. People smile from time to time, and the place looks clean. Young girls are sweeping and dusting around the rooms.

As I'm dozing off, I feel a hand on my forehead. The light is dim, and I see a man in a white uniform standing by my bed and looking at me. I open my eyes wide, and I see my Uncle Henry's tall and healthy body. He bends toward me, hugs me, and kisses my forehead with profound empathy. I sob, holding my face as he talks, "I have a plan for the five of us to reunite again. You must be brave, my dear, because we will all go together to see your mama. There is no way out of this infamous place of torture. I have made a deal with an SS official. I told him about our grandfather clocks at Sternberk, and he's going to have them all in exchange for his help in reuniting us. I will tell him where the grandfather clocks are in Sternberk if he manages to send us to Heaven at the same time. I trust him because he's from Sternberk. Your father, my brothers, you and I will be called on the same day and time to be killed. We're going to the same gas chamber, and together, we'll depart. It will happen in a few weeks."

Uncle Henry explains that they assigned him to work in the infirmary because he has managerial skills and fundamental knowledge of treating mild wounds. I know differently. He's talkative and jovial. Uncle Henry somehow manages to be likable among a bunch of egregious men and women, the Nazis.

As he steps away, my stomach turns in severe discomfort. I don't know if the pain is related to the poisonous liquid or my uncle leaving me.

RETURNING TO TORTURE

It has been two weeks since I arrived at the infirmary, and the doctor is letting me go now. It's breakfast time; hence, I'm going to the cafeteria. To my surprise, there is someone else working in my spot. The SS officials have already replaced me, and I don't have a job anymore. That girl is much taller than me; hence, she doesn't have any problem reaching the countertops. She, of course, is a Jewish girl like me, and one of the camp barbers has shaved her head. I wonder what her story is.

I'm spending the day waiting on the street until it's time for the SS officials to open the barracks doors. I'm hoping with all my heart to see Imelda. Unfortunately, there is another woman on her bed. That lady doesn't talk to me, maybe because she's hungry, sad, and tired.

THE SHOWER OF DEATH

The SS lady is announcing the schedule for the morning. They're telling us to line up to go to the "shower" room. We're walking at the pace of the SS women and follow them, fast and stern. Upon our arrival, I notice there aren't shower heads in the room's ceiling or walls.

That place is austere and packed with a wave of awful muddy energy. We begin to suspect something is wrong.

The women enter the sinister room one by one.

Suddenly an SS guard pulls on my arm with his large hand, as he tells me, "Same destination, different location." He waves my arm as if I were Ollie. I stroll because my innate survival instinct tells me that it's up to me to delay my arrival to the end of my life.

I'm entering a small room where my family is waiting for me. Everyone is wearing the prisoners' uniforms.

Papa sees me and comes to me as if he were trying to save me again. Uncle Mark is not approaching me because he's weak and on the verge of dying; Uncle Patrick stands tall in a defiant pose and doesn't come close to me either.

Uncle Henry comes and kneels next to me as he tells me, "My dear angel, you deserve to know. They're going to poison us with Zyklon B, a fumigant. It will not take long to kill us. You will experience the smell of anise, like almonds. Then, you will feel suffocated and fall. Soon, it will be over."

My father walks a few steps away and stops touching me. He humbly returns to his position. They line up, facing me.

Papa and Uncle Mark look very tired and ready to give up. Uncle Henry looks serene and completely conscious of what is going on. My Uncle Patrick looks angry because he doesn't have any power over the situation.

The SS official orders them to undress. They do so in perfect obedience. My Uncle Henry murmurs something to the SS man in charge.

My uncles and father are in front of me, and they're naked. I don't see them very well because the light is dim. The SS man tells us that we have to undress because it's easier for the officials to dispose of the bodies. He allows me to wear the top of my uniform; he has listened to Henry's last request. The man also has some compassion for me and my dignity; so, I want to believe that. My shirt is long enough and covers my private parts. Thank God for that.

There is a dim light, and I can hardly sit down. My legs are losing their equilibrium. In the next moments, I begin to smell what my Uncle Henry told me. It's indeed a bitter smell of almond essence. He also said that the scent is produced by Zyklon B, the gas they're using to kill us.

DROPPING MY BODY

I'm hearing the noise caused by the falling of each one of their bodies crashing onto the cement floor. My Uncle Mark falls first. Then, Papa.

When my father falls, I reflect, *Papa didn't learn much by sharing his life with Hilda, me, or anyone else in our family. None of the people he met during his life were able to help him find peace. Alfred lived in shame because of his treason to his people and loved ones. He also brought issues along from past lives.* I'm fading away, and this is my last thought of this life.

Yahim is talking now, "It's taking Alfred a while to learn that we all make mistakes, and each needs to forgive his/her intentional or non-intentional wrongdoings before others can forgive those actions. That is the first step toward soul growth."

Patrick follows, and then, my beloved Uncle Henry falls. They are all on the ground, lifeless, gone, and I'm still here. I have healthy lungs and body because I'm much younger; therefore, my youth keeps me from dying. Nevertheless, the youthful feeling of immortality is fading away within me. I cannot breathe, and it seems my lungs are not holding oxygen anymore.

I keep some air in my mouth, but eventually, the gas goes down into my lungs. They're begging for air, and I cannot help it. My lungs are dying. I'm still resisting leaving the planet Earth for good. My little body is bending toward the floor, and it falls, lifeless.

I'm indifferent because I don't feel anything for them, my uncles, or my father. Their souls abandoned their bodies and are ascending above the ceiling.

Mystical notes: Martyrdom

Right here at the portal of the spirit world, I see Yahim wearing his purple tunic, and Tarboo his green one. They're holding Hilda's hands as they wait for me. I see her in radiance. Her face is shining over my dead body; then, she lets go of the Masters and reaches to my right spirit hand. We leave together, but soon, she lets go of my hand and disappears from my sight.

My father and uncles are going toward the sky and are traveling together.

Uncle Henry conveys a message to my soul, "I did what I promised. We are all departing together."

At this point, I'm deciding to follow them. The words of hope come from Uncle Henry's vibrations, "We must go now because the Masters are calling us."

I'm changing my mind and have decided to stay on Earth for a little while.

It's sundown, and the SS officials leave our bodies at the edge of the pit. My body is facing downward, and the strong breeze has lifted my shirt. My body is naked from the waist down, and my buttocks are exposed. I don't feel shameful anymore. I'm at peace and released from all the atrocities I endured in Auschwitz. I see the way other souls are letting go of their flesh. I don't know where my family is anymore, and I'm transformed.

Suddenly, I sense a current of warm air all over my energy. Yahim is with me because he knows how much I have wished to travel around Germany and Europe to see all the devastation of the bombing. I know the American and the Russian armed forces are fighting for us. Even though it's too late for me, I want to know how they're doing in Europe.

Yahim is wearing an American army uniform, and his skin tone goes perfectly with the camouflage uniform.

He holds my hand and asks me, "Are you ready to explore with the freedom of being just in the spirit and without the flesh?"

We fly away, and I see Berlin. There is nothing but devastation, ruins of what was once the pride of Germany. There are dead bodies in the streets and there is a foul smell all over the place. Yes, I have my five senses.

Next, in Hamburg, I see pain, suffering, and the rumbling sound of the bombs that are still destroying the city.

We're in Dresden. Here, I'm seeing how people are running fast in search of shelter. They know the bombs are about to explode. It's the Germans falling now. Most of them are innocent people standing in the time and place of the infamous history written by the Third Reich.

I want to go to Warsaw, my father's town. Yahim takes me there in a split second. I'm seeing devastation, poverty, and misery in what was once a prosperous city.

Yahim is ordering me to leave. He's trying to guide me to my eternal home, but I want to continue my travels. I want to go to Czechoslovakia, to my hometown, Sternberk.

The town looks dark gray, and all we see are the two steeples of the town's cathedral. Its steeples are in perfect symmetry on both sides of the building. The streets are empty, and I don't hear a sound. The town is in ruins; hence, I want to leave right now. My Master listens to my wish and grants it.

FINDING UNCLE RICHARD

We're above the enormous waves of water wrapped in strong winds. It's the ocean with its splendor at dawn. We arrive at the port that my father mentioned so many times while I was growing up. It's "Puerto Montt" in southern Chile. I cannot find my Uncle Richard around here. Then, my Master retakes my hand since he had let go of it while we were over the ocean.

We arrive at Santiago. Yahim and I peek through the window of a tall apartment building. I see him, my Uncle Richard. I recognize him, even though I have never seen him before. I know who he is by the magic of intuition.

He looks just like my father, short and dark. He's bald and is smoking from a pipe. There is a Hebrew woman with him, and she's his wife. They're communicating in Hebrew. The couple seem content, talking and enjoying their time together while sitting in their living room.

While living as Marlene, I learned Czech, Hebrew, and German. But it doesn't matter because there is no such thing as language in the spirit world. Here, people communicate with a wordless expression of intuition, and since I am in spirit form, I don't have language barriers.

She tells Uncle Richard that the war is raging in Europe, and many people are dying, Jewish people. My uncle looks sad because he thinks about his brother, Alfred, and his three nieces. He has always yearned to meet my sisters and me because he never had children.

I let Yahim wait for me at the window frame, and I go inside the flat. I blow warm air into Uncle Richard's right ear, and he thinks the wind is coming from the open window next to him. He's asking his wife to close it.

Next, I stand in front of him, and he ignores me because he doesn't sense me. I move his right arm up and down, and he's surprised but doesn't question this movement.

I want Uncle Richard to feel better about losing all his family in the Holocaust; hence, I have decided to do something for him. I see a glass of Chilean wine on top of the living room end table. Oh, he will feel better if he drinks a glass of wine. My Uncle Henry always feels better after drinking it. I swing to the bottle and, with a blow, remove the cork. It flies across the room.

The woman says, "Goodness, funny things are happening tonight. It may be a ghost from the ocean coming to haunt us."

He replies with kindness, "Woman, serve us some wine." They both drink their wine happily, and as they do; I go through the window and join Yahim. We go ahead with our journey.

I realize that his wife is too old to conceive children. She would not be available to wish me as her child even if I wanted to choose her as my next mother. Besides, my uncle is too old to have a baby.

I'm telling Yahim that I want to visit the woman who was once called Darsha, my mother when I was a little boy in Mahashan. She is now known as Donelia, and I have unfinished business with her. Suddenly, we're at Donelia's house in Bucaramanga, Colombia. It has a square patio inside the premises, with rooms surrounding it. Donelia is enjoying her children while she combs her little girl's hair and braids it. She's an ambitious person who wants to leave the town and go to Bogotá in search of a better life for her children since she just became a widow.

SAN GIL, SANTANDER

Yahim is rushing me, but I still want to go to the place where Donelia grew up. San Gil is a colonial town with cobblestone streets. There is an old cathedral that was built by the Spanish conquerors a long time ago. Yahim and I continue going through the streets, floating on air, and he's still rushing me. My Master wants us to go home to the spiritual plane.

I'm seeing a gray light waving like a dog's tail in motion. It's ascending from a big old house. Then, another ray of light, just like the first one, shows up. The two lights leave from the same home, mount to gray clouds, climb to the sky, and then disappear on the horizon. They come back and station themselves on the roof of the old house and submerge again in the place. It's as if they're playing a flying game.

Yahim says, "Those two souls are ghosts because they refused to leave the world when it was their time to do so. They did not listen to the Masters and have remained on Earth to roam around this place. At this point, they don't know where to go. They don't know the way to the other plane and have become accustomed to being on Earth as ghosts, without a body or a purpose.

"The reason I want us to leave soon is that being here without a body can be fun. However, you may become attached to this world without any accountability. This condition will deprive you of growth, and you will regress. The universe itself will deprive your soul of finding the Ultimate Force, God."

As I listen to Yahim's wise insights, we go through a dense configuration of clouds. Soon, everything starts to become dark. Then, Yahim tells me one final message.

"You're about to enter the tunnel that will take you to a place of rest and reflection. There is nothing to fear, because you have done this many times. Once there, you will remember the connection between soul and body. If the soul refuses to let God and the Masters nurture it there, it won't be ready to resist temptations when it reincarnates. The bodily instincts will take over, and the desires of the flesh will cause significant damage to him/her and others."

GOING THROUGH THE TUNNEL

The tunnel is thick and dark gray, and there is just a little light filtering through some crevices. Dogs' faces appear in the crevices as if they're witnessing souls going by. They seem at ease, and the only thing they want is to see the souls of those who were once their owners. Birds are standing in smaller crevices trying to go back to Earth in new birth bodies. I softly fly over a beautiful, radiant, golden light, and I'm experiencing complete peace.

Next, I sense a vibration of love and comfort, and a deep desire to see what is waiting for me.

I look to the other side of the tunnel, and I see souls in despair, growling in pain and distress. From what I can tell, these souls are the ones of SS officials, Nazis, and others who have committed atrocities against my people and me.

One soul floating at my pace tells me not to look over there because they're the obscure souls, and their muddy energy is poisonous, and it may be contagious. I know I should stay away from that sickening energy. I look the other way, and I wonder what fate is waiting for me.

We make it through the tunnel, and there is a beautiful golden light shining all over the place. All is peaceful, and the air is filled with an atmosphere of wisdom, understanding, knowledge, and love.

Yahim is here waiting for me right at the exit to the tunnel. I'm in bliss. It's my time to rest, reflect, and slowly prepare to return to Earth. I arrive at my permanent/eternal home, and Yahim is leaving me at the doorsteps. Some of my everlasting family members are here. Others are living on Earth and on other planes.

To my surprise, Henry is here. My other uncles and my father have other clusters/homes near mine.

I'm back to "life between lives" to cohabitate with souls I know from other clusters, other communities, other worlds, and we develop ties with souls we don't know from before. At any rate, we enjoy meeting all these souls in a place I think of as Interlife. It's the same feeling as when we reunite with people we care about while we're living. In other words, we may cross paths with souls we have met on Earth or other planes while walking the avenues of eternity.

THERE ARE SCHOOLS IN THE SPIRIT WORLD

I'm in my eternal home now, and I'm in bliss. The beautiful light colors of all shades are illuminating the path I must take. These are what people on Earth call auras. We're on a patio inside a large building. It reminds me of Donelia's house in Bucaramanga because, as in her home, the inside deck has potted plants in each corner. One of the plants smells and looks like the prosperity plant my mother gave me when she traveled from New York to Chicago to visit me.

I'm in a large room that resembles an Earth classroom. There are other souls at my developmental level. We connect very well, and the learning begins.

I become aware that this is the school where I return every time I arrive at the spirit world. Yahim and Tarboo are my teachers. Yahim's curly hair resembles the curves of the roads in this plane.

I don't talk much; instead, I pay attention to my teachers. All of us pupils, about twenty, are projecting the same celestial purple light. My Master Yahim is wearing a translucent purple tunic that helps him float from student to student. No one is sitting since we don't have the burden created by the flesh. Instead, we find ourselves in a position close to Yahim or Tarboo.

Tarboo is wearing a brilliant green tunic. He is telling me to get one of the long books from a shelf on the wall. I float there, and he instructs me which one to take. The book is thick, yet not heavy. When I open it, I read all that happened to me in my past lives.

In an early life I was Robert de Ros, a cruel English nobleman who died in 1285. I killed commoners with my sword and without compassion for no valid reason. De Ros lived to please his flesh and for prestige and money. As De Ros, I decided to be reborn in destitution to purge my sins; as Pijush, a young skinny homeless boy. Later, as Abraham, I lived during the potato famine in Ireland, but overcame the ordeals of the land and was triumphant, despite living in a range of servitude and not prestige. Most recently, as Marlene, I didn't have the chance to commit many mistakes. The oppressors victimized me. And I endured suffering without many lamentations and no anger.

Yahim wants to talk to me in private. We go outside the school and sit on a bench. He tells me that it's time for us to reflect and says, "From extreme pain and sorrow comes reflection, wisdom, understanding, humility, endurance, and above all, purification of the soul and closeness to God. He, at times, chooses some of us to live a life of sacrifice for the benefit of humanity. The Chosen

Souls are loved and honored by God. Some souls are chosen to be the redeemers of lost spirits who have been corrupted by heavy, obscure, and muddy energy."

Yahim continues talking and says, "I want to hear from you, my dear Marlene. What is the most important lesson that is resonating in your being from this life?"

Tarboo has shown up looking sad and impatient because all the pain he has seen from Earth has devastated him. I remain calm and quiet for a few moments and ask Tarboo to do his task, to speak for me.

"I paid my dues, and I'm at peace. The sacrifice of my flesh was worthy because humanity is now aware of the consequences of being biased against a group of people. It's unspeakable to hurt our fellow human beings because of their ethnicity, race, creed, sexual orientation, or any other difference we consider variations from correct and acceptable norms. We're children of God, and He gives us the gift of life on Earth. If an individual has a problem with the looks, beliefs, or personal behaviors of others, then they have a problem with God because He has created each one of us in His likeness."

I want to utter something else from my soul lips. "I will forever be honored because I took part in the awakening of souls lost in the perverse satisfaction of seeing other humans fall in pain and despair."

Tarboo says, "May Holocaust victims remain alive in the conscience of humanity." He is ready to recite the poem he composed from the pain and suffering he experienced through me:

MARTYRDOM

I need grit, but where to find it?
When the oppression is immense, and compassion is absent
When prayers are kept from reaching Heaven
And the only thing that is present is the torment
Of knowing that life is brittle, and it will disappear

How am I condemned to such brutality
Just because I'm what God once made me
A Jewish girl with wealth in history
Punished like Job was, for being righteous

Then, what is the purpose of my martyrdom
Perhaps the cleansing of souls in darkness
Or the awakening of those whose instincts are too brutal
It's stained by an evil force that forever is roaming

All I know today is that I'm growing weaker
And as Jesus did before dying
Ask for clemency and change of history
When He begged His Father at the Mount of Olives
To spare Him pain from malignant evil

CHAPTER ELEVEN

PERSEVERANCE

EUGENIA, 1976

HOPE

I'm leading my spirit
To the place of some hope
Where my life will be guided
by the Masters who I know

HOUSTON WELCOMES US

Sophia is eighteen months old, and Violetta is six years old. We're leaving Chicago for good, and I have managed to put the root and a few branches of my prosperity plant in my purse. I also have three hundred dollars in a baby sack deep down in the purse as well. This money is what I managed to save from household items I sold to some neighbors.

The apartment is new and beautiful. I have a place with central air conditioning, a dishwasher, a new wall-to-wall carpet, and an inviting swimming pool in front of our apartment.

I have just realized that there is no source of public transportation in this city like there is in Bogotá, New York, and Chicago, cities where I have lived. I don't have a car; neither do I drive.

VIOLETTA IS IN FIRST GRADE

Violetta is going to first grade at Saint Paul Catholic school. I need to get a car as soon as possible with the three hundred dollars I have in my purse. Andreas is riding the motorcycle his Greek boss let him use, but he tells me that he found a car for three hundred dollars. That must be divine intervention because that is what I have. I tell him I want to buy the car, and he agrees to help me with the transaction. It didn't take me too long to get my driver's license because he taught me how to drive with a good disposition.

MY MOTHER IS ILL

We have lived in Houston a couple of years now. Today I just received a phone call from Lucy, my sister in New York. She's telling me my mother just had a mild heart attack. I'm traveling with Sophia, and Violetta is staying behind with Andy because she's at school. I'm getting the plane tickets tomorrow because I have a thousand dollars saved from the money I have managed to keep from my paychecks.

Sophia and I are in the plane now, and I have a funny sensation all over my body. I am seated next to a priest and I try to tell him that my mother may die today. He is quiet and ignores me.

I go to the restroom and sit on the commode with my child on my lap. I cry and ask God to release my mother from pain and suffering. I'm feeling an endearing, sweet energy all over me that affirms He's listening to me. It's 6:00 p.m.

Soon after that, the plane arrives at La Guardia International Airport. Kathy Delakas, an old friend, is picking me up from the airport because my two sisters, Lucy and Marie, are in the hospital with our mother.

An hour has gone by since I arrived at my friend's house, and my sisters are just coming. Marie told me that our mother died at 6:00 p.m.

My desolation is infinite; I'm falling to the floor as if I don't have any control of my body. I know God answered my prayer when I was in the plane because He allowed her to make her transition at 6:00 p.m., at the same time I was praying for her peaceful departure. Today is April 2nd, 1978. I will remember this day forever.

We're at our mother's apartment. I light the wick of a candle on the kitchen table. Marie is preparing some tea. I'm taking a deep breath, and I deny my mother's passing; I know deep in my essence that she moved on to a better place where pain doesn't exist.

Marie serves the tea while I stare at the candle's wick. My right arm moves from side to side in a rhythmical way. I place my right wrist on my chin. Suddenly, I feel a force moving my arm up and down.

My sisters notice the odd movements and tell me to stop doing that because I'm making them nervous, but I cannot control my arm. They look at me with disbelief. We all notice the candle's wick moving from right to left without any breeze.

I sob and know my mama is present at this time in her kitchen.

RETURNING TO HOUSTON

Sophia and I just returned from New York, and Andreas is surprising the girls and me. He bought a little frame house at 1101 Belshire in Pasadena, Texas. It has three bedrooms, a living room, a kitchen, and a garage.

I'm pleased about it; unfortunately, my mother will never see our little frame house.

I have an abdominal pain that keeps me from being completely happy about our new home. It started about a year ago. I have two pains, one on the right side of my lower chest and the other also to the right side of my lower abdomen. I went to the doctor, but he only prescribed over-the-counter medications.

The pain in my stomach and my mother's passing keep me awake at night.

Right now, I'm in a hypnagogic state, lying in bed with Andreas. Suddenly, the hair on my head is rising straight up, and an abundance of energy comes from the front door, crossing the short hallway and arriving at my bedroom.

While the energy is passing by the hallway, I know it's my mother's. She's showing up with at least three or four more identities, other spirits. She sits at the corner of the bed next to me.

I'm lying down, and she speaks to me, "My darling daughter." She conveys to me without words that I'm going to suffer even more while living with Andreas. She looks at him with reproach while accusing him of causing past, present, and future misfortunes to me and the children. Mama extends her right hand, which is adorned with the diamond ring she wore throughout the last years of her life. I hesitate to take her hand since it's transparent.

Andreas shakes my body and brings me back to this reality. He says, "Woman, what are you trying to do? I just bought this house, and I might have to turn around and sell it."

I look at Andreas and grab his steady hand as hard as I can. I tell him Mama just visited us.

He responds, "I saw her. Of course, I saw her." He turns his head and falls into a deep sleep. I toss and turn.

I get up from bed and go to the living room to sit on the sofa beside the front door. I pray to God with all my heart to send me an insight. I want His confirmation that what I have just experienced was indeed true.

"Dear Lord, my mother died at 6:00 p.m., and soon it will be 6:00 a.m. Was that my mother visiting me? Please, send me a sign at 6:00 a.m. Let the front door be opened by itself."

I fix my eyes on the wall. Sure enough, the house entrance door opens by itself and closes all the way at 6:00 in the morning.

I'm breaking into tears as Tarboo stands to my right, beside me. He says, "You must let go! You're disturbing your mother."

It has been several months since Mama died. Andreas is going back to his old ways, disappearing and not having money all the time. I am terribly upset because he's working as a bartender in a strip club. I feel humiliated and disrespected. When I look at my little girls, I think their father doesn't have any conscience.

I have a job that also brings money into the household. But I fear for my girls; hence, after eighteen months of normalcy I'm quitting my job. I have chosen to do so even though I desperately need the money I'm making; I understand that my priority is the children's well-being.

We're in poverty because we depend only on Andreas's income. I manage to feed my family with forty dollars a week if he doesn't gamble away our grocery money.

The only hope I have is the priest's letters from back in Colombia. The Father writes flowery letters to me all the time, promising that when he dies he's going to leave a fortune to me. I don't care about the money he offers, but having some income, besides the little bit of cash Andreas wants to give me, would be nice.

REMEMBERING ANOTHER LIFE

Several months have passed and I no longer dream of my mother, but a weird dream keeps appearing during my slow wave sleep (SWS).

I'm looking at a short, stocky man with a red face and an authoritarian demeanor. A big blue eye takes his place and swings from side to side of me.

Last night a name, De Ros from England, kept on being repeated in my dream. It also reiterated the year is 1285. Then, another voice kept repeating the exact words, "De Ros, De Ros, De Ros."

In order to distract my mind from the weird dream that occurs every night, I have decided to enroll at the junior college and enrich my academic skills.

My efforts help me because not only am I not having the disturbing dream anymore, but I have obtained my high school equivalency diploma (GED).

THE FATHER

I continue receiving letters from Father Perico. I'm writing letters to him and letting him know about my life and how graciously my children are growing.

I'm trying to create some kind of bond with him because I need to find out if he's my natural father. When I receive letters from him, he writes about his money and considers me in his will. Here is one of the many letters I have received from him.

January 13th, 1979
Eugenia,

I have sent you money before with people who travel to the States. I also have sent you money by mail. For example, I sent you a letter for Christmas last year with some cash. It was returned to me without the money.

I understand the terrible sadness that you're experiencing because of the death of your mother. However, what I cannot understand is that you didn't let me know when it happened. I had to find out about the unfortunate news from a third person. I cannot forgive you or your family for not sharing Donelia's passing with me. I forgive you for the Christian love I preach. But I cannot excuse you as the man I am. I suffer from your indifference and continuously tell myself, "She doesn't know who I am. She has forgotten about me. She has not corresponded to the love I have for her."

I correctly understand the deep anguish that you're experiencing. It was a deep wound, hard to heal. I share with you the emptiness and fathomlessness Donelia has left in your heart. But nothing, absolutely nothing, excuses you from the marginalization that you impose on me. You're an orphan now; hence, I should have known about it before anyone else due to the long friendship that links us.

When I bought the house in Bogotá, I made the mistake of not letting you know that I bought it on your account. I did so because your mother told me that letting you know how I helped was not the right thing. I bought it because of the many difficulties your family was going through because of the lack of shelter. I will leave you a savings account here in Bucaramanga, and I'm trying to send you money through some banking services. But that is almost impossible to conduct because that is way too risky.

Cielito, I want to share with you that on September 22nd, I had the golden anniversary of the priesthood. There are celebrations all over the place, including in the regional history building in Santander.

Padre Genaro Perico.

From what I understand after reading the letter, the man doesn't have any feelings or emotions. He teases me and goes around with a lexicon that is confusing and indirect. I have decided to go to Bucaramanga to confront that man for my own sake.

I want him to tell me why he doesn't practice what he preaches from the pulpit. Where has he been throughout my life and during all the trials I have to endure? I'm always alone, bearing my broken dreams and hopes.

FINDING THE TRUTH

It's the end of 1979, and I plan my trip to Colombia for the summer of 1980. I managed to save some money while working at Gray Tool Company, and Andreas doesn't know about it. My sister Mariela has lost her husband and wants to come live in Houston. Upon our arrival at Colombia, I let her know I have all the paperwork needed to sponsor her and her two minor sons to move to the United States.

On the road: Bogotá to Bucaramanga

Mariela and I are traveling together to see the Father. My daughters are staying in Bogotá with Lilian because the Father doesn't like little children. It's fun going through the Andes Mountains from Bogotá to Bucaramanga, and we admire the wild and magnificent scenery. The mountains look high and steep; it seems risky to be a passenger on those narrow roads.

I look down the cliff to see the virgin land that has been untouched by humankind; I think about my ancestors and how much I want to know about my paternal roots.

The Father is waiting at the bus stop in downtown Bucaramanga. He looks at me with intensity and is talkative. He's telling me that this is the land where I come from and not to forget my origins.

I'm observing him, and I see how much I look like him. His hands are replicas of mine, small with long fingers. He portrays an air of superiority, which he struggles to hide from me. We're now at his house, and two older women greet Mariela and me with a friendly disposition. They live here, attending to him all the time. He owns this house; hence, he doesn't live in the church. The house has a patio where he says they occasionally celebrate Mass. The dining patio has a ceiling made of glass.

We have a comfortable humble bedroom. We wake up early in the morning, but the Father is already gone; hence the ladies cook for us, and we eat by ourselves.

Breakfast is good, arepas, changua, and hot chocolate with cheese. The Father is joining us for lunch. He shares with me that he's not in the best of health and has difficulty sleeping. I'm showing him empathy and promise to send him a bottle of expensive B complex vitamins. He's surprised at my offer because he thinks I'm there to get, not to give.

The Father is taking us around the city for sightseeing early in the afternoon. We're at his house now. He's showing us his office. It's full of people waiting for him for consultation. He's an ecclesiastic attorney; hence, he's the priest assigned by the dioceses to evaluate petitioners who want an annulment to their marriage. Father Genaro Perico recommends and authorizes the evidence that goes to the Vatican for further analysis.

It's a new morning again, and he's gone by the time we wake up.

Another priest from the parish is here looking for him. He's asking me what kind of kinship I have with Perico because our resemblance is incredible. He's answering his own question with a mischievous look, "I know. You must be one of his nieces."

VISITING WITH THE FATHER

It's early afternoon, and we're seated in the living room. I notice the portrait on the wall is of an older woman. It affects me because I'm looking at photography of one of my ancestors. It's a pretty woman dressed in an outfit of the 1800s. I ask him about it. He tells me that she was his mother.

To evaluate the love for me that he has expressed in the many flowery letters he has written to me, I ask him if he would let me have that portrait. He's not answering.

Then, I ask him if he would let me see a photo of his father. He's not answering that either.

Finally, I ask if he has pictures of any of his relatives, and all he replies is "Many."

I need to ask a final question, "Where did you meet my mother?" He is still quiet.

I'm disappointed, and I feel that my trip to Bucaramanga was a waste of time.

We're waking up very early because I want to go home today. I'm frustrated because I didn't get what I wanted, the truth from the Father.

If he's my father, he doesn't dare to tell me.

RETURNING TO TEXAS

I'm back home in Houston, and the first thing I do upon my arrival is to send the Father the vitamins I promised. I'm frustrated today because I failed to find out if the Father is my father. My trip to Bucaramanga didn't help in finding a definite answer to the old question. I have decided today never to respond to his letters anymore because they're confusing and misleading.

I'm distracting my mind because I just received a letter from my sister Mariela. She tells me not to worry about Genaro Perico because I don't need him. He's not a good man.

She also tells me that the American ambassador in Colombia has granted her and her two minor sons permanent residency to live in the United States. My children and I will not be lonesome anymore because we will have extended family around us.

LOSING MY BABY BOY

The years march on and I'm pregnant again. I can barely make it with my two girls, twelve and seven. I visit Galveston Medical

Center for a checkup and am instructed to rest because I may lose the baby.

After returning home, I fall asleep. I dream of a lady floating in the air dressed in black, telling me that the baby in my womb will part from me because he has decided not to have me as his mother.

It's morning again, and I'm in pain and having a miscarriage. Andreas is leaving me home alone because he says he has to go to Louisiana to pick up some mirrors for the strip club. He leaves me alone at home while I am going through the process of losing my unborn child.

Marie and her husband are living in Houston now. They take me to the hospital. It is Saturday, January 7th, 1984, and I'm having a miscarriage. The doctor tells me it was a boy and that I will not conceive again.

A NEW BABY

The doctor was wrong because I'm pregnant again. It's Sunday, July 21st, 1985, and my baby girl is arriving in this world. My daughter Violetta helps me choose the baby's name. She and Sophia have assumed the role of little mothers to my baby. I have Elizabeth Ashley on my bosom, and I promise her as I did the other two: they will always have my love and protection.

GOING BACK TO SCHOOL

Andreas is back to full-blast gambling, and I have only one choice; I need to go back to school and get a formal education. If I do so, I will be able to support my girls.

Going back to school is going to be challenging and rewarding at the same time. Besides, learning is therapeutic to me. I often feel stuck without the tools to overcome the barriers that will give me freedom of will. But when I engage with the books, I disengage entirely from my pain, sorrows, and frustrations. Fortunately, I'm finding out that learning distracts me from my worries and the severe pain in my stomach.

Mystical Notes: Perseverance

I am in Sophia's bed, and I'm dozing off. Suddenly Yahim shows up and says, "You have tried so hard, my dear one, and you need to nurture yourself because you too are a miracle, and as such, you need to treat yourself.

"Your mother lived her journey and graciously completed it. The Father is your natural father, and his pronounced indifference is on his agenda and will be written in his scrolls. Let it be, and let it go for now. You need your strength to raise your daughters on your own and will be fine. And your husband is a forgettable soul who cannot remember the goals that brought him to his current life; he has his journey to live, and you cannot live it for him."

Tarboo is wearing his green tunic and looks radiant. I'm smiling as I look at my Masters. I'm thinking about Yahim's words and realize that each soul learns through the lessons lived, but some souls get wrapped up in the flesh and take the most straightforward way, the way of carnal pleasure.

Yahim pops the question he often has for me, "Besides what you're thinking at the moment, what is the most important lesson you have learned up to now?"

Tarboo looks enthusiastic and ready to answer the question for me. "I have learned to deal with the issues presented to me throughout my story. But I feel lonesome, unloved, vulnerable, and unprotected.

"I believe that we must stop tolerating other people's wrong behaviors when they take away our happiness and peace of mind. We may set a goal to free our-

selves from this pain by using guided perseverance; that is, to plan and stay with a plan of action to disengage from the people who take away our ability to enjoy life. In addition, it is wise that at the time of decision-making, we invoke God and the Masters to help us with the task to let go and let God guide us through the process of setting strong boundaries.

"Opportunities to new horizons will be handed to you from the Masters because God instructs them to help us get out of blocked roads on the paths we walk in life."

Tarboo has his scroll in his hands because he has been taking notes. He says, "I understand you, my sentimental one. You feel lonesome and sad. I took all you just said and made it into a poem. I'm reading it back to you, but at the same time, I want you to be aware that you have been a good pupil, and you will harvest what you have planted. These are perseverance blessings."

LONELY

I'm lonesome as the wind that is looking for a place to settle
I'm searching for the paths that will free me from my sorrows
From oppression and the disillusion of impending doom
In search of the sun rays of light that are hiding in the shiny moon

I'm lonesome as a tender butterfly
I'm lost in an illusion embedded in hope
To find some nourishment for my flesh to have
And the gift of wisdom for my soul to guide

I'm like a dove searching in the spacious sky
Striving for a place called mine
But it's late; the stubborn storm has come
It has broken the fragile branches that were held by the trunk of life

I'm lonesome in this world, I feel
My home on the other plane, I find
Deep down, I know I must stay
To fulfill a purpose that is somewhere in my walk through life

I'm lonesome; I'm looking for love and acceptance too
That will give me strength on the days to come
With serenity, take me to a better path
For me to encounter the sweet taste of staying alive

My warm hands, companionship want
From a father who decides to stay apart
And a husband who refuses to keep our unity alive
Because my soul and flesh companionship want

I'm lonesome like the shining moon
Its destiny is to be without love
Its brightness is for her to show
Only to hide from her beloved sun

I cry my solitude; I cry alone
And many times, I don't even know
That pain and suffering are my spirit's parts
I need my father's acceptance of his parenthood
And my husband's love or his departure at last

Marlene and Me

CHAPTER TWELVE

TRUSTING

DE ROS, 1237

CONSCIENCE

Oh, my life is marked by wealth and status
My ear is deaf to the needs of others
My hands possess ephemeral richness
That by default, one day, will vanish
And I'm missing the gift of charity

WEALTH, NOBILITY, AND PRESTIGE

It's 1237, and I was born into wealth and prestige. I'm considered nobility because I'm a baron. My name is Robert de Ros.

Feudalism is declining since the Magna Carta was signed in 1215. But I still have a lot of power over the serfs who are on my land. I have plenty of money, prestige, and status; therefore,

I'm not compassionate toward those who suffer from poverty and marginalization.

My grandfather, Sir Robert de Ros, took part in the signing of the Magna Carta, and I still don't feel compassion for the serfs that work the land for us. I work for the king, not for the sake of loyalty, but for prestige. At times I abuse the rights given to me when I became a baron. I kill innocent bystanders because I feel superior to everyone around me, and one of the ways I satisfy my thirst for power is by robbing the helpless of their lives.

It's 1258, and I'm working in Scotland aiding King Alexander III. He's in danger because people who oppose him want to hurt him and kill him. There are invasions from people who want to take away my king's power. I'm cruel and kill without any shame because I want to be in the king's favor.

I have another secret; I indulge my power by inducing women to satisfy my sexual desires. I find them among my serfs' families. At times, the family's patriarchs notice my behavior; other times, they're not aware of what I'm doing.

I usually take women whose husbands have died or have left them. I honestly don't know how many children I have. Even if I get to know who my children are, I will not get emotionally involved with them. I believe I have done them a favor because I gave them life. My wife knows about my affairs, but she looks the other way.

I live two lives: the one as a devoted Christian and a faithful husband to my wife Elizabeth and the only father to my five boys; the other as someone who chooses to let his flesh take charge of his soul. Deep down, I know I'm doing wrong, but I don't have any remorse. I believe that I deserve to have all I need and want.

I notice a beautiful woman who is eighteen years old. She's the daughter of a man who is my serf, and he knows that I'm courting the girl. I often go to her house to drink mead with her father. He likes to talk about the Magna Carta. I know all about it because my grandfather signed it in 1215.

This serf is a smart man and wants to converse with me. I tell him that he has the right to leave or stay to work on my land. He says he's never going to leave because he loves it. Sometimes we talk very late into the night, and when I leave, I wait for the light of the oil lamps to go off; then, his gorgeous daughter comes out, and we go into the field to be together.

The girl gets pregnant twice, and I have two daughters with her. I'm making her promise that no one will ever know of our secret. She agrees to it. Her father knows the kids are mine, but he doesn't say anything.

A few years have gone by after the affair with the young girl. Now, I'm having an affair with another woman. She's thirty-five, and her husband recently died. I tell her that she has to give herself to me if she wants to stay on and not be kicked off my property. She agrees. She has six children, and the oldest is only a fourteen-year-old girl. The two youngest are boys, and they are mine.

Later, I'm selling the same property to another baron. I don't even consider that my lover is a widow and has no one to protect her and her children.

Years later I have moved on, but my two little boys are begging to see me. I'm calling them to my castle, and they look dirty, skinny, and ill. I don't have any heart for them and ignore their pain, denying any responsibility because Elizabeth, my wife, is with me, and I cannot confess that I know they're my children. My wife throws some coins to them, which they rush to grab. They leave the castle, and I will never see them again.

I'm dying, and the five children I had with Elizabeth are by my side. The only person who can awaken my soul is my grandchild, who is only five years old. He's holding my right hand and looking at me with a sense of endearment. His deep blue eyes are moving my soul to its core. I'm reflecting and admitting to myself that I was not loyal to my king because I often abused my authority to meet the wants of my flesh and kill innocent people I did not like. But most of all, I feel guilty that I brought children into this world only to disregard and abandon them.

I'm not happy with myself and don't have any more time to repent. I look at my five-year-old grandson and tell him, "I will find some way to make amends." He understands, because he's smiling.

Mystical Notes: Trusting

Master Yahim is here, helping me to depart from the Earth. He talks with eloquence as is proper in 1285, the time of my death.

He says, "Each life you live is a gift. It's a fresh beginning granted to you by God. It has many joys and many challenges presented to you with the purpose of soul training on becoming a master of the flesh. Always trust in the optimal desires of your heart because they are linked to God's heart. They are forever connected. Follow your inner calls when they come with the sweet voice of peace when they benefit you and the members of your family constellation. Do so because you are not in this journey alone. All is reciprocal, mainly when you are dealing with your loved ones. It's also essential to look after the new lives you create. Children come to this world with the need to be protected. If we conceive children, we're responsible for their upbringing. Protect your seeds and nurture them. If we fail to do so, great pain will come to us in our future lives. It's also true that shedding innocent human blood is an aberration. God is the life giver, and He is the only one who has the right to take it away."

I, De Ros, reply to Yahim. "I'm a sinner. I lived for prestige and money and to please my flesh."

Yahim looks at me as I prepare myself to transition.

He says, "De Ros, what is the most important lesson you learned during this life?"

Tarboo is behind me, and I sense his hand on my forehead. He is talking for me, "Nurture my seeds and don't let them be adrift. Be mindful of what I do because all acts have consequences. Treat my fellow man applying the Golden Rule—'Treat others the way you want to be treated.'"

Tarboo pauses and is letting his own thoughts float. He is telling me, "You have finished a life of rudeness and deception. You took the lives of innocent people, robbed them of their dignity, and took young girls' innocence. You abused vulnerable women, disgraced them, to later abandon them with your children. You lied to your wife Elizabeth, making her believe you were a loyal husband, a Christian man who followed the Bible's teachings. You have learned to deceive your consciousness because you have let the pleasures of the flesh take you over. The good news is that you're learning, and you will succeed at it."

Tarboo has a violin in his hands and plays it while he recites a poem to Yahim and me. We listen and pay attention to its words.

INSTINCTS

Children are born in innocence and candor
They cry when discomfort is encountered
They smile and learn that pleasure is trusting
Lies and its ruthless, abstract understanding
The infant in purity all good perceives

As children grow older, their speech is improving
They say what they feel, tangible realities

Soon they witness the facts when distorted
The truth is skewed by those who are good at harming

Eight winters they've lived, deceits they're understanding
And the strength of the truth sometimes becomes fragile
Lies are the fleeting salvation, a temporary escape
Honesty is the principle in consciousness guarded

The frame of both actions, good versus evil
The axiom is complex; the spirit has two choices
Lies are the escape that attracts wrong actions
Truth is courage, manifested in honesty and rightness

Wisdom detects the tricks that hide evil
Sometimes ruthlessness is veiled and becomes facts
The truth, with its strength, the lying will shred
We're allowing goodness to remain forever shining

Why do we lie, knowing it hurts trusting?
Human behavior, uncertain and complex
Lying we do for power or pleasure
For hate or revenge, for envy or arrogance

The worst form of lying that usually happens
When one constant guile becomes the whole truth
The words convey a compelling message
Which even persuades liars themselves

The soul in captivity for the flesh, its pleasure
Ruthless is to obtain what the human desires

Power and the taste of carnal desires
And lie becomes a habit, and reality becomes quiet
While truthlessness defeats the honoring of trusting

CHAPTER THIRTEEN

ACKNOWLEDGEMENT

EUGENIA, 1987

LIFE CHALLENGES

Is it destiny, or is it choice? That is my question
I let destiny aside, and I make my own choices
Allowing with my voice, loud and clear!
The desires of my heart that I'm so much wanting

FINDING A JOB

I have seldom been able to give myself the luxury of staying home with my girls. I have worked as a clerk in several places. The last job I had was with the state as a temporary clerk at the Texas Employment Commission, but my boss, Mr. Wilkerson, hired someone else for the permanent position.

I'm crying because I feel inept. However, another job has come along that will help me conquer my goals and allow me to spend summers with my children.

Tom Hancock has offered me a job at Pasadena High School as a bilingual teacher's aide. This job is opening the door to my academic career because I can take classes at the junior college after school hours and during the summer.

I still sometimes dream of being trapped in a library, but now I'm finding words I can read from these books. I know the Masters have been sending me this dream to alert me that I have to find a way to a formal education.

ATTENDING COLLEGE

The work is arduous, and the patience is solid. I work forty hours a week at the school and attend classes twice a week. When I return home, I feed my children, prepare them to go to bed, and I sleep. When in bed, I set my alarm clock to go off every half an hour; hence, I sleep for half an hour and study for half an hour. That goes on for the next six years.

THE DIVORCE IS IMMINENT

I don't cry over the failure of my marriage anymore; instead, I have decided to lift myself up, let go of my sorrows, and continue living with the affirmation that I will overcome all my misfortunes.

I'm not allowing Andreas to disturb my goal and the enthusiasm to take my kids and me away from poverty. I have a great opportunity, and I'm determined to take it. I know that neither my spirit nor my flesh can stand much more suffering and abandonment from my husband. Being married to Andreas has been torturous since day one. Since I don't have any money to pay a lawyer for a divorce, I'm contacting United Way to see what legal aid the institution offers. All I'm paying for the divorce is 177 dollars.

My Master Yahim has been with me all the way, and Tarboo has always tagged along. Sometimes, when they want to manifest, they blow in my ear or make me laugh at something silly, such as a cat that often appears at my front door. They have said with unspoken communication that they will back me up in all I wish to accomplish.

Despite all the impediments I have found along my way, I have carried out my goal. I have graduated with a Bachelor of Arts from the University of Houston, Central Campus. My degree is in Spanish and English Arts. Mr. Hancock has hired me as an English as a Second Language (ESL) teacher and a Spanish teacher. The money I make is not enough to support my family; hence, I'm also teaching ESL to adults.

MY SISTER'S TRANSITION

It has been fourteen years since my sister Mariela moved to the United States with her two younger sons. It's Saturday evening, and she's visiting me. I'm fixing coffee and fresh bread like we usually do when we meet. We're talking about how she feels blessed because I sponsored her and her boys to come to this country. They own a house with a pool, which I enjoy a lot with my daughters. On her way out she asks me to take her to the store tomorrow.

While I'm in a deep sleep, I dream Mariela is pacing the floor because she cannot breathe. My nephew is trying to convince her to go to the hospital, and she's refusing. The pain is severe, and she gives in. Next, I see her leaving in an ambulance, and my phone rings. My nephew tells me that his mother has been rushed to the hospital because she just had a heart attack.

My heart trembles. I know the Masters were preparing me with the dream I just had. She dies six months later from complications due to her weak heart.

MOVING TO ANOTHER HOUSE

I'm selling our unpaid home, but the equity money will give me a down payment to buy another one in a better condition and location.

My future home may be located next to Space Center Houston. This place may become my dream home soon. I could be a proud owner of a luxurious town home, all through my own effort. If this happens, I would be breaking barriers created by my gender, ethnicity, and nationality, a timid Colombian woman who speaks with an accent, who has endured the pain and alienation of an immigrant.

The Masters helped and listened to my prayers.

I invoke God and the Masters while meditating in the guest room at my Belshire home in Pasadena. The Masters are giving me the affirmation that my wish will manifest. I will sell the old house and buy another one. I'm worried because of the two loans Andy left on the property. He took out loans on the house during some of his gambling sprees. I'm not going to sell it if these debts do not clear. Fortunately for me, someone at the courthouse has forgiven the loans, and the house can be sold. We will move to our new home in three weeks. I consider this divine intervention.

GOING BACK TO NORMALITY

Elizabeth, my youngest, is excelling in sixth grade; my middle daughter Sophia continues putting herself through college while working a full-time job at the bank. Her career plan is in teaching (eventually, she will become an elementary school principal). Violetta, my eldest, is a stepmother of three children and a mother of one, with another on the way. She's busy working and attending to her new family.

HEALTH ISSUES

I divorced Andreas, and I'm still suffering from abdominal pains. I have been experiencing that ailment for nearly seventeen years. It's a throbbing pain that attacks me all the time. I take Mylanta, magnesium water, Tagamet, and Ranitidine to alleviate my pain. But nothing helps.

It's Monday evening; I'm still waiting to complete the purchase of my house. I go to my safe place, the guest room at my Belshire home, because I have severe pain in my abdomen.

Yahim and Tarboo are present, feeling sorry for me because they can feel my stomach on fire. They guide me to the living room, and I turn on the television.

A *20/20* television documentary is being aired on ABC. The program host is interviewing an Australian doctor, Barry J. Marshall. He's talking about a bacterium that sits in people's stomachs and produces severe pain that, with time, may cause ulcers and even cancer. The bacteria's name is *pylori stenosis*.

That is interesting because when I first developed the pain, I went to Galveston Medical Center, and they told me I had a peptic and a duodenal ulcer.

On the program, Dr. Marshall is saying he ingested the bacteria, and when he got the symptoms caused by it, he cured himself by taking the proper antibiotics. Bingo, I have that bacteria because I have the symptoms.

MEDICAL CENTER HOUSTON

I'm at the doctor's office at Saint Luke's Hospital at Houston Medical Center. Upon my request, the doctor tests a sample of my blood. Sure enough, after a long waiting period at the doctor's office, the nurse tells me that I have it.

What is next? I'm thinking.

Before I ask the nurse any questions, she hands me a prescription and tells me to follow it for two weeks. I will be religiously taking my medication.

Two weeks have gone by since I went to the doctor, and I'm pain-free and cured. Science is based on human discoveries. Then God and His Masters convey messages that may help us overcome illness and emotional tribulations. God gave Dr. Marshall the strength and intelligence to discover and defeat the bacteria, and the Masters guided me to find the way to get the cure.

TRAGEDY IS ON THE HORIZON

Violetta has a stepdaughter named Marcy, from her husband's first marriage. The eleven-year-old girl has leukemia. Violetta wants to take the child to a place in Blanco, Texas, where the Virgin Mary's icon performs miracles.

Violetta has invited me and her eleven-year-old sister Elizabeth to go to Blanco with her and Marcy and her one-year-old son Ian to pray for a blessing for her stepdaughter. Elizabeth and I are enthusiastic about visiting the Virgin Mary's icon at the Greek church in that community. According to what Violetta tells me, the Virgin Mary's eyes cry real tears and perform incredible miracles.

I'm staying at the hotel with my one-year-old grandson and Violetta's stepdaughter, Marcy. Violetta and Elizabeth drive to town to see the icon. It's a dark evening, and I'm sleeping with the children under my care. It's midnight, and they haven't made it back. There is a knock at the motel door. I'm opening the door to four men wearing Texas Ranger uniforms.

I'm being informed that my two daughters were in a terrible accident. Violetta is having surgery, and Elizabeth is in intensive care. I scream frantically, and Ian is crying out as well. Once in the Rangers' car, the baby doesn't stop crying, and he returns to my arms.

I don't remember at what point my grandson was removed from my care. I feel as if my soul and spirit are away from my body. Marcy is being returned to her mother.

I'm at University Hospital in San Antonio, Texas, and a nurse is taking me to see Elizabeth. Her head is open, and she's bathed in blood. Her forehead has many lacerations caused by the windshield's broken glass. She suffered an extended cut on her jaw, from side to side; her left knee is wide open.

A middle-aged male doctor tells me, "Be glad you were not in the car. Only a child could stand such injuries." I try to touch my daughter, and the doctor doesn't allow me. I realize that I am not in a dream.

It's morning. I discover that my oldest daughter Violetta had only minor injuries and will recover well, and she did not lose the baby she was expecting. This is a great relief to me. However, the doctor tells me that Elizabeth is in ICU with closed head injuries. He still doesn't know if she's going to make it. I'm losing equilibrium in my legs and almost faint. I have to grab hold of the chair and find the armrest so I can rest my head.

It's been two days since the accident. I'm asking the nurse if Elizabeth will be okay; she replies in affirmation to my question. People come to pray for my child from all kinds of Christian denominations. I help when nurses wash her injuries. She has two tubes coming out of her head. I'm here waiting for the nurses to finish removing the tubes that drain the fluid from her brain. I sleep on the floor by her bed while Elizabeth is in ICU.

This goes on for two long weeks.

Elizabeth is out of ICU and is resting in a room by herself. Before being dismissed from the hospital, one of the doctors comes to the room to see her. He says that she needs physical therapy (PT) and has to learn to walk and speak fluently again. She's discharged from the hospital and has an appointment to return for a checkup in a month.

We are at our home, and we go to bed early. I wake in the middle of the night to the sound of the three crystal music angel globes. Their music chimes at 1:00 a.m. every night. It's soothing, and I'm not scared. The Masters will send good people to help us overcome the tragedy.

People in the community are bringing me food. This morning, I found an envelope in my mailbox with dollars and coins. Every little bit of money helps because I am the only one bringing in an income for my family. I don't have a clue about who sent that money. It helps me fill my car with gas since Elizabeth needs to go to the medical center twice a week, and we live twenty miles away from Hermann Hospital, where her physical therapists are.

We're back at University Hospital in San Antonio for Elizabeth's follow-up. The doctor's surprised at her progress and says that children with this type of injury usually take six months to show improvement, and yet she's okay. We don't have to return to that hospital, and she doesn't need physical therapy anymore.

MIAMI AND A LOVED ONE FROM MY EARLIER LIFE

It is six years later, and Elizabeth doesn't want to go to college in Texas because she wants to go away for a while. She's still traumatized by the accident. I'm in Miami, leaving Elizabeth in college. My four living sisters—Sara, Lilian, Marie, and Lucy—are here for a family reunion. Lucy's apartment is small; therefore, I have to share the bed with Sara.

I'm into a deep dream, and I see a man wearing a white uniform with blue stripes from the Holocaust. He speaks a language that is neither English nor Spanish. For some reason, I know it's Czech. The tall, stocky man tells me he loves me, and asks if I remember him. I tell him I don't. He says, "I'm about to be reborn into a Jewish family in this city. I was your Uncle Henry when you were Marlene."

I'm agitated because I'm watching snapshots from that life. I scream at the top of my lungs, "I don't want to die like this. Please, Uncle Henry, save me from this death! Please don't leave me."

My words don't make any sense, but I know what I'm saying. My sisters are alarmed because of my screaming. I'm experiencing sleep paralysis and cannot come back to this realm. I'm aware that my sisters are around me. I open my eyes, and the four of them are trying to wake me up. Sara says, "I recognize that language from the store in Chapinero, that old neighborhood in Bogotá. It was a Czechoslovakian shoe store."

Mystical Notes: Acknowledgement

I'm meditating in my bedroom at the University Green Town Home. All is quiet. Suddenly, the music from the three globes that house the angels begins to play. I feel a wave of energy on the right side of my body. Yahim comes with Tarboo, and they want to manifest their acknowledgment on my physical presence. Yahim talks. Tarboo and I listen: "Eugenia, go back to the time when your sister Mariela died. You dreamed about Mariela having a heart attack, and she was having one. I prompted Mauricio, your nephew, to wake you up with the ring of the phone call, and he did. You were confused for a little while, but it did not take you long to acknowledge the message that your sister was in imminent danger of losing her life."

I'm looking at Yahim, and he looks peaceful. Tarboo is behind him now. I do not have anything to narrate because they know everything that happened the night my sister had the heart attack.

Yahim becomes larger and tells me, "I also sent you another dream about your sister because you were very close to us during that time." I respond, "Yes, you did, and you probably know all about it." Yahim smiles and says, "Narrate it anyway." I talk now, "It's Sunday, and I'm just returning from church. As I lie down on my bed, everything turns gray. Mariela tells me that the place where she is now is just like planet Earth. There are schools, universities, recreational parks; suddenly, two Masters who look like you grab her and take her away as they scold her for her lack of prudence and for talking too much."

Yahim and Tarboo smile at each other and comment that I am intuitive. I don't like labels, but "intuition" doesn't sound that bad. It implies that I know that in the afterlife there are communities very similar to those on Earth.

ELIZABETH'S MIRACLE

My two Masters have similar energies and are smiling at me. Yahim comes closer to me, and I feel his celestial energy. He tells me he was with me when my daughters had an automobile accident in Blanco, Texas. He says that my words of desperation vibrated in Heaven in a way that Jesus and His angels heard them.

Tarboo wants to declare my statements with grace as Yahim and I listen to the prayer I sent to Heaven at the time of the accident: "Dear God, I need my baby Elizabeth alive. If anyone must go, let it be me. If she makes it, I promise I will always be there for whatever she might need in life. I want her to be normal, and as she was before this awful accident."

Yahim is reinforcing what Tarboo just repeated, "The Lord listened to you and granted you the gift of having your daughter back."

Yahim has his question, "What lessons did you learn during these times of havoc in your life?"

Tarboo talks with eloquence for me as if he's reading my thoughts, "Acknowledge the Masters and trust them. Don't feel discouraged and faithless during times of trials and tribulations. You're never alone, because we're the ambassadors of God, and we're with humans to give them hope, resilience, and acceptance. Humans grow stronger with each strike in life. Remember that everything happens for a reason, even though we don't always know the reason. We have to accept the inevitable. Remember the Masters, invoke them, and they will descend to help during those hard times."

Yahim states now, "Use the five senses to find us, because we also assist good, transitioned souls to communicate with their loved ones. We also send messages in dreams that alert people to what is coming or to watch for signs that may prevent tragedies."

I agree with my Masters, and I see how they softly dance to the music of the globes that rest on the top of my tall dresser in my bedroom. Tarboo has composed a poem from the thoughts I have engraved in my eternal memory and he recites it for us.

MASTERS

Our Masters are planning and waiting
For returning to our lives
We humans are busy searching
For the ones who wish to guide us
Through anguish and sorrows, they help us survive

While souls wait for their new bodies
To wear when we shall return
We see a glimpse of unfinished business
And find our closure as we march through many lives

The Masters with us once planned
On the where, when, why, and how
We would solve the troubles we left once pending
in another life, place, and time

If we fail to learn the well-planned lessons
Returning is the forever payback
Living with the same conflicts and same sorrows
That we created sometime in a far past

Life is nothing but a circle that continually rotates
One experience after another, coming, going with a variety of vibes
We bring knowledge, wisdom, strength, and understanding
To help us decipher issues pending from past lives

The Masters are in the midst, seeing and helping all the time
They're wise at understanding and diligent when they need to act
To give us tools and wisdom that, at times, we do not grasp
While we find our place in the enormous web of life
Living, dying, and with purposes which are hard to finalize

Marlene and Me

CHAPTER FOURTEEN

HEALING

PIJUSH, 1311

HEALING

Masters are present to open the veils
That reveal the issues we experienced in the flesh
They're ready to share their wisdom with us
That reminds us of lessons that we agreed to before we arrive

THE LITTLE BOY IN MAHASHAN (PRESENT-DAY BANGLADESH)

While meditating in the guest room in our tiny house at Belshire Street, I remember events from another past life. My dark brown feet reveal I have not worn any shoes for a long time. They look hardened from walking on hard surfaces.

I'm fourteen years old, since I make sure to count my age with the passing of the moon cycles. I'm alone, homeless, incredibly skinny,

235

in poverty, and constantly need relief from gasses and fecal elements from my sick stomach because I have rotting guts.

My lips are dried, and my big eyes are trying to find shade under my copious eyelashes because they're tired. The year is 1325.

A HOMELESS BOY

I'm Pijush, living in the street, and my soul is connected with this flesh. When I want to rest or sleep, I curl up in a fetal position, avoiding contact with the disgusting rodents that go by us boys. It's scary when they run in front of me as if they have the intention to harm my friends or me. Shop ladies put out leftover food from previous days to feed us, but often wild birds and rats get it before we boys do.

Among the women, there is a new face. This diligent woman shows a lot of interest in helping and insists on being the one who helps me. It seems there is a personal reason, because she gives me more care than she gives the other boys. She brings fresh water only to me from a clear stream that is in the nearby forest. I drink from the metal cup she offers me, then she takes it back home with her to wash it and bring more fresh water the following morning.

Eventually I'm too weak to even use my hands to eat. My long black hairbands fall in the way when I reach for the water she offers me. She tries hard to help me eat and drink, but I'm not responsive anymore. She insists, and finally, I swallow a few drops. I become exhausted from my drinking efforts and collapse to the ground.

The woman shows remorse when she kneels to lift me. She reveals feelings that only a family member, such as a parent or caregiver, might experience. I manage to sit down again but refuse to take a piece of fresh bread she's offering me because the pain in my guts is very intense.

The woman looks at me with tenderness and finally tells me, "I'm Darsha, your mother. I have walked many kilometers from a faraway land to come back to you, my son. I love you."

I, Pijush, reflect. If she is indeed my mother, where has she been all this time? My grandmother, her mother, told me she was dead.

She continues talking with a voice of endearment, "I've been looking for you ever since I left you with my mother. I wish I could shelter you, but my landlord doesn't want you in my place since you're ill. He's afraid you may infect other tenants."

Her words are beginning to fade away. Everything that happened to me in this life appears in my mind. Yahim, the wise Master, arrives and stands near me. The Master is helping me with my final departure from this plane.

REMEMBERING MY LIFE AS PIJUSH

My weak, fourteen-year-old body is ironically fading in the arms of my long-lost ma, the woman who abandoned me when I was an infant.

Yahim knows I'm looking for closure. I need someone's words of permission to leave once and for all. Rahul, a twelve-year-old and one of my friends, gives me the assurance it's in my best interest to leave in peace. I'm barely breathing, and I'm looking at the blue sky. Rahul comes closer to me, pinches my right forearm, and says, "Don't be afraid; death is better than living a dying life."

I'm not breathing anymore and still can see my ma with my soul's eyes, and I sense a connection with her; however, I still don't understand my ma's abandonment.

Yahim tells me that it's okay to wander around for a bit once I let go of my last breath. I want to say my goodbyes to the people and places I encountered during this life. I also want to remain on planet Earth for a little longer because I want to be with my mother for a short time before departing forever.

Suddenly, I let go of all my feelings. I'm free, and don't suffer anymore. My soul sees how my body is inert, lifeless. Boundless energy is present.

Yahim is here, sharing his restorative power with me. The Master tells me, "I have been your companion throughout many lives. You will find an answer to your question. What prompted Darsha, your ma, to abandon you? Accept it, Pijush; it was the love she felt for the man she ran away with when you were an infant."

FINDING THE TRUTH

Darsha is a fourteen-year-old when she gives birth to me one afternoon. She's unable to attach or attend to my needs. Because the love she has for the man who is not my father has blinded her, she's abandoning me without any guilt.

I have known Darsha since I reincarnated as Robert de Ros in the early twelve hundreds. Darsha was De Ros's wife, and her name was Elizabeth. De Ros was a cruel man to most people but loved Elizabeth, the woman of his life.

My ma's lover killed my father before I was born because he wanted Darsha. It's late at night, and my father is walking on a road. On his way home, he's happily singing ballads because he had a good day at the market and because he's going to be a father for the first time. Suddenly, ma's lover attacks my father from behind with a sharp blow to his back. He pierces my father's heart with a spear. I feel my father's heart fading away while I move in desperation in my mother's womb.

Life is good during my first eight years of life. If I don't go to school, I go to the market where my grandmother has a booth. She's a good shoemaker and sells shoes made from snakeskin. Grandmother and the other vendors are always alert because thieves are all over the place. I pull on her apron when bandits are around. She understands the message, takes her sharp knife out of her apron pocket, and with the help of other vendors, runs the bad guys out of the market.

I'm eight years old, and my grandmother just died. I'm an orphan now, and my home is on the street assigned to destitute children like me.

Mystical Notes: Healing

I'm floating above my inert body, and I'm on the ground in the street where I was homeless for several years. Ma covers me with white linen and stands in front of me. Darsha is wearing a soft silky tunic and a veil over her head that resembles aristocracy.

My soul is ready to depart from Earth. I swing back and forth from a thick strip of energy that links me to the heavens. From there, I see what is going on throughout times past, present, and future. I see how my life as Pijush begins with the death of my father and Darsha's abandonment. My grandmother tells me she's my mother, and I believe her.

I'm nine years old now and have the understanding that I don't know it all. I'm very intuitive but don't grasp abstract concepts of matters related to the flesh. My mother is alive in another city because I hear that from people in the market, especially women, who cannot resist gossiping. They tell me how Darsha abandoned me for a man. I'm too young to confront the gossiping women.

The strip of my soul's energy briefly transports me to the future. I'm with Yahim. The Master is preparing me for future lives yet to come. I see myself floating in another plane, being attentive and enthusiastic about new experiences on planet Earth. It could be that at some point, God may assign me to live in other faraway planets and different dimensions.

Yahim and Tarboo know what is going on in my soul's future, and they're waiting for me to give them the sign that I'm ready to depart. The strip of my soul's energy briefly transports me to the future. My companion Masters, Yahim and Tarboo, prepare me for a future life that one day will come. The life of a little Jewish girl in Europe.

PIJUSH'S BURIAL

My mother's guilt is unbearable because she doesn't have any other children, and I have transitioned; hence, she wants to bury me with dignity and a beautiful ceremony. She has prepared an ornate burial. Ma brings clean white outfits for my homeless friends, and they are all marching and saying goodbye to me, Pijush, at the cemetery. The women who attend to the orphans go to the funeral as well.

As the procession to the cemetery takes place, the pallbearers march with elegance. The elephants are wearing fine silk, and they display their rhythmical walk along the cobblestone streets. Several women cry because Darsha has paid them money to bring dignity and grief to the burial. She's announcing to the people's congregation that she's my mother. As she cries over my tomb, she tells me that I will always have flowers. The pretty birds and doves will forever keep me company as they will fly over my grave.

I, Pijush, am disappearing from the face of the Earth, and now I have unfinished business with my mother. At this point, I have a more realistic way to connect with her. I'm planning to be her child in some future life. Darsha and I combine our energies, and without realizing it, make a contract with each other. She will have the chance to be my mother sometime in another life, another place, and in another time.

Yahim looks at me in my energy body and tells me, "You will go to the afterlife and disengage from this world's affairs for a while. Sometime in the future, you will be Darsha's son or daughter again and under better circumstances. You will find your mother in a country across the continents. You will have six sisters and one brother."

I refuse to leave at this moment because I want to experience how the soul reacts once the body goes to the grave. Nothing happens. I feel relief and am ready to leave.

Yahim asks me, "What lessons did you learn in this life, my dear Pijush?"

I'm not answering, and Tarboo comes along with his hands holding a harp. He has a solemn look and, as usual, reads my mind and talks for me.

"I learned that we heal when we remember past injuries and we allow good vibrant light energy to be the source of our energy. All we do, good or bad, vibrates for eternity. I learned that karma follows us from life to life, and at times, we come back to Earth to experience the suffering we caused other people in the flesh. I came as Pijush because I needed to purge De Ros's wrongdoings.

"I have healed as I remember these lives, as well as Marlene's and Abraham's. I have been remembering and healing as I am living as Eugenia."

I recognize the Masters' wisdom because they are ambassadors of God. They have the tools to guide humanity through hardships of life.

Tarboo has something to say on his own. "When we're in a position of wealth, prestige, and of being able to help, we should keep a posture of love and kindness toward people who are walking the roads of life without any of these life tools."

Tarboo is ready to play the harp, but instead he recites a poem he found in my eternal memory that only he, Yahim, my mother, and I can hear.

ETERNITY

It will be a bed of flowers; it will be a bed of roses
The blanket that will cover me when my flesh surrenders
To ashes of deep memories embedded in the unknown
While mischievous seagulls will rest over the solid stone
Singing, mewing, and dancing under the shining moon

The nocturnal wind sounds will run across my grave
While my pale face will resemble the sadness of fainting Lili
My hands in inertia will pose like rocks that were just carved
And my withered lips will quiet the words that were before

The vibrant flesh will become the august emblem of perfect solitude
The world that I'm leaving will soon forget my passing
If by luck one memory manages to stay
The arrogance of time will vanish with its steady fast steps

But all I wish to keep when my flesh surrenders
Is a bed of many flowers just lying over me
To warm what was once my essence
Though their gorgeous beauty soon should also fade away

The ephemeral existence of those beautiful flowers
Will see how the tears of my loved ones will vanish from the Earth
But their beauty I want, even if my eyes don't witness
Their glorious splendor, of colors of all kinds

It will be a bed of flowers; it will be a bed of roses
The blanket that will cover me when my flesh surrenders
And my happy, joyful spirit to another plane will go
Where angels of all fragrances wait with music and their singing
To hold me and to guide me to a new life to grasp

Chapter Fifteen

ACCEPTANCE

Eugenia, 2003

Farewell

Oh, my soul that my heart embraces
In moments of solitude and sadness
My three offspring have marched away
And with grace, I must celebrate as they take their routes
For the world is claiming their service
As I stay behind, holding just the memories

Coming home

I'm returning home from Miami to an empty nest. I have decided to move from a high school teaching assignment to a kindergarten position. No longer do I have to send students to the office for not behaving; instead, I ask them for a time-out at their desks.

Several months have gone by, and I'm adjusting to my new life. I sometimes date, but finding the right man is a challenging task. My experience and belief system are durable guards that protect me from mistakes when choosing a man for a relationship.

COUNSELING CALL

It's time to go back to college and achieve a master's degree. I'm in front of the counselor's office at the University of Houston–Clear Lake (UHCL), ready to inquire about a master's degree in writing.

A lady professor who is passing through the hall where I am standing says I should apply for a counseling scholarship since I'm bilingual. The university has just received a grant for bilingual teachers to help them achieve a master's degree in school counseling. I'm going for it because I will not have to take student loans.

Unfortunately, Dr. S, the professor in charge of the scholarship, doesn't approve me, and other teachers receive the scholarship. I don't know what prompts her to decide to deny me the opportunity to obtain the scholarship. However, I have already made up my mind, and I will achieve it. I will take out school loans, resign my evening ESL teaching position in order to cover all my expenses and have more time to take care of my children, take classes and study.

MASTER'S DEGREE AT UHCL

The UHCL counseling program offers free counseling to students in their core. I'm going to try it. The Masters are my support, but I often have to wait for them to come in a dream or by telepathy.

They alert me with the messages they send me; however, I'm ready to get counseling from a human being in the flesh, just like me.

Receiving counseling from a therapist is concrete and in a complete human form. Ms. B is my counselor, and I can utter all my insecurities related to my origins and feelings of abandonment from the Father. On top of guilt from my heritage, I also have an inferiority complex created by my ex-husband's disdain toward me. Andreas's indifference toward me has hurt my self-esteem and the core of my existence.

I have discovered throughout psychotherapy that I'm injured because of my father's abandonment, and my awkward behavior reveals my insecurities. Learning about my emotional injuries related to Genaro Perico is painful, and I often cry during therapy. All those open wounds are so much part of my identity, and revealing them to someone in the flesh is very painful.

Psychotherapy has gone well, and the counselor has helped me see the world differently. There are issues caused by negative cognitions I have created about myself. It's my task to replace them with positive ones. There are many approaches in counseling, and hers is person-centered. I understand the therapist's point of view, and she makes sense. She's giving me human techniques to improve my mental health. I'm following the counselor's directions.

She suggests that when I think about Andreas, to visualize him on a large imaginary movie screen. Ms. B recommends slowly shrinking his image on the screen until he becomes tiny. I'm doing the exercise, and the approach is working.

The therapist has commented that the priest abused my mother because she was vulnerable. Women didn't have much of a voice during those times in Colombia. Mama's lack of money and education prompted her to believe the man who merely wanted to please his flesh. He didn't take anything seriously, not even his priesthood vows. How could he take his offspring seriously? He had an air of superiority and disdain for his own offspring.

MEETING ROGER

I'm an empty-nester parent and I live alone. I'm using solitude to connect with the Masters, but I also need human companionship. I don't want to die without experiencing the feeling of being loved by a man.

The chances for me to meet someone are few since I hardly go out, and at church, most men my age are married. Hence, I'm joining a dating website.

Something funny just happened. I'm signing up for one dating service, and to my amazement, another one is welcoming me to their services. Oh, well, I stay with it because I just don't want to bother. It will be what it will be.

It's Saturday morning, and I'm just getting up from bed. As I stand in front of the bedroom door, I'm declaring these words, "God, send me a man who will love me and won't frown at my beliefs. I want a professor with lots of wisdom."

Right now, I'm seeing the man in my mind. He speaks with wisdom; Yahim's light radiates all around me, and there are books and papers floating around him.

Tarboo is also in my mind. He's smiling and carrying a tablet in his hands. He's telling me he's composing a poem for my new man and me. I'm puzzled. I realize that Yahim played a trick on me. I signed up for a website I didn't know about because my future husband was there, waiting for me.

I'm at Starbucks waiting to meet the man from the "unplanned" dating service. It's Wednesday, April 16th, 2004. Roger, a professor from a local university in the School of Economy, shows up at Baybrook Mall. As the evening goes on, I'm noticing we have many affinities. He likes to read and learn; I do too. He has a sense of humor, and I enjoy his jokes.

Roger and I continue dating and have found out that we care for each other. It's the time of our lives, our golden years. We both are looking for a peaceful relationship where we can grow spiritually; hence, we have decided to get married.

WEDDING BELLS

Bells are tolling for love on this day
An embrace of dreams and wondrous joy
As flowing rivers of harmonious bliss
Bathe two hearts in glorious hope

Bells are tolling for love on this day
Winter has allowed spring to bloom
Aging trees have been made strong
By the miraculous force of love

Bells are tolling for love on this day
As laughter beset yesterday's sorrows
When smiles overcome pain
Bright days will attract sunny tomorrows

Bells are tolling for love on this day
God's unexpected blessing of a second chance
The oil of joy with beauty for ashes
Heart's delight in the beauteous romance

Bells are tolling for love on this day
We're forever dissolving solitudes past
We're building a path for two united souls
Weaving dreams that will forever last

NEW HORIZONS

It's the spring of 2005, and I have graduated with a Master's in Behavioral Science. We are also having a June wedding at the church, with a DJ, dancing, and good food. My grandson Ian is walking up to the altar with pride and optimism for a better future.

OUR MARRIED LIFE

Life with Roger has been good. I don't feel lonesome any longer. He gives the love and care that nurtures my soul and spirit. We talk for hours, and we have many affinities, including our firm belief in the afterlife. We visit places of common interest, such as art museums and presidential libraries. I go with him when he presents his economic papers at various cosmopolitan cities in the country and overseas.

GETTING A SCHOOL COUNSELING JOB

My husband helps me apply for a counseling job in several districts in and around Harris County. It's tough to find one because I'm no longer that young; however, Roger's support and perseverance constantly lift my spirit.

Finally, I get a job as a counselor in Channelview ISD. The job is not easy, but I have my Masters and faith in God to become a good and efficient school counselor.

Every morning at dawn, I had invoked the Masters while manifesting visions of myself in a large school helping children with their emotional issues. The intention has worked, and I have a job in a school with students who come from severely dysfunctional families.

A REAFFIRMATION ON REINCARNATION

I'm still having sporadic flashbacks of earlier lives. No longer just Abraham, Marlene, De Ros, or Pijush, but other lives I lived in different places on Earth.

I'm reading about Ian Stevenson and his intense studies at "The Reincarnation Division of Perceptual Studies" at the University of Virginia. Roger is interested in the subject, and after reading data on the subject from Stevenson, he embraces this belief.

We read Brian Weiss's books and listen to his CDs to enhance our meditation skills and focus on finding our old memories. We're up for a new learning adventure. It's so lovely to transfer from the pronoun *I* to the pronoun *we* when talking about the journey of life.

THE FATHER, MY FATHER

It's Martin Luther King Day, and on Monday morning, January 16th, 2012, I'm opting to drink my coffee before leaving for work. The students are not at the elementary school today, but the faculty has ongoing training throughout the day. As I'm drinking my coffee, I reflect on the mystery of my natural father. I need to figure out something to get closure on the subject that has puzzled me for so long: Is the Father my father without any doubt? I don't know.

I remember the Father's letter I never opened. It has been in my dresser drawer for over a decade. I take it with me and promise myself I will be able to read it. It's probably another letter without any real meaning like the ones I received before.

A couple of teachers drop by my office and invite me to go to lunch with them. I decline the invitation; instead, I'm staying at school to read the old letter. I figure I will not be emotional about it because many years have gone by since I received it. I'm wrong. The letter is moving me to the core of my being. It says the following:

April 2nd, 1991
My dear Child,

The words I'm writing are sending sad news to you. I have been bedridden for four months with an illness named "brain sclerosis." Its symptoms are weakness, cerebral palsy, and lack of appetite. I have consulted with several doctors, and they have all told me there is no cure for this condition. I ask you to pray for me with all your compassion to God so He will cure me with His infinite mercy. You're my daughter. There is not anything else to say at this moment.
Yours Truly,
Padre Genaro.

He wrote that letter exactly thirteen years, to the day, after my mother's death. She died on April 2nd, 1978. I want to cry, and I can't because I'm at work. I'm sweating, and my hands are cold. I want to go home and hide under the blanket in my bed. However, I'm doomed to continue living in the shadow of my parents' secret.

ROGER AND I, DESTINATION MUNICH

Roger met Peter Leibl, a German professor, during some of his presentations in Paris while we were in Europe in 2009 and 2010. Dr. Leibl is inviting Roger to teach at the Munich University of Applied Sciences for the summer of 2011. We're excited about the opportunity to visit Germany and go on a tour of some other countries on the continent.

DACHAU

While we're in Germany we're visiting Dachau, the concentration camp near Munich. I'm closing my eyes and remembering that my two sisters, Abigail and Ruth, died here. I'm remembering that Marlene's father, my three uncles, and I died in Auschwitz. My heart trembles, and I have to cry.

CAREER GOALS

I'm thinking about retiring from the school district; hence, I'm working toward achieving Licensed Professional Counselor (LPC) credentials. The college work and the internship are not that hard, but I have found that the exit exam is challenging.

Nevertheless, I just passed it, and I'm ready for a new way to serve humanity.

UNIQUENESS, POWER, AND MAGNIFICENCE

I'm retiring from the school district in the spring of 2017 because I need more time to focus on finding sources that will help me understand the science of parapsychology.

It's fascinating to discover the wonders of the subconscious mind. I have been reading about Michael Newton's teachings and still don't know much about formal hypnosis. The reality is that I need to find out more about it and learn about the mysteries of the subconscious mind.

After looking on the web to find the right training on hypnotherapy, I have found Paul Aurand. He's training individuals with counseling credentials at Pietrasanta, Italy.

As I join the training, Dr. Newton dies. He was a real Master teacher on Earth. Dr. Newton was the founder of the Newton Institute of Life Between Lives. He specialized in hypnotherapy. His main asset was helping humanity heal through spiritual regression. His books are *Life Between Lives*, *Journey of Souls: Case Studies*, and *Hypnotherapy for Spiritual Regression*.

As I read his works, I become more fascinated with his research and findings. I have decided to focus on his teachings to enhance my God-given ability to understand matters related to the afterlife.

LEARNING TIME AT PIETRASANTA

Roger and I have rented an apartment in Pietrasanta. I'm attending classes daily from early in the morning to late in the afternoon. I'm learning about the essential components of hypnosis while I'm receiving training in *clinical*, *past-life regression*, and *parts therapy*.

I'm also learning that by discovering past lives, we may heal from old wounds. One topic that impresses me a lot is the power of the subconscious mind. If it's activated, we can cure unexplainable ailments that physicians sometimes have problems finding and healing.

FOUR YEARS LATER

It has been four years since I opened my practice in Clear Lake, Houston. My goal is to help people of all ages and walks of life with issues related to mental health. I can attest that the solutions to our problems are within. Each of us has a unique universe, and becoming knowledgeable of our inner self gives inner peace and happiness.

Mystical Notes: Acceptance

While meditating alone in our new home's bedroom, Yahim takes me to a safe place in a dream. It's a faraway plane with many different shades of light. I observe his enormous face framed in cumulus clouds where Tarboo is standing to his right side.

Yahim says to me, "You have lived most of your life, and you have learned most of the lessons you have yearned to experience. Now, Ms. LPC, tell me about the most important lessons you have learned up to now?"

Tarboo as always speaks for me, standing behind a pulpit made out of a pileus cloud. He takes the position of a professor who is reviewing an interesting book.

He says, "I have learned that **talents** are God-given gifts that are at times healing tools. We heal when we **remember** experiences we have in each life. When we return to a new life, we bring memories that may help us find closure with issues of the past. The leaders of the family life are both the mother and the father. Loyalty is the manifestation among human relationships. It strengthens family **ties**. It would be wonderful if we could learn to practice **loyalty** not only with our family members and friends but with our neighbors, country, and nations all over the world. The key is in the Golden Rule, 'Treat others as you want to be treated.' I would add, be honest to others as you wish they would be honest to you.

"It is vital to nurture our strengths to overcome unhealthy matters of the mind. **Strength** comes with the ability to create positive talk to replace negative thoughts and cognitions we have about ourselves. If you have the strength to be disciplined with your thoughts, you will come out of the trials of life that come from negative thinking.

"By another token, it is important to recognize the quiet voices of the Masters that filter into our minds. They alert us by sending **predictions**. If we listen to this delicate voice, we will learn to avoid sufferings and calamities. When we rush into decision-making and allow impulses to take charge of our life, we need to take a step back and **reason** before acting. This will also help us to avoid problems. We can avoid having to make amends for impulsive wrongdoings that lacked reflection and reasoning.

"We should **honor** and love our family members unconditionally; however, it is vital to accept that loved ones at times do not honor us. Set your emotional boundaries, because no one should hurt or take advantage of our kindness of heart. **Tolerance** is a crucial quality for our peace of mind, but only when boundaries are established around it.

"**Martyrdom** is a quality of just a few beings. They are the 'chosen ones' who suffer a great deal to cleanse humanity's soul. They are rewarded with wisdom and the blessing to ascend closer to the Masters and to God.

"We should also learn to be brave during difficult times. Always remember that there is going to be a fresh morning to begin anew. **Perseverance** is the ability to find the tools to endure challenges and become triumphant in the end.

"We cannot go through life without **trust**. It is imperative to trust others, including people who have earned knowledge in their professional arena. If we are sick, we should look for medical doctors. If we need any other kind of aid during challenging times, let others help us.

"If we are in the position of helping our fellow men, let's do so, and we will be generously blessed. Masters are our helpers, and we should **acknowledge** them and allow them to become our guides throughout life.

"I learned that karma follows us from life to life, and when we return to Earth, we may experience the suffering we caused other people as we heal from the guilt we carry from having hurt someone in the far past. We also **heal** when we remember past lives and understand that the other flesh is long gone. In the end, we will understand that **acceptance** is surrendering to what is inevitable and admitting that we can also change the route of our paths if they cause pain, sadness, and despair. We may change our destiny in any constructive way our soul desires."

Today, as the three of us, Yahim, Tarboo, and I finish this book, we're sending the reader a note of fortitude from the Masters' teachings. They have departed now; but they will be back.

Yahim's face vanishes in the cumulus clouds, and Tarboo takes his position. He wants me to recite one last poem because he likes it since it talks about my absent father, and he has always felt sad about my fatherless story.

Yahim is going to listen to the poem from someplace above the skies because he is flying away as I begin to recite it.

TWO SETS OF HANDS

God once carved two sets of hands
Father and daughter, they look alike
They weren't united, never were held
Not even when little, when I wished to take

His hands' purposes claimed
Noble missions the Good Lord will give
Time went on, never came the day
His hands and mine, always far away

His hands and mine looked alike
Missions on Earth God assigned
His, strong paired with Mars
Mine, Venus warmth, motherhood kind

On that day, when thinking of his hands
They were gone, matters of the past
His actions for others they spiced
For me, their tenderness was denied

One given day, when thinking of his hands
For the last time, I confirm
From the outside, mine and his look alike
Long are our fingers, bronzed our surface

His are bigger; the lens to a pupil is mine to his
My father's hands and mine look alike
His are ready to let go in grace
Rejoice on the day; Heaven is celebrating

The mission's done with others, and I was left behind
God once carved two sets of hands. His were the tireless tools
That diligently worked to meet God's will
From now on, my hands I will look at to think of his
No resentment I have. He lived his life, and I'm living mine

Marlene and Me

Epilogue

TIME

We are here for a reason. When we decide to live again, we come to Earth with a specific purpose. When we arrive in the world as infants, and while we are still little children, our minds are alert, and our subconscious mind is open to bringing back old memories. In addition, our subconscious mind stores painful events that are too hard to bear. However, in order to achieve healing, it is necessary to activate this part of the mind. Fortunately, our subconscious mind is ready to awake at any time if we allow it to do so.

As a result of my life and experiences, I have found fifteen qualities that we must discover to live happy and enriched lives. These fifteen qualities are explained in each of the fifteen chapters.

1) Finding our *talents* with the art of self-discovery.

2) *Remembering* past lives is healthy.

3) *Family ties* begin with our parents.

4) *Loyalty* is a unique human quality.

5) *Strength* is the key to survival.

6) *Predictions* are useful when we recognize they are the inner voice of the Masters.

7) *Reasoning* is an act that should overcome impulses.

8) *Honoring* our loved ones is essential to happiness.

9) *Tolerance* is one of the keys to achieve peace.

10) *Martyrdom* keeps the victim's spirit present after he/she drops the flesh. These individuals are chosen to suffer while cleansing humanity's souls.

11) *Perseverance* gives us hope and opens avenues to better tomorrows when we are stuck.

12) *Trusting* science and the ability of professional helpers to assist us when we need them.

13) *Acknowledging* that Masters in our lives make life much easier for us.

14) *Healing* occurs when we remember our pasts.

15) *Acceptance* is a gift that comes from humility. It is wise to surrender things we cannot change and give them to God to manage the issues.

We have the ability to remember past lives and the ability to contact the Masters. It is important that if we decide to accept this reality, we remain grounded in our current existence and don't let those memories affect our "here and now," because this is the beauty of our present time.

Think about a rose. Its splendor is in its radiant petals, and the sorrows are the thorns. The rose with all its parts is beautiful. Allow yourself to be the rose and enjoy its magnificence.

As a final word to the reader, I want to affirm that my earlier experiences are subject to my own reality. This is not advice for anyone to follow. Consider your universe, your uniqueness, and start from there. You know yourself better than anyone else. Be aware of "healers" that may be tampering with the art of self-discovery and hypnosis. If you decide to go this route, do so, but please look for respected professionals in the field. It is better to manage your situations staying in your current reality than to trust unreliable healers or practitioners.

If you choose to start the journey to self-discovery, you may want to imagine a real or unreal self-place. It will be your sanctuary, a perfect place to go to be in union with God and His universe. Practice meditation, because it can become a door to self-hypnosis. You could use other methods, such as the art of mindfulness, or yoga.

In great humility, I declare that I am blessed because I have found my call on Earth. I am where I belong, serving others to help them discover themselves and how they can heal from past and present injuries of their spirit and their soul.

My road to intellectual success was paved with laughter and tears because my responsibilities were many as a single working mom. My three daughters gave me strength through their laughter, and I overcame many obstacles with the taste of my tears. I pursued my academic call and became a teacher and a counselor, and the Masters helped me carry out my goals. I am a certified teacher, and I have my license as a professional counselor in my state. I have a certification from the International Association of Counselors and Therapists in Hypnotherapy. My final goal has been achieved, and that is to inspire others with the message of this book; hence, my great hope is that you find it heartwarming, inspirational, and helpful on your journey of self-discovery.

TIME

Oh, time, you run just like a fugitive
Leaving your print on a permanent seal
You shadow the shining of cheerful hearts
And away, you blow the flames of real love

The past is your partner that mocks all people
You give sorrow, and bliss is so short
Why, with your pace, destroy all my dreams
Why don't you wear out, oh time, you eternal walk by

Why, when I sob, you never console me
My tangible goals, in pieces you make
Instead, I do hear your laughter and laughter
You encrypt the sound of your arrogant walk

Why am I asking? Speak, you don't know
You laugh at those who know how to cry
Stop! I have told you, and I'm telling you now
But you will never listen; your walking will go on

Oh, your wisdom and knowledge you have shared with me
And with blows and strikes, you have helped me withstand
The challenges and trials that life brings along
Your purpose has been noble, and I didn't know

ABOUT THE AUTHOR

Eugenia Afanador is a Licensed Professional Counselor and a Certified Hypnotist. Her formal education and life experiences have provided Eugenia with skills to help clients with issues related to their physical, emotional, intellectual, and spiritual imbalances. She helps individuals to identify the nature of the barriers that prevent them from finding the true meaning of life and living. Eugenia helps the client discover and validate the subconscious mind to reach a flow of self-healing.

In the academic arena, Eugenia Afanador received a Bachelor's Degree in Arts at the University of Houston. She earned certifications in teaching English as a Second Language (ESL) as well as an elementary/bilingual education teacher. She also has a Master of Science degree, with a specialization in School Counseling, and has attained the requirements for counseling as a Licensed Professional Counselor (LPC).

Due to her own experiences and academic and life training, Eugenia decided to become a hypnotist. She traveled to Pietrasanta, Italy, where she received instruction from Paul Aurand, an award-winning Master Hypnotherapist from the Holistic Healing Center. She received training on Past Life Regression (PLR), Parts Therapy, and Clinical Hypnotherapy. Upon returning to the United States, Eugenia completed the hours and documentation needed to receive the credentials necessary to practice in this field.

Eugenia Afanador counsels in English or Spanish, according to the client's preference. She's a member of the International Association of Counselors and Therapists (IACT), the American Counseling

Association (ACA), and Texas Counseling Association (TCA). She's often contacted for services at *Psychologytoday.com.*

Website: *https://www.spiritualityandbeyond.com*

Instagram: @spiritualityandbeyond

Publication: The poem *"Time"* was published in *The Colors of Life: The International Library of Poetry* (2003), page 1.

Printed in Great Britain
by Amazon

34035062R00155

Gallery Books
Editor: Peter Fallon

THE SHAPE OF METAL

Thomas Kilroy

THE SHAPE OF METAL

Gallery Books

The Shape of Metal
is first published
simultaneously in paperback
and in a clothbound edition
on the day of its première,
29 September 2003.

The Gallery Press
Loughcrew
Oldcastle
County Meath
Ireland

© Thomas Kilroy 2003

ISBN 1 85235 350 3 (*paperback*)
 1 85235 351 1 (*clothbound*)

A CIP catalogue record for this book
is available from the British Library.

  The Gallery Press acknowledges the financial assistance of An
Chomhairle Ealaíon / The Arts Council, Ireland.

Characters

NELL JEFFREY, *a sculptor, aged 82 and 52*
JUDITH, *her daughter, aged 47 and 17*
GRACE, *her other daughter, aged 25*

Time
The years 2002, 1972 and, again, 2002.

If there is to be an interval it should occur after page 39 in the script.

Suggested music: *Cello Concerto, No 2,* by Alfred Schnittke (1934-1998). Slow movements 1, 3 and 5.

The Shape of Metal was first produced in the Abbey Theatre, as part of the Dublin Theatre Festival, on Monday, 29 September 2003, with the following cast:

NELL   Sara Kestelman
GRACE   Justine Mitchell
JUDITH   Eleanor Methven

Director   Lynne Parker
Design   John Comiskey and Alan Farquharson
Lighting Design John Comiskey
Sound Design   Gareth Fry

Darkened stage. NELL JEFFREY's *studio, now like a tomb. High ceiling, large windows, sky-lights, all now heavily curtained. Large, garage-like doors, centre, upstage, now closed.*

The back wall has an elasticated or other opening to allow a ghostly entrance, a device where the wall opens and closes behind the figure.

NELL JEFFREY *sits huddled to one side, sleeping, eighty-two years old, a forbidding presence, enthroned on a sculptor's model's chair, wearing several, oversized, torn sweaters and, on her head, a coiled, brightly-coloured turban. Her hands are hidden in an old-fashioned fur muff on her lap.*

A crane with tackle hangs from the ceiling but is now pushed to one side. Otherwise the studio has been cleared with the exception of a single piece of sculpture now covered completely in sacking or cloth. There are also shelves, benches and piles of 'found objects', typical of a working artist's studio, but these, too, are covered.

NELL   (*Stirring in her sleep, agitated*) Grace! Gracie!

> *She sinks back into sleep again. Suddenly, through the back wall, the head of* GRACE *appears, illuminated. She is in her twenties. The effect is of a mounted head, speaking.* NELL *remains asleep throughout.*

GRACE   (*Out*) I'm here, Mummy. Your own Gracie, over here. Can you see me? Are you going to sculpt my head, Mummy, as promised? In the studio? Busy fingers pressing and shaping, lump of stuff, stone or metal to be transformed into Grace finally at peace, head still and quiet, no terrible dread anymore, no mad panics to run out into the fields screaming, no dreadful terrors for Gracie anymore, Mummy kneading the head, Mummy's fingers on skin, nose, eyes, ears, all head sick, worms at work, stuff pouring out of me, through nose, eyes and ears. Mummy stop everything, head on pedestal, absolutely still. Grace inside the silence. Safe. (*Distress*) Don't be cross, Mumsie. Won't let you down this time. Promise. Know exactly what you're going to say. (*Imitating mother's voice*) Gone off on one of her walkabouts again, has she? Gone off on the Dublin bus, has she? With her blue handbag and white hat and fair-isle cardigan and no overcoat in the midst of rainstorms. Off to nowhere. Not to mention the sleet, slicing down. Soaked to her skin, the silly little bitch.

NELL (*Disturbed sleep*) I — I — I —

GRACE (*Down, inner voice*) Everything's so terribly heavy, pressing down. Like weights or bags. Sky heavy above as well, louring, I believe is the word, but also dead weight in the crutch between legs, soft heap on shoulders. (*Cry out*) Back soon, Mummy! Ta-ta! Won't be long! Back in a jiff! In time for tea in the conservatory, five on the dot, with Mummy and Judy. (*Down*) Load like soft, dead flesh, weighing a ton. Pressing on back of head, neck, shoulders, tits and genitals, soft heap, heavy. (*Cry out*) I'm waving cheerily from the bus window, Mumsie! Look! Bye-ee! (*Mother's voice*) Where's she gone to this time, for heavensakes? Gone for days at a time. What's she up to, the little trollop, on street corners, who's she meeting, the little tramp, in pubs, casual pick-ups! (*Own voice*) So heavy! Can't breathe. Mustn't dilly-dally now, run to front gates, bus late as usual, got to fly —

The head disappears suddenly and NELL *jerks about, very upset, struggling to wakefulness.*

NELL (*Great roar of grief*) Grace! Grace!

JUDITH *immediately rushes on. She wears a coat or outdoor jacket which she will take off during the exchanges that follow. She hurries to* NELL's *side.*

(*Puzzled*) Is that you, Grace?

JUDITH No, Mother, it's me! Not Grace, it's me, Judith!

NELL (*Puzzled*) Judith? Where are you?

JUDITH Right here, Mother. I just stepped out for a moment

into the garden.

NELL   Garden. I was outside, too. Back now, though.

JUDITH Yes, of course. (*Beat*) You were calling out for Grace just now —

NELL   (*Furiously*) No I was not! That little bitch! The suffering she has caused —

JUDITH And what about *her* suffering?

NELL   Don't wish to speak about it.

JUDITH Well, I wish to speak about it. One of the reasons I came, actually — talk about Gracie — after all those years —

NELL   Thought you said earlier that you came about Eddie's death?

JUDITH Yes, that too. But also Gracie. Both of them.

NELL   (*Accusing*) Did you come here in the motor car?

JUDITH Yes.

NELL   Not take the train to Greystones? (JUDITH *shakes her head: no*) Fool! More poison. My mind is perfectly alert, you know. As we go on you will think otherwise but don't be deceived. Can't concentrate! (*Shout*) I said it's just more fumes in the atmosphere! (*Completely different tone*) Actually, I adore the motor car. Simply love the idea of all that concealed power under the whatchamacallit. So he's dead at last, is he, old Eddie? Isn't that what you were saying to me just now? Haven't forgotten, you see. Took everything in first time round! Got all me marbles. Died in his sleep, you say? What an extraordinary phrase that is, when you think of it. Wasn't the worst of them, Eddie. Sleep, dying, entirely different things. Trust me. Eddie wasn't the worst. But they're all shits, men. Every man jack of them, one way t'other. But you wouldn't know anything about that, would you, darling, given your taste in sex?

JUDITH Oh, dear God, here we go again —

NELL   Had these magnificent muscles in his back. Yes, Eddie. Wouldn't think it, would you, in the latter days? Played tennis without a shirt. In the old days.

Hot stuff. Hard to believe now. But he had this zump when young, younger. Like one of those sumptuous niggers on the telly, running and jumping and throwing balls about the place. Have you eaten?

JUDITH You simply can't speak like that anymore, you know. Not these days, not about black people —

NELL I'll speak any which fucking way I choose, m'dear. There's no food in the house.

JUDITH It's appalling —

NELL (*Yell*) I said there's no food in the house!

JUDITH Just elementary respect for other people —

NELL (*Banging fist*) No grub! No grub!

JUDITH That's fine. I'm not hungry.

NELL Why are you always so bloody polite? It's excruciating.

JUDITH Why have you become so ugly and aggressive?

NELL Good! Now we're getting somewhere!

JUDITH Oh, no, we're not! Not playing that game!

NELL Go on! Go on! Tell me some more about my wretched behaviour —

JUDITH What is it? All this foul language? Being one of the boyos. Doesn't shock anymore, you know. That sort of thing.

NELL I can do without your penny analysis, darling —

JUDITH Why *do* you behave like this? You didn't use to. Different, you were —

NELL You forgot to say 'behave like this at your age'. (*Explosively*) I don't want to die, that's all, I don't want to die!

She actually tries to throw herself out of the seat but collapses back into it again. JUDITH *takes all this in, shocked.*

JUDITH Sorry. Didn't mean to — do you want me to fetch you something?

NELL Nothing. Dammit! It's not true, by the way. I do respect every thing that lives. I don't respect what's dead. Deadly politeness. Living dead. All that deadly correctness. Choking rectitude — Are you still queer, darling? Or have you finally taken up with the males? Only asking.

JUDITH You have a truly pathetic sense of relationships —

NELL Really? But you'll set me right, will you?

JUDITH Oh, dear God!

NELL Do you realize how often you refer to the deity? Not something you picked up in this house. They're coming to take away the last of my pieces, you know. Carted off. Going to put them into that museum in Kilmainham. A Nell Jeffrey Room, no less! What a lark! Used to be the old military hospital, Kilmainham. I've seen too many uniforms in me life. Get a man to do the unspeakable, first put him into a bloody uniform. Stick a badge on him. Off you go. Shoot a few gunks. Father shaking hands with Uncle Norman, with that formality that is only possible between brothers. Must have been '37, '38. Certainly before the Hitler war. Year before I met Giacometti on the Rue Hippolyte-Maindron. Do you think women will fight differently in war when they take over the mess? Because fight they will! Oh, yes! (*Towards piece of sculpture*) Never wanted the world to have this one. Know why?

JUDITH Because it's a failure —

NELL Thank you! How well you learn! (*Puzzled*) What have we been talking about? Just now?

JUDITH That piece there. The Egg Woman. Unfinished.

NELL Hate that name, hate it. Nickname. *Woman Rising from Water*. That's its title. I've spent a lifetime trying to create finished objects. There is no meaning if it isn't finished. While all around me the bloody place is disintegrating. The young gather bits and scraps nowadays and call it sculpture. Bloody rubbish, that's what it is. Anyone can do it.

JUDITH Grace gave it that name — Egg Woman —

NELL Remember the *Rondanini Pietà*, darling? Milan. Michelangelo? The three of us went to see it. (JUDITH *nods, distressed*) What happened to their

15

faces, Mummy, Grace asked. They're only half there! Half there! Indeed! That's what makes the piece so unbearably — human, the failed touch, the unfinished carving, something which could never, ever be completed successfully. That wasn't what we were talking about — dammit, my mind's gone again! (*Discovery*) Eddie! Is that why you really came? Simply to tell me old Eddie's kicked the bucket?

JUDITH There were two other reasons —

NELL Two! How splendid. Goody! We'll have enough to keep us going all afternoon, at this rate. You were always the secretive one when you were a gel. You were always — lurking. Not like that other little twit. Turn around and there you were. In a corner. I'm leaving everything to you, you know. Last farthing. Just keep enough to pay the crematorium man. Light the match. Whoosh! Going to knock the studio when it's emptied. Always wanted to work a wrecker's ball and chain. Whammee! Balderdash! Just look at my hands. Couldn't even hold a bloody teacup now. Wasn't the worst, Eddie. Made a bloody fool of himself, though, with those greyhounds. Always thought he was on to a winner tomorrow, next day, next week, next year. Whereas he carried this tremendous failure around with him everywhere he went, like a wet crombie. Tell you one thing, darling, failure is like the damp. Seeps into everyone and everything nearby. That's why I had to throw him out in the end, old Eddie. Off you go, you dim fucker! Before you drag me down with you. Missed him. Terribly. Did he say anything? About me? Before he you-know-what? (JUDITH *shakes her head: no*) I forgive him, the splendid bollocks. (*Pause: distress*) Not even my name? Perhaps he mentioned my name? Last gasp? (JUDITH *shakes her head: no. Turning aside*) I can't believe this, not even my name. Even if I did throw him out.

JUDITH (*Very upset*) Well, it's true!

NELL Under his breath, maybe? Hard to hear? Always

mumbled, the adorable shit, even when he was twenty-two and singing in the choir in Arklow. Maybe he left something for me? Written? Always a whore for scribbling notes, Eddie, here, there and everywhere, sometimes to himself, reminders, 'Don't forget Aunt Mildred, 3 pm' — sometimes what appeared to be reprimands to — Huh! —the deity. There! Another mention. Never mentioned the deity so often in one day. Caught him once, Eddie, that is, not the deity, passing a note to a waitress in Roberts' Café. 'Meet me at six outside Hibernian Hotel.' Harmless ride, the deluded prick. (*Pause. Anxiety*) Nothing at all? He must have said — something?

JUDITH There was no message. As such —

NELL Yes, but something — ?

JUDITH Yes.

NELL Well? Out with it! Speak up, girl! What the hell did he say?

JUDITH (*Shout*) He said two things to me which I find extremely disturbing —

NELL Two things! That precise number again? How very mathematical! Did he use his fingers to count? One, two —

JUDITH (*Blurted out*) He said he wasn't my father!

NELL (*Long pause*) Did he now? Well-well-well.

JUDITH All those years — there I was — is it true, Mother? Is it? And if so, who is? Was?

NELL This is a bit of a shock.

JUDITH Bit of a shock! You? What about me?

NELL Give me a moment. Did he actually say that?

JUDITH You heard me the first time.

NELL You talk like that cowboy in the pictures. Eastwood.

JUDITH I'm looking for an answer. You are my mother, aren't you? Good God, I hadn't thought of that! Maybe you're not!

NELL But why would he say that now? (*Discovery*) He was lying!

JUDITH Lying! The man was on his deathbed!

NELL   That, my dear, is precisely where the biggest lies are told. Actually, there are times when I could snuff it meself. Yes. Close up the garage, block the exits, get into the old Jag, turn on the juice, and Whoof! Kaput! But then all that energy starts pouring through everything again, great flood of spunk and pulse and blood and wet, organs bursting like billy-o, the fucking excess of it all, and I know I can't die! Not today, dearie, thank you very much. Not today. Pass the salad and on we go! Found some photos, by the way, rooting in the drawers —

JUDITH   (*Yell*) And don't change the subject, damn you!

NELL   Oh, my gracious goodness gracious! Oh, my!

JUDITH   And stop putting on that ridiculous act! Simpering!

NELL   (*Insulted*) I've never simpered in me life, damn you! (*Appeal*) Judy! I'm on me last legs — Do you remember? In the old days. During our battles? One of us would call out: Pax!

JUDITH   A truce —

NELL   Time out! — as our Yankee friends would say — I need a little pax just now, darling. I need it rather desperately, as a matter of fact.

JUDITH   You're not just avoiding the subject, are you?

NELL   No — I am trying, darling. Promise.

JUDITH   It's too important for me, this. I tended that man for years, washed him, fed him, nursed him — cared for him! — because I thought he was — There were things I didn't like about him, particularly, his shiftiness, for instance — maybe there weren't too many ways I could connect with him, but there was always his good manners to fall back on, his blazers and cold hands, but at least I believed he was my father!

NELL   But all this is as much a surprise to me, darling —

JUDITH   I tried to love him! And now this! You always thought I'd put up with anything, didn't you? Abuse!

NELL   Not true —

JUDITH   I was always the one who stood about, waiting —

18

NELL   (*Pleading*) Judith —

JUDITH Well, this time is different, Mother. I'm not just
        hanging about this time. Oh, no! (*Pause*) Well?
        Aren't you going to tell me? Eddie and you — ?

NELL   Can't.

JUDITH Can't what?

NELL   Have to think about it.

JUDITH Think about it! What're you talking about? My
        birth —

NELL   You know the worst thing is seeing your mind go?
        Legs bad enough, but seeing your mind quite un-
        able to add things up anymore — Let's see. What is
        it? Forty years ago?

JUDITH Forty-seven! You can't even remember my age!

NELL   Such a long time ago and B, at the time, my life was,
        well, rather — crowded —

JUDITH Crowded! Good God!

NELL   Yes, you could say that. (*Bright idea*) Could look up
        the diaries. Forty — Nineteen fifties, nineteen fifties.
        Lots of chaps around.

JUDITH Lining up to service you, were they?

NELL   (*Very quietly*) Now that is coarse, dear. Not you. Not
        you at all.

JUDITH Do you know, I become a different person when I
        come back here. A kind of slut or something. That
        has to mean something. I'm not like that anywhere
        else. Can you explain it? Is it you? Sort of adoles-
        cent rebellion? Certainly makes me feel degraded.
        Maybe it's this place? I feel this sort of — bile,
        welling up inside me and out it pours.

NELL   I *wanted* him to be your father!

JUDITH Wanted! Wanted? Did you just stick pins or some-
        thing? Eeney-meeney-miney? Have this one!

NELL   I thought he would be good to you. There are so
        many shits around. Don't you want to see the
        photos? They're in the house. On the dining-room
        table.

        JUDITH *sits for the first time, on the floor, cross-legged.*

19

JUDITH   (*Guardedly*) What of?

NELL   Hols, mostly. We did take hols, didn't we? The three of us. Summer after summer. Paris. Vienna. Florence. Rome. Three females. I was determined there would never be a male on board. No wonder you're queer. That's where the essential spine is. Paris. Vienna, Florence, Rome. Down through the continent. A marble spine! All gone now with all this pathetic rubbish masquerading as art. Lots of pics of you and that other little turd.

JUDITH   Her name is Grace, Mother.

NELL   Turd! Turd! Turd!

JUDITH   Grace! Grace!

NELL   You should eat something, you know. Could always ring up the pub. Send up that boy Mick on his bike with spiffy sandwiches dripping with Colman's. I adore watching that boy on his bike. Wonderful buttocks going like billy-o.

JUDITH   Don't you have anyone in anymore? Where's Birdy?

NELL   Only comes in on Fridays and Mondays now. She's even more ramshackle than I am. I said to her, Birdy, we're both on our uppers, let's just drop all this rubbish. Let's just be pals, Birdy, from here on in to the hole in the ground. Oh, I couldn't do that, Miss Jeffrey, says she. Why ever not? I said. Oh, I could never be the same as you, Miss Jeffrey, that sly, lying, peasant look on her face. You and me is different, she said. Different? I said. Different? We're not different! We're simply two upright, female apes with a highly developed brain-box and a fondness for Jameson! Actually said that to her. Upright apes. Should see her face! Ho-ho-ho-ho!

JUDITH   (*Smiles*) Poor Birdy! With her endless apple tarts! Have another slice, Miss Judith, 'twill make ya blossom, so i'twill!

NELL   Read somewhere that the human embryo passes from slime to rodent to reptile to human in a few weeks! Think of it! Millions of years of evolution in a few weeks! That's you, Judith —

JUDITH How generous of you, Mother —
NELL (*Quietly*) And Grace. And I myself. And all of us!
JUDITH I'm not going to let you off the hook, you know. I
want some questions answered and that is that!

*NELL suddenly gets to her feet in a scrambling,
staggering motion and quite rapidly scoots off.*

(*Calling*) Mother! Where are you going? Come back
here! (*Beat*) Need to talk to you. (*Beat*) About Grace!
Are you listening out there? (*No answer*) Eddie said
something about her. When he was dying — don't
you want to hear what he said? Mother! (*No answer*)
Oh, hell!

*She bows her head on her arms, hunched over her
knees.* GRACE, *aged twenty-five, steps through the
back wall behind her, dressed in coat and hat, carrying
a suitcase and purse. It is 1973. No reaction from*
JUDITH. *A voice of memory.*

GRACE No, not a word, Jude! Please! I'm perfectly fine now,
and I'm off. Mustn't try to stop me. Promise? Need
to get to where she can't find me and bring me back
again. Dr McKinnon says I'm — restored. Rather
like an old chair or something, what? Terrifically
restored. His very words. Do you think he might
have been lying? Am I lying? I mean I feel OK.
'Cept for those headaches. Can't dilly-dally. Got to
run. Sometimes I think everyone is lying. I mean in
the whole wide world — Imagine! If no one ever,
ever, ever told the truth! Ever! Cleared out my
room, always the one for clearing out, aren't I? Left
some keepsakes, if you want, my albums, books,
also my sketchbook. Might send for some things
later. When I get settled. Simply can't live without
Procol Harum. I'm so terribly frightened, actually.
Don't know where I'm going except that I must.
Why did she do that to me, Jude, why? It's all so

terrifically sordid. One's own mother! What did you do to her, Grace, I ask myself? What is it about you, Grace, that made her do such a thing? To do that. No, don't answer! If you were to say anything I would just collapse in a heap! Must go! Ta-ta!

She makes a quick exit through the wall. JUDITH *raises her head. She has been weeping.* NELL *comes shuffling back in, carrying a brown, stuffed envelope. She thrusts this at* JUDITH *and sits in the chair again.* JUDITH, *dazed, stares at the package on her lap.*

JUDITH What's this, then?

NELL It's for you, dammit.

JUDITH Yes, but what?

NELL Cash. Loot. Notes. A few thou. Lying about the place. Here! Take it!

JUDITH What on earth for?

NELL Take a trip. Maybe with one of your galfriends. Go wherever. Enjoy. A bit of mindlessness. You need a break. A bit peaked. Have fun, damn you!

JUDITH Do you know something? You're generous with all the wrong things. Very odd, actually. It's like a — deficiency or something.

She stands and carefully plants the envelope on the covered piece of sculpture.

NELL Really? Has it ever occurred to you, m'dear, how utterly priggish you are?

JUDITH You can never be generous about things that really matter —

NELL E g?

JUDITH Well, what other people might need — really need — feelings —

NELL Oh, all right. I know I'm a bit of a beast. Sometimes. Go at things with a hatchet, I do. Sometimes. Can't help it. Can't be bothered with niceties, never had much time for good manners and all that tommyrot.

Get to the point quickly. Engage! Engage, that's all that matters. Besides, B, I'm dying. Dead before Christmas. Promise. I meant that, Judy. That loot there. Go have some fun. Dammit! If only I could work — just one more time. My head teems with stuff! Hands dead. Do you know, Eddie used work in the quarry with me? Not many know that. Stone is pure before we touch it. Marks, daubs, cuts, scratches. I think we're trying to blend into that purity. Possible? (*Desperate tack*) When Sam took Betty Jones from Monkstown and I to visit Giacometti in 1938 —

JUDITH I stood at one of the centres of the modern world —

NELL (*Quietly*) Damn you!

JUDITH In that dilapidated studio with its homemade chimney pipe sticking out of the roof I learned how to *see* for the very first time —

NELL (*Loudly*) Damn you!

JUDITH He wore a white coat, Giacometti, leaning on a cane, after that crazy accident he had. More like a lame chemist than sculptor, shrouded in dust with brother Diego beside him. A furnace, a melting down, nothing ever the same again —

NELL Have you quite done? Mockery!

JUDITH Of course, Mother, anything you say, Mother —

NELL Something else. Dammit! Can't remember — what was it? — numbers — my mind — There! A few moments ago. What was it? What was I talking about? One, two, three, four! Fuck it! I'm finished! One, two, that's it! It's come back to me! Not basket-case, you know. Perfectly capable when I want to — you'll see! Eddie! That was it. One, two. Second thing Eddie said, deathbed revelations and so forth. Well? Out with it, girl!

JUDITH (*With difficulty*) Grace —

NELL What about her?

JUDITH (*Distressed*) Eddie —

NELL Eddie? Grace? What has that sublime shit to do with Grace? Certainly not *her* father. That would

23

have been Bertie. Herbert, the neurosthenic son of the bishop of — Where the fuck was he bishop of? Leeds? No. Wolverhampton? Burton-on-Trent? Sounds like something lost on the railways. Bishop-ric, indeed!

JUDITH He and I — we'd been talking about her. Thirty years ago.

NELL Herbert loved me.

JUDITH Eddie loved Grace. Loved her!

NELL Sometimes I was attracted to decent people.

JUDITH Told him, yet again, about my search for her. Years and years of my banging on doors, showing photos, useless phone-calls, polite, indifferent strangers, half hopes, all dead ends. The trail always ended up back there. Back in that two-roomed basement flat, number eleven Colville Crescent, Notting Hill. It's as if she just stepped out of there one morning in 1975 and disappeared into thin air. Just like that. Eddie listened. Odd, since he seldom listened much to anything.

NELL Thing about dear Herbert was that he had a foul mouth. I mean his teeth —

JUDITH Then Eddie, choking, gasping, Eddie croaked out, 'Ask her!' 'Ask who?' I said. 'Ask her! Ask her!' spitting, gasping, as if there was only one her in the whole world which I suppose at that moment was true for him. Then I realized he was talking about you, Mother. 'Ask her what really happened be-tween her and Gracie.' Then he sank back, wouldn't say anything else. Looking at me with that stare of a dying man.

NELL But he had beautiful hands, Bertie, like a woman's, in fact. I am suddenly extremely depressed.

JUDITH What was he talking about, Eddie? When he said that — about you two, Grace and yourself? (*Beat*) Mother!

NELL (*Struggling to get up once more*) Time for me nap, Judy. Beddy-byes.

JUDITH Don't you dare move!

NELL   (*Menace*) Don't you dare tell me what to do.

JUDITH   I'm not afraid of you, Mother. Never have been. Gracie was the one who was afraid. Not Judith. Judith is the one who never left your side through thick and thin. Remember? Those awful times? That was me at your elbow. Afraid of everything, really, Gracie was. Well? Aren't you going to tell me? What was Eddie talking about? I'd always thought she left because of that row between you two. Over that boy in the village. What was his name? Very Irish name. Seán or Seamus, something like that. Not our kind of person — dear! NOKP, that's what you used to say to us when we threatened interest in one of them. Not suitable, darling. Worked in the garage. It's still there. Saw it in the murk as I drove here. A broken-down garage with one old pump and a broken Esso sign. At the corner of Sea Road. She loved him, that boy. All that love and nothing to show for it. Except loss. Why is that? (*Pause. Yell*) Answer me!

NELL   (*Almost to herself*) I was trying to save her! In the only way that I knew.

JUDITH   Said she had lost him. Because of you. That's what she said. I've lost him, Judy, Seamus or Seán or whatever he was called —

NELL   Breeding every year. Rest of her life. Dirt. Stuck in that dreadful house with that gang — that deplorable mother — those thuggish brothers —

JUDITH   I remember saying to her, 'For heavensakes, Gracie, you're an adult!' She just burst into floods of tears — as if I had said something intolerable to her —

NELL   Now, look here! I'm not a snob. Never was. All apes at the end of the day. It's simply that I saw her life stretch out ahead of her. Grim. I know this bloody country in all its quite spectacular capacity for squalor. Gracie was terribly immature —

JUDITH   She was sick, Mother!

NELL   Immature! A child in a woman's body! Didn't know what life was capable of inflicting on one.

JUDITH Why can't you simply accept the fact? Dr McKinnon said she was manic depressive with schizoid tendencies.

NELL Nothing to do with the boy *per se*. Happiness. Survival. Could never stand up to that life — never, she was utterly unaware, fragile, weak. There's a bloody draught in here! I'm freezing!

JUDITH She's lost! Lost! At least she might be here if she'd taken up with him!

NELL The boy was an idiot. Handsome, but an idiot. She escaped.

JUDITH Can't get it out of my mind. She and that boy. And now Eddie's dying, Eddie's talk. It keeps coming back. Thirty years ago — that day. Do you remember? Here in the studio. 1972 it was. Did I miss something that day? (*Pointing*) Sitting over there, I was —

NELL What the hell are you nattering on about?

JUDITH That day —

NELL Day? What day? Are you trying to confuse me again? Interrogations, all these damn details, can't remember half! You mustn't do this! You're confusing me, damn you — you mustn't do this — I can't function — can't remember, when you go on like this —

JUDITH (*Seeing everything*) You were working. (*Pointing*) Over there. She came through that door. Grace. With her bicycle. I wasn't paying all that much attention —

> NELL *staggers to her feet once more and makes another, crab-like exit, her version of running away.* JUDITH *makes as if to follow her, but stops.*

Mother! Oh, what's the use —!

> *She stands undecided. Then goes and picks up the envelope, opens it and pulls out a wad of notes, shakes her head, looks about, goes and opens a drawer and puts the envelope and money into it and closes it again.*

*She takes a deep breath, then makes a decision and
begins to circle the studio, stopping, pointing, remembering it as it once was. As she speaks, the studio is
put into working order around her, as if at her behest.
It is 1972. Vitality returns to the studio.*

*A wall opens and pieces of sculptural work slide in.
Work-benches appear and covering is taken off the
shelves and cupboards revealing sketches and carved,
African heads, found objects etc. This is not an exhibi-
tion but a display of work-in-progress, so what is
suggested is a general style, a sculpture-signature of*
NELL'*s middle period of work. The dominant image is
the circle, versions of the circle in coiled springs of
metal, cones, undulating ribbons of metal, vortices,
gyres, ovoid-shaped balls, perhaps a few large indus-
trial springs.*

*The covered piece, the Egg Woman, is uncovered.
A marble piece entitled* Woman Rising from Water.
*The shape is ovoid, beautifully carved and polished to
a high finish. One side is as if it had been attacked and
out of the rubble, this powerful, female face emerging
from the stone. This piece was inspired by Michelangelo's* Rondanini Pietà. *See, also, Brancusi's* Sleep,
although NELL'*s head is far less benign, more witch-
like with wild hair.*

*Leaning to one side are several huge metal rings of
different sizes for a projected, outdoor 'Ring Garden'
that* NELL *is currently working on.*

*Curtains are thrown open on windows and sky-
lights and light pours in. Upstage, the sliding doors
slide open and sunlight plays upon a splendid garden
beyond.*

JUDITH   (*Picking up a chair*) 1972. That day. The sun shone
brightly outside. I was over here. No, further away.
There! (*Puts down chair*) Reading. (*Looks about and
finds a book*) Always reading. Seventeen years of
age, oh my God! Novels mostly, but also biog-
raphies, one of Virginia Woolf, I remember, stones

in her pocket, entering the water for the last time. Nose in a book, that's why I think I only half heard things that were said in this house. Everything half passed me by. Seventeen years old! But was it ever otherwise? Half present, half absent, all my life. (*Points*) Let me see. Yes. Doors open. Then, yes, Mother was over there, working.

> NELL, *aged fifty-two, comes on briskly. She's dressed in her work outfit, a dusty blue boiler suit, another tight turban on her head. She immediately grabs the crane and hoists a piece of metal onto a bench, then puts on a protective head shield, picks up a welding iron and sets to work welding.*
>
> JUDITH *has taken her seat to one side and at an angle to the proceedings, both in the scene and outside it at the same time.*

NELL (*Towards* JUDITH) Don't look in this direction, darling! Finished soon, promise!

JUDITH And Gracie! My poor lost, damaged, probably deranged sister!

> GRACE, *aged twenty-five, a delicate, nervous figure, appears at the open door with her bicycle and stops to watch. She is dressed in a bright summer frock. There's a large bunch of wild flowers in the carrier basket of the bicycle. She hesitates, about to enter, changes her mind and quickly disappears again. Neither* NELL *nor* JUDITH *notices this.* NELL *stops welding, turns welder off and pushes the protective visor up.*

NELL *Visione*, Giacometti said, to see things whole one has to see them from a distance, a remove. He showed me some small pieces and, yes! odd thing, when you held them in the hand they looked an absolute mess. But then when you looked at them from a distance they had this — how would you say? — yes! quite appalling — presence! You're not listening, Judith!

JUDITH (*Playing her young self*) Yes, I am, Mother — you're talking about when you went to visit that famous sculptor in Paris —

NELL Sam was childishly pleased to be able to show his two Dublin gels, Betty and yours truly, the artistic sights. All the Becketts are like that. Always immensely attentive to others, the Becketts. Put that book away, darling. Get out into the air. Beautiful day.

JUDITH But you're working, aren't you? I love to sit and read here when you're working. It's so — complete, somehow.

NELL And I love having you, darling, you know that. Finished, actually. Ready for anything now. Are you game?

JUDITH (*Gaily*) Oh-oh, I can see it coming —

NELL Something utterly extravagant together! I have this sudden compulsion to spend money, lots of money! Where's Gracie?

JUDITH In the garden, I think.

NELL Let's powwow when she returns! Us three!

JUDITH Last time you said something like this we ended up in Algiers.

NELL And why ever not! I want to have some crushing adventure with my two gels! I want to close up shop, get in the motor car and hit the boat to Holyhead. Maybe drop by the cousins Hackett at Tewkesbury, call by old Nathan's gallery in London and see if he's sold anything of mine recently, squeeze a few shillings from him or, who knows, ignore all and sundry and simply keep going to Dover and beyond — onwards, into the heart of that battered, beautiful continent — us three! We do have good times, don't we, darling? Us three! Why, you both keep me young! Young!

An uncertain, timid-looking GRACE *reappears in the open doors, without bicycle but carrying the bunch of wild flowers.*

GRACE Hello, all!

NELL Why, darling! Are these (*flowers*) for me? How splendid! Where did you get them?

She goes and sweeps the flowers from GRACE, *giving her a big hug and kiss.*

GRACE (*Helplessly*) Well, I — (*Pause, to* JUDITH) Hello, sis.

JUDITH Where've you been all this time?

NELL Yes, where've you been, darling? We wondered.

GRACE Oh, out and about. Garden, mostly —

NELL (*Hugging her*) Have you taken your pills, darling?

GRACE Yes, Mummy.

NELL Good! Must be in good nick for the trip!

GRACE (*Panic*) Trip? What trip? I can't —

JUDITH Mother's just finished something and hit one of her post-natal highs — you know what to expect!

GRACE Can't —

JUDITH We're off to Timbuktu! Apparently.

GRACE Impossible —

NELL But of course it's possible. If you two have learned anything in this house it's precisely that. Everything is possible. First, there is belief. Then there is engagement. Engage! Engage! Then there is execution! Get out and do it!

GRACE (*Outburst*) I saw that man again!

A long pause. GRACE *looks about, frantically.* NELL *looks at* JUDITH *but she looks away.*

What I meant just now, impossible, it's simply impossible for me just now, go away, that is, so much to do — here —

NELL What did you say, Grace? Just now?

GRACE Really terribly busy. Also, my job.

NELL Grace — !

JUDITH Don't, Mother!

NELL (*Very gently*) Come here, Grace —

GRACE *approaches and* NELL *takes her head in her two hands,* GRACE *with her head raised, eyes closed. What follows is a fairly elaborate head massage. At first* NELL *uses her fingers delicately, almost shaping the face, eyes, ears, hair. This progresses to a more specific kind of kneading, cheekbones, forehead, chin, back of head. This in turn gives way to* NELL *using her two powerful hands to caress the young woman's head. At this stage* GRACE *has gone limp, drawn into her mother's body for support and the two of them sway together. Almost in dance.*

JUDITH who, up to now, has been taking part in the scene from her angled seat, gradually stands and turns to watch all this as an intense, fully involved spectator, the older JUDITH looking back.

NELL (*Whisper*) One must take care of our dear, sweet Grace, mustn't one? So lovely, so precious, drive all those worries away, all those awful heebie-jeebies, all gone —

Suddenly, GRACE *breaks out of her listlessness, snaps out of her mother's arms, wild and struggling, someone escaping immense danger, flailing about. Both NELL and JUDITH are shocked by this.*

GRACE Stop it-stop it-stop it!
NELL Gracie — !
GRACE You are killing me! Trying to kill me — you —
NELL Kill! Don't say that, Grace!
GRACE (*Her own hands like claws*) Hands — fingers — pushing!
NELL Why, you alway love when I rub your head. Please, Mummy! Rub my head, you say. Isn't that so, Judy?
GRACE (*Cry*) My head, my head is — leaking —

She sinks in exhaustion, NELL *rushing to hold her again.*

NELL Grace! (*No answer, sing-song*) Gracie!

GRACE I'm so — heavy — so heavy —

NELL (*Desperately*) You're not heavy, why, you're as delicate as a butterfly! Isn't she, Judy? Our Gracie, wandering about like that in the garden and giving herself all kinds of unnecessary panics, flitting from flower to flower, just like a butterfly —

GRACE A sort of heavy softness, smothering — What does it mean? All that soft heavy?

NELL Do you want to sleep, darling?

GRACE No-no-no — I really have far too much to do — my sketching, my room needs to be — also my job in Mr Pender's office —

NELL I know, dear, we're so proud of you — why, Mr Pender says you're terrifically helpful about the office. Doesn't he, Judith? (*Wake up*) Judith!

JUDITH (*Sunken*) Yes.

NELL Judith! Tell Grace how much Mr Pender values her work.

JUDITH (*Tonelessly*) Mr Pender values Grace's work.

NELL (*Prompt*) In his office —

JUDITH In his office —

NELL (*To* GRACE) There!

GRACE (*Frightened*) That man. He was sitting in a car at the west gate. Just sitting there. What was he doing if he wasn't — ?

NELL Grace!

GRACE No reason for him to be sitting there — except to watch — follow — me —

NELL Now you listen carefully, Grace! Are you listening, Grace? (GRACE *nods*) Very well. The last time. Who was it the last time? Answer me, Grace! Who was the man the last time?

JUDITH (*Exasperated, anxious*) Mother —

NELL No, this is important. I want an answer from Grace. No answer, is it? Not going to own up, is that it?

JUDITH (*Angry*) Please, Mother!

NELL Very well. Judith will answer for you, won't you, Judith?

JUDITH God!

NELL Who was the man, Judith? Who was the last man that Grace was frightened of? (*Beat*) Can't hear you, Judith! Grace wants to hear what you have to say. Out with it, girl!

JUDITH Surveyor.

NELL Who? Say it clearly because Grace must hear this, it must *sink* in!

JUDITH (*Yell*) He was a County Council surveyor doing his — measurements!

NELL Did you hear that, Grace?

GRACE (*Low*) Yes, Mother.

NELL And the time before that, Judith? Who was the man that Grace was frightened by?

JUDITH (*Almost under her breath*) Commercial traveller.

NELL A commercial traveller. Coffee and tea, I believe. Different man, Grace, absolutely, utterly different creature. Not the same one back again. No. Different lad. Perfectly sensible explanation, you see. No need for panic. (*Familiar routine*) Now what do we have to do, now, Grace?

GRACE Fix —

NELL Go on!

GRACE Fix —

NELL In place — facts — fix — Say it, Gracie!

GRACE (*Miserable*) In place. Facts in place. Fix in place —

NELL Remember what Dr McKinnon said — Grace has to learn facts as if they had never existed before. She has to hold them in her head against all the turbulence. Signposts, he said, Dr McKinnon, like signposts. Facts. Showing the way forward. Oh, darling, I know how awful it is for you. But we're here for you. Aren't we, Judy? And always will be! Come, give Mummy a big hug!

GRACE *offers a weak hug but* NELL *seizes her and lifts her into her own arms.*

Oh, I do love you so much, dear, dear Grace! (*Pause*)

Besides, B, we're about to hit the road!

JUDITH And, C, live happily ever after —

Slight, tense pause, then NELL *bursts out laughing.*

NELL Ho-ho-ho, oh, you are a card, Judy! Did you hear that, Gracie? Isn't she a devil! Our Judith —

She goes quickly and touches JUDITH *on the head, then spins away again.* GRACE *tries to join in the mother's laughter but doesn't get very far. She then drifts away towards the piece* Woman Rising from Water, *standing, running her hands over it.*

Do you know, girls! I actually get the tang of the Mediterranean miles before seeing the sea! So that when it actually opens up it seems so much vaster than it actually is, really a space within oneself, limitless, within the senses —

GRACE (*Childlike recitation,* NELL *and* JUDITH *troubled*) Oh, Egg-woman, Egg-woman, where have you been?
I've been to the bottom of the ice-cold sea.
Oh, Egg-woman, Egg-woman, what have you seen?
I've seen all the monsters
That are there to be seen.
But now I've come back to Judy and Grace.
Feel my cold forehead,
Feel my cold face —

NELL Your poem is lovely, darling, but can't say I ever cared very much for that name, Egg-woman —

JUDITH I like it!

NELL You would, darling.

GRACE I dream all the time. Of her finally stepping out of there, rising out of the stone.

JUDITH Anyway, I love listening to what Gracie sees —

GRACE (*Breaking*) I see nothing. Nothing! Except — except —

NELL Now, really, girls, we should be having one of our powwows, the three of us — so much to plan — decent food and wine — what am I talking about?

34

Scrumptious food! And everything open and clear in the white Italian light! Don't you remember it? Girls! I'm almost giddy with the very thought of it! Oh, my goodness, look at those flowers! They're positively wilting already. Let me fetch a vase!

NELL *swiftly takes up the flowers and sweeps off.* GRACE *turns towards* JUDITH *who is quite crushed by what has happened.*

GRACE Jude —

JUDITH Yep.

GRACE Do *you* believe me?

JUDITH I believe everything you say, Gracie. Everything. Always. No matter what.

GRACE I know she means well but she doesn't know. He *was* watching me. From that car. I know he was watching me, even with my back to him. It was quite the most dreadful sensation — like something boring into one. She's so — so certain, Mother, isn't she? Certain about everything. I often think about that. How could one be so certain? Why doesn't she ever question things?

JUDITH Oh, I think she does, rather. Question things. It simply comes out differently, somehow, I mean with her. Are you all right?

GRACE I think so.

JUDITH No one's going to harm you.

GRACE (*Nervous laugh*) Don't say that!

JUDITH Why not?

GRACE Brings bad luck. Say good, get bad, say bad, get good. Everything's a question, really, isn't it? Questions, questions! (*Giggle*) Do you remember, Jude? How we used joke about Mummy moving the Sugarloaf Mountain? Lying awake in the dark, when we were small — ?

JUDITH (*Demonstrating muscle*) Two-ton-Tessie and her bisseps —

GRACE (*High*) You simply must join Duffy's Circus, Mummy!

JUDITH Hit the big hammer in the carnival and ring the big
bell! Mummy-Ding-Dong-Dell!

They laugh together for a moment.

GRACE (*Shift*) You know the most dreadful thing is that I —
do you ever feel this way, Judy? It's awful, really,
quite unnatural, I know, but I can't — What I mean
is, well, I sometimes feel I couldn't possibly be her
daughter. Do you feel that you're her daughter? All
the time?

JUDITH Oh, I feel I'm her daughter, all right. Alas! Well, not
really alas. Say — sometimes alas.

GRACE I feel absolutely fine now, really do, no shakes or
anything — It's just super to be able to talk like
this —

JUDITH She's right, you know. I mean about facts et cetera.

GRACE All I need, really, is not to be rushed or pushed or
anything. If everything could just — slow down,
somehow. Do you know what I mean? Everything's
over before one can pick up the pieces and one is —
confused. Somehow.

JUDITH Grace — do you actually have trouble hearing what
people say to you?

GRACE Now, don't you start!

JUDITH Well, really!

GRACE I will simply have one of my headaches again and
that's that.

JUDITH You make it sound like a threat —

GRACE (*Urgently*) Promise not to tell —

JUDITH Tell what?

GRACE Promise first?

JUDITH Oh, promise — God! What is it now?

GRACE I met Shay at half-twelve, on the dot!

JUDITH You mean that boy in the garage?

GRACE He's not just that boy in the garage, Judith!

JUDITH Where? Where did you meet him?

GRACE In the village.

JUDITH People see you?

36

GRACE   No. We have a secret place.

JUDITH   Secret place! Oh dear God! Mother will have con-
niptions. You know the village is *verboten* for you,
just now, and as for that boy —

GRACE   Promise!

JUDITH   But what on earth do you see in him?

GRACE   He makes me feel — normal.

JUDITH   Doesn't your — family — make you feel normal?

GRACE   Normal is about not feeling — different. Isn't it? I
hate feeling different.

JUDITH   Oh, Gracie!

> As GRACE *speaks,* NELL *comes in behind, carrying
> the flowers in a large vase. She stands there listening,
> unbeknownst to the two girls.*

GRACE   When I was very small I thought I might be a change-
ling — You know? — something swapped in the
crib, and that was tremendously comforting and
not in the least threatening or iffy or anything like
that despite all signs to the contrary, I mean for a
very small child and all, somehow, because one
could think that somewhere, over whatever rainbow
or other, there was this possibility of, no, certainty
of being in one's own place and when I tried to
think of what that magical never-never place might
be it was always somewhere perfectly ordinary, no
magic casements and dress-ups in quaint outfits or
any of that fol-de-rol but ordinary, like the street in
the village, for example, where everyone went
about doing the most incredibly everyday things
like shopping or sweeping and stuff. That's what I
felt, anyway. When I was very small, that is.
(*Turning*) There's Mother!

NELL   (*To* GRACE) Where did you find these (*flowers*) — ?

GRACE   What?

NELL   Flowers.

GRACE   What do you mean? (*Appeal*) Judith?

NELL   Grace! I've asked you a simple question.

37

GRACE Don't know what you mean.

NELL You know perfectly well what I mean. Where did you pick these flowers?

GRACE Out and about —

NELL Out and about. Did you pick them in the village?

GRACE Not village —

JUDITH Grace!

NELL Judith! Kindly stay out of this, if you please.

GRACE (*Very nervous*) Maybe near the village.

NELL Maybe near the village?

GRACE One cannot keep answering these questions — dreadful headaches — it is intolerable. (*Appeal*) Judith!

JUDITH Mother! Please!

NELL (*Picking and holding a flower*) Harebell. *Campanula rotundifolia*. I know where you picked this. You crossed the old stile into the field behind the RC Church in the village — Didn't you?

GRACE It's a secret —

NELL And look here! (*Another flower*) You went among the trees. *Digitalis purpurea*. Wild foxglove. You've been seeing that boy again!

GRACE No! Yes!

NELL Which is it to be, Grace?

GRACE I hate you! Hate you!

NELL Oh, Grace, Grace! Can't you see the danger?

GRACE I hate you! Who are you to tell me what — I will see my own danger, thank you very much!

> GRACE *rushes away through the open doors and* NELL *follows her.* JUDITH *stands and watches.*

NELL Grace! Let me talk to you! (*Going out*) Grace!

> JUDITH *stands a moment in silence. Lights down on everything else as she is pooled in light, looking off, lost in her own thoughts. Behind her, the wall re-opens, the sculptural work and benches slide out, the covers come down once more and the studio is returned to what it was at the beginning of the play.*

JUDITH Wherever you are now, Grace, would it matter to you? Even if I were to find out something? Whatever it might be. It's all so incredibly sordid. That's what you said, wasn't it? I never really listened to you, Gracie. Really listened. Did anyone ever listen to you? And that boy? Did anyone ever listen to him? Sordid. Why did she do that to me, Jude? That's what you said, back then. (*Remembering Eddie*) Ask her, ask her! Secrets.

She moves quickly, finds her coat and puts it on.

(*Discovery*) The answer isn't to be found here at all. It's to be found — somewhere else.

She turns and leaves quickly. Lights down. Music.

Lights up. Same day as at the beginning, late afternoon light. The eighty-two-year-old NELL *staggers on with a heap of old diaries/journals. She uses a battered pair of spectacles, reading.*

NELL   *(Calling)* Judith! Yo-hoo! Are you back, dear? Where on earth has she gone to all this time? *(Goes to chair, looks at a diary)* Hmm. 1956. *(Reading)* What's that word? 'Bedded'! Yes! Date? 'March 12th, '56. Booked into hotel as Mr and Mrs. The flunkeys in front hall grinning at us, knowing perfectly well who I was. Finally bedded the divine Charlie in Room 217 looking out over Stephen's Green.' *(Looks up)* Divine Charlie? Who the fuck was that? Charlie Prendergast? No! Impossible! That dope! Charlie? Charlie? CT what-the-hell-is-his-name, in Trinity? Never! Not with that nose, never mind that smell — *(Back to reading)* 'March 12th. Off to Shelbourne after endless drinks in Arts Club and Davy Byrne's with pretty CM.' *(Looks up)* CM? And pretty, for Godsakes! *(Disgusted)* What a dreadful little shit I was! Pretty Charlie! Divine Charlie! *(Reading)* 'Booked into hotel as Mr and Mrs. The flunkeys in front hall grinning at us, knowing perfectly well who I was. Finally bedded the divine Charlie in Room 217 looking out over Stephen's Green. *(Beat)* Two out of ten.' *(Looks up)* No wonder I can't remember him! Divine Charlie my royal Irish appendage! Down the Sewanee, Charlie, whoever you were. *(Examines cover)* 1956. Wrong bloody year. Let me see. *(Checks other notebook)* Judith Agnes Swaine Jeffrey, born March 12th, 1955. March. *(Counting)* February. Oh, my God, I can't even remember the months anymore! Mind fucked. *(Checks diary)* Nine — nine! Mmmmm. October, September — July! June-July 1954! *(Frantic search of diaries, finds the right one)* Let me see, not that! Aha! April, April — ah, August! *(Back to reading)* 'August 5th. Preggers again, sickness not as bad as last time.' *(Reflecting)* Miss Moral Judith has arrived! *(Reading)* 'This morning Gracie came into my bed as per usual.

She did not look at me. She put her tiny hand on my tummy, her daily touch, now. Then she said: Mummy, will it take my place when it comes out? I said, nothing dearest, nothing will ever take your place. Promise? Promise.' (*Looks up, very distressed*) Promise. (*Forces herself to move on with great effort*) Eddie! (*Hunting through pages*) Aha! Eddie! (*Reading*) 'Eddie swimming, wet arms cutting air, not water. Pablo's *Bathing Woman* but without the tits, of course.' Pablo! That's a bit rich, I must say. What an arrogant little bitch I was! (*Turning pages*) Pablo! Actually, Eddie had the most astonishing nipples. 'Strue. (*Savours word*) Tum-escent! Always found them — getting in the way. Here we go. (*Reading*) 'August 10th. Can't remember much of last night after the Roundwood party. Eddie in his nightshirt doing his Lonnie Donegan act, round and round the floor making me dizzy. Says he's starting a skiffle band, the adorable lunatic. Nightshirts soon off with 'Rock Island Line'. I said shouldn't we be careful of our baby.' (*Stops, shocked*) Our baby! (*Reading*) 'He said our baby will welcome a visit from me, meaning him, says baby's going to be a front-row forward, play rugger for Ireland. I said our baby is a princess and will be a Spring wonder child. Just you wait and see, Eddie-mutt!'

> *She stops, disturbed.* JUDITH *has come on, silently, behind her, standing and listening to* NELL *as she finishes. As she listens, she discards her coat.*

A princess. Spring wonder child. Poor Eddie. Dead. The adorable shit. (*Sees* JUDITH) Darling — (*Gestures*) I was just — You're back! What time is it? Where've you been all this time? I had begun to worry. Aren't you going to say anything? (*Beat*) It must be nearly night. Where did you go?

JUDITH (*Takes breath*) Out and about —
NELL Out and about. (*Diaries*) See!

41

JUDITH What?

NELL Old diaries and — guess what? — I've got a secret to tell you!

JUDITH (*Deadpan*) You tell me your secret, Mother. (*Beat*) And I'll tell you mine.

NELL Now, look here! I know I've been an absolute beast to you. It's this living alone. Never could live alone. Work best when someone's around. Do you know, I actually asked that awful O'Brien woman to come and sit with me the other day. Then she drove me bananas, turfed her out. What one does, actually, with one's pieces, I mean, is add one more, yes, presence. That's what we do in sculpture, we — populate. I'm beginning to babble, aren't I?

JUDITH Secret?

NELL Eh?

JUDITH You said your secret?

NELL Yes, well, it's no secret, really. Simply that it's very clear from reading this pile of rubbish that, yes, Eddie was your father. Never doubted it, meself, actually. But there you are. He was really quite wonderful in his way, greyhounds and all.

JUDITH I see.

NELL Don't understand. You were in such a state before, who your father was and all. Now you seem — indifferent —

JUDITH Not indifferent, oh, no —

NELL Well! Not particularly — moved —

JUDITH Look. I've changed!

NELL What on earth do you mean? Changed? In a couple of hours?

JUDITH Let me ask you something. Do you think a parent has to earn the love of a child? Well, do you?

NELL What a dreadful word that is, earned. Quite, quite inappropriate —

JUDITH Well, I do. Believe that. And, yes, earned. I don't believe in this blood kinship mumbo-jumbo stuff, Mother. Not after today. Not anymore. If I ever did. All that sickly, sentimental rubbish, parents, children!

NELL   What has happened to you? Where've you been?

JUDITH (*Fiercely*) All love has to be earned! Yes, earned!

NELL   You've been hurt, darling, terribly hurt.

JUDITH (*Prowling about*) Why did he say that? Why? That he wasn't my father? If he was?

NELL   Can't be up to them, men — Besides, B, you may have — misheard him —

JUDITH I heard! He was quite — vehement about it —

NELL   Never know what they're up to, those bollocks —

JUDITH I don't know what to think. Why would he have said such a thing? Why? Why? If it wasn't true?

NELL   (*Thought*) Perhaps it was a final — sundering —

JUDITH Sundering? From me?

NELL   No. From me, actually. It is entirely possible that he wanted you to hurt me. I was quite impossible to him, you know, over the years. I see that now. Impossible. I am sorry, dear. I mean that you should have been hurt so.

JUDITH God, you're unbelievable, you are!

NELL   What? What?

JUDITH My father! — The question of my father and you! You have to insert yourself into the middle of it. Sundering from you! Typical! Me! Me! Me! Do you ever think of anyone but yourself?

NELL   I'm trying to address the bloody question, damn you! (*Beat*) I can understand why you're upset.

JUDITH (*Upset*) I'm not upset!

NELL   Let me ask you something. Can you remember anything else that he said? Eddie?

JUDITH No. (*Shift*) Wait! Yes. He did say something else. I found it very odd at the time. He said he wanted me to be free.

NELL   Free? How very odd. I can't think of anyone more free than you, darling.

JUDITH (*Working it out*) Maybe he wasn't talking about — biology — biological fatherhood — maybe —

NELL   What's that? Didn't hear. Could you — ? Judith!

JUDITH (*Pursuing it*) Maybe he knew my real feelings for him all that time we lived together. That I didn't

43

like him all that much. Maybe he was — letting go, letting me be free. Of him. (*Very upset*) That he and I were not — part of one another! And never could be. That that's what he meant, not my father in that way! Relationship. Not there. (*Suddenly pulls herself together*) That's it, so. That's the end of that.

NELL What is it? What's going on here?

JUDITH Yes. Just a few hours ago it all seemed so important who my father was — not anymore — not with what happened to poor Grace —

NELL (*Surprised*) Grace — ?

JUDITH You see, Mother, I've been thinking about all this. Out there. Walking about the village.

NELL Village? Down the village, were you? See anyone? Haven't been down there for months.

JUDITH And you know what I decided? About all this parental stuff? Fathers, mothers, children. I decided the time comes when you know you like or dislike your parents as people. As human beings like any others. And whether you actually like them. Or dislike them. And that this is stronger than blood. No, I didn't particularly like him as a person, Eddie. And that's not going to change. And right now I don't like you. Particularly. The person you are.

NELL I see. Failure. It really is just a question of how great are one's failures. That's all. And how one lives with them.

JUDITH (*Exasperated*) Mother!

NELL (*Lost*) 'The piece of sculpture must embody its own particular failure.' '*Son propre échec.*' That's what Giacometti said that day on the Rue Hippolyte-Maindron, in 1938, or at least some time before the Hitler War. 'Indubitably,' Beckett answered from a corner of the room. 'Indubitably,' Sam intoned once more, being clearly attached to that particular word.

JUDITH (*Outburst*) For God's sake, this isn't the time to be talking about bloody artists!

NELL Bloody artists! Well, I never!

JUDITH (*Rush*) There are more important things now — I

44

want to talk about Grace —

NELL Grace?

JUDITH What happened to her back then — right here!

NELL (*Moved*) Oh, Grace! (*Stop*) Judy?

JUDITH (*Coldly*) What?

NELL How do you remember her? Gracie?

> JUDITH *is about to say something very different in her* *anger but then decides to go along with* NELL.

JUDITH I remember her with her suitcase. I shall always think of her with a suitcase.

NELL I remember her before she became — you know. She was such a serious little gel. Everything, always, had to be just so. Dress, hair in place. Ribbons and bows. Everything had to be — exact, at age two. Everything in place. Before she could go out. And face the world.

JUDITH You know, you're capable of monstrous things, you are —

NELL True —

JUDITH Don't say that! Damn you!

NELL What do you mean?

JUDITH That's too damn easy to say — true — after the event. Owning up when all the damage has been done. Closes the book, does it? By God, it won't this time.

NELL You're confusing me again, Judith! Can't think straight when you go on like this —

JUDITH Confusing you!

NELL Can't — sometimes I can't — follow — it's like something switched off —

JUDITH Oh, you can follow, perfectly well — when it suits you.

NELL (*Examining her closely*) Something did happen to you?

JUDITH Yes.

NELL In the village?

JUDITH Yes. And that's why the stuff with Eddie seems so — irrelevant somehow.

NELL   He had an immense sense of life, Eddie. That's what I loved about him. Never earned a bean in his life. Didn't matter. Knew how to spend it, though. With him you wanted to seize every second, wring every drop of juice out of it before letting go! When he walked into the room and started his mick-acting one simply downed tools and hit off with him to god-knows-where to do god-knows-what. An adorable shit!

JUDITH   (*Pause*) I went to see that man in the village.

NELL   Man? What man?

JUDITH   Grace's — I almost said boy! Not a boy anymore, oh, no! Man in garage. Aren't you going to ask, Mother? What we talked about? No? The whole place sinking, roof with holes, so much rusted junk, wheels, axles and mysterious bits of broken metal, the stink of oil and grease. The odd thing is that I immediately thought of this studio. Very different, of course. But somehow — connected. And I had this sudden immense — sadness at all that human effort in the world to — make things. Could this really be the slim blond boy that Grace loved? This heap with his gut spilling out over the old jeans? He sat slouched at the back. Had he been — waiting for me? All those years? Bald head bowed, straggle of white hair over his ears. Shay, he said, I'm Shay. I know who you are, he said. You're the second daughter.

NELL   The second daughter —

JUDITH   That's right. The one who brought up the rear. What do you want? he asked, still not looking at me directly. What are you after? As if I were some kind of extortionist which, I suppose, I may have appeared. To him, that is. At that moment, I mean. What are you after, he said?

NELL *staggers to her feet and tries to make one of her exits but this time* JUDITH *holds her and forces her to sit down again.*

46

NELL Have to —

JUDITH No!

NELL Go — pee —

JUDITH (*Yell*) You're staying right there and you're going to hear everything I say —

NELL (*Almost childlike*) Why? Why are you doing this to me?

JUDITH Wasn't even sure I'd be able to go there. But I had this premonition that I was going to — learn something. I mean, I didn't even mention Grace to him. All I said was that I wanted to hear his story. What story, he asked? I've no story, and looking at him I could believe that. A man with no story. But he did have a story. Bit by bit it came out. How one day, in the middle of his affair with Grace, you took him up to this house and seduced him. She fucked me before I knew what was happening to me. That's how he put it, in his charming fashion. Did Grace know this? I asked him. I never told her, he said. Sure, how could I tell her a thing like that, he asked? Wasn't she weak enough as it is? For an instant, I saw the face of the boy he had once been, looking out at me tearfully from beneath the layers of age and drink. You are a monstrous person.

NELL I asked him to pose!

JUDITH You told him to strip!

NELL Pose — !

JUDITH You're disgusting!

NELL He became excited — aroused —

JUDITH In that chair, was it? Or on a bed?

NELL Wasn't at all like that.

JUDITH Then what was it like?

NELL You're being prurient, dear!

JUDITH Prurient! *I'm* being prurient! And what about Grace? Did you think about Grace in all this?

NELL I was trying to protect her! In the only way I knew how!

JUDITH By taking away what she loved? Is that your sense of helping? Oh, my God, it's beyond belief!

NELL By showing him up for what he was! It had to be blocked, however it was done! Besides, B, the boy was an idiot —

JUDITH So you destroyed Grace, too —

NELL I did not destroy her!

JUDITH You wanted and you took —

NELL (*Cry*) It was like — violence!

JUDITH (*Stopped*) Like what!

NELL (*Rush*) Have you ever surrendered to the animal? Have you? Of course you have! When nothing matters but what's in front of you and it has to be seized, come what may! The living pulse —

JUDITH (*Yell*) But what about Grace and that boy?

NELL Grace knew he was going to pose for me! Why, it was her idea! It's come back to me! You must shape a statue of him, Mummy! That's what she said. I remember because of her use of that word. Shape. (*Deep distress*) I was unable to stop myself! It's true! I seized him. Yes. In this chair. A monster? Possibly. But there was more. I also knew I was trying to show what he was really like. For Grace.

JUDITH You told her what had happened?

NELL She knew. She was perfectly calm.

JUDITH Calm? Calm? Oh, for Christsake!

NELL She saw what he was, knew she was well out of it —

JUDITH Because you said so? You satisfied yourself — and then persuaded her to accept it! Manipulative!

NELL Stop trying to make it what it was not!

JUDITH Your monstrous ego — young people — you couldn't stand the sight of them together — I want, I want, I take, I take —

NELL She agreed with me, saw he was trash!

JUDITH Saw yourself ageing, did you?

NELL Ageing? Nothing to do with that!

JUDITH Proving yourself, were you? Like some middle-aged stud?

NELL (*Roar*) Get out of my fucking house!

JUDITH I'm going nowhere, not until you face yourself.

NELL I face myself every hour of every day in ways you

couldn't begin to comprehend —

> JUDITH *is struck by this for a moment but renews her attack.*

JUDITH You may wrap it up in whatever way you choose. You may find your twisted excuses but it all comes down to the one thing. Ego! Monstrous ego! The same ego that drove your work —

NELL What are you talking about — ? My work!

JUDITH The way you gobble up other artists that get in your way —

NELL (*Great roar*) My work has nothing to do with this!

JUDITH Spitting them out behind their backs — I'm the only one that matters! I'm Nell Jeffrey! I'm top of the heap! I'm going to wipe the rest of them off the face of the earth! I've heard you talk like that behind people's backs! So-called friends of yours. Other artists! Competitors! That's all they mean to you!

> NELL *pushes herself up, standing, at first unsteadily, groaning, moaning. Then it is as if the years roll away and she is a powerful figure once more. For a moment it looks as if she is about to launch herself at* JUDITH. *Then she subsides, sinking into herself.* JUDITH *watches this, half afraid, half moved.*

NELL (*Quietly*) I am very tired now. I've had enough of this. I've heard all that I want to hear. And you know something? Nothing you have said is new to me. I know all this. I have to live with all this, day and night. Because I am what I am. I'm not angry with you, darling. You've said what you have to say. Besides, B, you look quite dreadful yourself.

JUDITH I think I'm — ill.

NELL Not surprised, considering —

JUDITH You've just wiped it all out! It's as if it were nothing!

NELL (*Simply*) That's what happens when you age. Your

response to things keeps getting shorter and shorter. I suppose that's what death is. The end of all response. No further answers. Or questions.

JUDITH You're quite, quite impossible.

NELL Better than predictable, don't you think? Pax. I need a little pax now, Judy. Draw breath.

JUDITH Why, it's just occurred to me! You actually hate men.

NELL Not true —

JUDITH Maybe all that sordid business with that young man was precisely that —

NELL Not in the least —

JUDITH Getting revenge upon the males.

NELL Perhaps you're thinking of yourself, darling? Sorry. Shouldn't have said that, should I?

JUDITH I don't hate men. Actually, I adore their company for the most part. It's simply that I don't find them in the least attractive.

NELL They are the most beautiful creatures on earth. And, B, the most frightening.

JUDITH It can never be the same again, after this. You know that?

NELL Nothing is ever the same again after anything, my dear. You won't have to put up with this much longer. Gone before Christmas. Promise. Made my mind up on that. Sex! Actually, do you know, I tried it myself. Once or thrice. With gels.

JUDITH (*Half shocked, half amused*) You what!

NELL Yes. Girl stuff. Did very little for me, I'm afraid. Do you think you could fetch me some Earl Grey, darling?

JUDITH Everything is so disposable for you!

NELL It was rather like going for a medical, come to think of it.

JUDITH It's person to person, Mother. Relationships. Ever heard of those? Relationships —

NELL All that — exploration down there. You know, we're so alike, you and I.

JUDITH What? (*Shocked*) I'm not in the least like you!

NELL Oh, yes you are!

JUDITH Rubbish!

NELL For one thing, we're both brutal truth-tellers —

JUDITH Brutal? Brutal?

NELL Yes, brutal.

JUDITH (*Cry*) I am *not* brutal!

NELL Choose whichever adjective you wish, darling. Same thing.

JUDITH (*Hysterical*) I am not brutal! *I — am — not — brutal!*

NELL What's the matter?

JUDITH (*Loud cry*) I am not in the least like you!

> *She looks as if she is about to strike her mother, much to* NELL's *astonishment, but then she rushes away out.*

NELL Judith! Judith! Well! What was that all about? I am so very tired —

> *She thinks about following* JUDITH, *then changes her mind and sinks back into the chair.*

(*Lower*) Judith. Grace — Grace —

> *She droops in the chair, almost overcome by exhaustion. The head of* GRACE *appears behind her, this time a bronze death head on a plinth, a bronze head which speaks, the mouth moving but the eyes closed over, metallic.*

GRACE Mummy shaped Gracie's head into metal. Mummy's fingers moulding eyes, ears, nose, mouth, head. Cold. Cold metal. Peace. Silence. All finished. Nothingness. No feel, no fear, no sight, no sound, no touch, no taste. All finished. Nothing-nowhere-no when. Grace's head. Not Grace's head. All finished. Mummy shaped Grace's head into metal. Cold. Cold. Cold.

> *The head quickly disappears.* NELL *staggers to her*

feet, panting, into the middle of the studio. For a moment she lingers by the shrouded piece, Woman Rising from Water, *the Egg Woman, touching the sculpture through its covering. Then she draws herself up, groaning and breathing heavily, centre-stage. As before, but this time even more pronouncedly, the years seem to slip away from her body and she moves with sudden, shocking power. At first she goes back and rummages through her working tools, hammers and chisels flying about. She finds a sledgehammer, comes back to the covered sculpture, raises the hammer and crashes it down, once, twice, so that we hear the splintering of stone. She raises it again, this time with great difficulty, crying with the effort, and hits the sculpture again, with less force, but, once more, we hear the damage she has done. She is now in a state of collapse.* JUDITH *rushes on and catches her as she slides to the floor and manages to get her back into the chair.* NELL *sits there.* JUDITH *rushes off again, returning with a mug of tea which she feeds to her mother. She looks towards the damaged sculpture and back to her mother.*

NELL (*Towards sculpture*) I have failed!

JUDITH No! I will not allow you to say that! Your work — not failed — no —

NELL (*Distraught*) What have we been talking about all this time, if it hasn't been — failure?

JUDITH Your work means everything to me, Mother, and to so many other people —

NELL All my life I have resisted that word, failure — never allowed it to even enter my mind —

JUDITH Do you want to lie down?

NELL Fuck lying down. I'll be lying down long enough, thank you. No. Talking about the life. Failure. Keep to the subject. Failure. And the worst kind of failure of all. Failure because I evaded failure. You see, to be human you have to live with failure —

JUDITH Are you quite sure you won't lie down?

Nell No, and this is not Earl Grey, dammit!

JUDITH Sorry —

NELL No. I want to finish — all this. All finished. That's
what Gracie said. All finished. Finish it!

JUDITH What on earth do you mean? When did Gracie say
that?

NELL Never mind. I have spent a lifetime trying to create
perfect form. The finished, rounded, perfect form.
Mistake. No, take that back. Colossal fucking blunder.
And, B, I knew it. All along I knew this. Knew what
I was doing. Knew it was an illusion. And still
persisted.

JUDITH Listen, Mother! Your work is going on permanent
display, a room dedicated to you —

NELL If I had the energy I would wreck every piece there
and set fire to the fucking room into the bargain.

JUDITH Don't say that!

NELL Do you know, the young are right. Put your urine
in a row of bottles and exhibit them. Arrange some
rubbish in a corner according to some design that is
only known to the rubbish artist. Art! So be it. There
is some extraordinary revelation in the times we
live in. Do you know why? Because this is a time of
relentless, artistic mediocrity. A great step back-
wards from what has gone before. So it displays, in
the most naked fashion, human futility, human
failure. Anyway. Scientists are the ones making
great imaginative leaps nowadays. Not artists.
(*Annoyance*) That's not what we were talking about!
What were we talking about?

> JUDITH *is touching the damaged piece of sculpture
> through its covering.*

JUDITH You know, funny thing, I always felt older than
Grace. Isn't that odd? Even when we were both
small. I wonder why that was. Can this (*sculpture*)
be — fixed?

NELL We were talking about something? I can't fucking

remember — my diaries — what are they doing here? What's going on? I can't remember. Judith? (*Appeal*) Talk to me! Please.

JUDITH Perhaps I've done quite enough talking for one day.

NELL Eddie — Grace — diaries — it's all so incredibly confusing —

JUDITH I think you should rest.

NELL You know he tried to kill me once. Eddie. Yes.

JUDITH Eddie? Can't believe it.

NELL Time he was going about selling toys. Toys! Meccano sets and jigsaws, cowboy outfits on cardboard, blonde dolls and magic kits. Door to door. I yelled at him that he was like a fucking spiv Santa Claus. White-faced, he got into that bloody van and quickly reversed in my direction. Jumped out of the way in the nick of time. What a sublime shit he was! (*Discovery*) And your father!

JUDITH Thank you, Mother.

NELL Shall I tell you what really happened that day? Back then with Giacometti and Beckett? My pal, Betty from Monkstown, got bored. Betty from Monkstown always got bored sooner or later. So she left, carrying her box of crayons. And Diego, the brother, Diego took himself off somewhere. So there I was, alone with Giacometti and Beckett. All afternoon and well into the evening. Sam had produced a bottle of brandy from his raincoat. It was consumed. Alberto produced a variety of half-empty bottles of Heaven-knows-what. Steady assault on same. I was tipsy. They were spifliated. They showed off, of course, as men of a certain age are wont to do before a young woman. And, then, they quarrelled. It started with arguments about their midnight walks through the city, up and down the boulevards, in and out of alleyways, down empty streets, walking, walking, punctuated by their encounters with whores with whom they seemed to be on curious fraternal terms. What is this? I yelled at them. What is this about tarts? They looked at me with that dazed puzzlement that you get from drunken men. Actually rather boyish and endearing. Then they quarrelled. About walking.

JUDITH   Walking? What do you mean, walking?

NELL   I mean walking! Walking! The putting of one foot in front of the other variety. Giacometti became quite lyrical on the subject. 'Look how easily one can walk on two legs,' he cried, prancing about with his walking cane. He cavorted, just like a little boy. 'Isn't it wonderful?' he called out to us. 'I shift my weight from one foot to the other, turning sharply without losing my balance. It is really quite the most amazing thing.' What a comedian!

JUDITH   And drunk.

NELL   Then they got on to the subject of shoes.

JUDITH   Shoes!

NELL   Beckett had been emphasizing the importance of sturdy footwear 'The-fitting,' he said, 'the-fitting-is-all-important,' like a bloody salesman behind the counter. 'Nobody,' Giacometti announced, 'nobody notices shoes.' Now this seemed to enrage Sam who was, indeed, given to very occasional outbursts of incomprehensible rage. But Giacometti didn't stop there. 'The foot,' he declaimed, 'touches the ground, so! And is frequently embedded there.' He demonstrated, his back to me, the torn white coat, the mop of wild hair, the cane to one side, like Chaplin in repose, and — do you know — his two feet, splayed, did seem to sink into the floor! Beckett *stormed* at this. To my astonishment he began to pull off his boots, a pair of prized Austrian or Swiss walking-boots with curious tassels which apparently he had brought back with him from Germany. He removed these treasured objects and held them aloft above his head like a trophy. His thin wrists and fingers looked as if they were made from fine wire. 'Regard!' he yelled and, as always happened when he was in a fit, the Irish brogue came out. 'Regard!' he cried, like some priest with some arcane holy objects in his uplifted hands, 'These! They carry us everywhere!' And that was my encounter with the two great artists. An argument about the relevance or irrelevance of footwear.

JUDITH Did you, and Betty from Monkstown, before boredom set in — did you two have any notion of what was really going on?

NELL I beg your pardon!

JUDITH That day? Two young women, hoping to be artists, bowing the knee before the two great male artists — how predictable!

NELL I tell you I have immense respect for those two!

JUDITH Not the point —

NELL Immense respect!

JUDITH Point is —

NELL Point of the story is that everything — no matter who or what you are — everything comes down to the ordinary, a pair of bloody boots —

JUDITH Kowtowing to male greatness! You've never done this! All your life you've struck a note of independence from men —

NELL Down to the banal. Down, down further, down to the common animal —

JUDITH You are a great artist! You don't need a male example, never have, which is why women look up to you! I know something of the battles you fought, Mother, remember —

NELL Snuffling and scratching and guzzling and breaking wind, that's the base! On which everything is constructed! Then you build and build! (*Fist up*) Build!

JUDITH (*Pause*) Do you ever listen to what I have to say?

NELL Do *you* ever listen to what *I* have to say? (*Pause. Snort of laughter*) Huh-huh-huh! We're so alike!

JUDITH (*Quietly*) I'm not in the least like you.

NELL Actually, I think they have little to offer us anymore —

JUDITH Who are you talking about?

NELL Giacometti. Beckett. All the rest of them! They're

dead. We're alive. What we know now comes to us from the future. And the future is rushing towards us with immense speed. Do you know, the human race has already created the conditions of its own extinction? Irreversible, they say.

JUDITH That's a dreadful thing to say!

NELL Dreadful but true. Imagine it! A withered world inhabited only by rats, voles and bats. And loads of microbes.

JUDITH Mother! We've had quite enough of this!

NELL But wait! The other fact of our time is even more astonishing. They're not saying it in public, of course, the scientists. Course not. Frighten the horses. But they know, oh, yes, they know. They know that, sooner or later, the human can be reinvented in the laboratory. Millions of years of evolution in a few hours on a laboratory slab! How amazing it all is! Extinction. Transformation. Choice. Will she have the courage to go with it, the woman of the future? Oh, how I wish I could be alive to see her. The new woman. Femina Nova. If only I could live long enough to see — her art! (*Struggles to rise*) I need to go outside —

JUDITH Outside? Now?

NELL Need to go out!

JUDITH At this hour?

NELL (*Pointing*) Door — Open the fucking door!

JUDITH Really, Mother!

NELL I need to get air! Besides, B, I have said all I have to say in here, thank you very much.

> JUDITH *goes and opens the door. It is dusk outside but even then we can see that the garden has been neglected in recent years.* NELL *tries to rise, again. She is quite feeble.*

JUDITH Here! Let me help you.

NELL Manage perfectly well on me own, thank you. Don't need help.

JUDITH Oh, don't be daft. Take my arm. (NELL *does*) I'm not in the least like you, you know!

NELL Oh, darling, we could be buddies, you and I.

JUDITH Spare me, Mother.

NELL (*Stops*) Can I ask something of you? Stay here with me, Judith. Just this one night. Please.

JUDITH If you wish me to.

NELL Need you to. (*Stops. Beat*) Judy. Do you think she's out there somewhere? Grace?

JUDITH Certainly not!

NELL Hiding from us. In the dark. Don't you remember, Judy? How she used to love to hide from us? As a little gel?

JUDITH She is not out there, Mother. She hasn't been out there for a very long time. Accept it. Get on with it.

NELL You know, you are tougher than I —

JUDITH Realistic. That's all.

NELL Tougher. You see, I need to — dream.

JUDITH It's frightfully cold. Do you want to take my coat?

NELL No-no. Into the air, the air!

JUDITH I'm not at all like you.

NELL Keep moving, darling, just keep moving!

JUDITH Are you quite sure about this?

NELL (*High*) Yes! I am going into the garden.

They walk out together through the open doorway, into the gathering darkness, and the play ends.